Shattering Orthodoxies

An Economic and Foreign Policy
Blueprint for America

A. HAAG SHERMAN

with a Foreword by Mark W. Yusko

EASTON STUDIO PRESS

Published by Easton Studio Press
P.O. Box 3131
Westport, CT 06880
ISBN-10: 0-9798248-5-0
ISBN-13: 978-097982485-2

www.shatteringorthodoxies.com

Printed in the United States of America

FIRST PRINTING: NOVEMBER 2008
10 9 8 7 6 5 4 3 2 1

Book design by Mark McGarry, Texas Type & Bookworks

To Millette, Carson and Julia

Contents

Preface

I completed much of *Shattering Orthodoxies* in 2006; it represents a compendium of papers, articles, and other materials that I wrote over the past several years. However, the last two years have seen a lot of change. Indeed, the last several months have been among the most turbulent since the Great Depression. Despite this, for practical reasons, I left much of the text intact. The book would never have been completed if I constantly updated it to address the most current events. Also, most of the broad themes in *Shattering Orthodoxies* are playing out as anticipated. And, the policies outlined in this book are more applicable today than when first written. The policy recommendations are grounded in prioritization and a more efficient allocation of this nation's resources, a must whether times are good or difficult. As a nation, we have been accustomed to "having it all", and we have accomplished this desire (both consumers and the government) by borrowing heavily abroad to finance it. Debt has piled up. Today, in late 2008, credit is necessarily contracting. As a result, consumers are being forced to prioritize and consumer spending is declining.

So far, the US government—due to a flight to "quality" (US Treasuries)—has been immune from it. However, a day of reckoning is coming for the biggest borrower in the world: namely, a downgrade of the

US treasury. When this occurs, borrowing costs for the US government will increase markedly and the US government will be forced to retrench. Even the US government is not immune from market forces.

The purpose of this book is to outline a series of policies that will allow the US government and consumer to emerge from the current crisis stronger, and to lay the foundation for another century of economic prosperity. I fervently believe that with modest sacrifice, the United States can develop a better, more coherent and more efficient economic and foreign policy that would better serve the American people and provide a strong foundation for decades to come. That is what I have outlined in the pages to come.

However, before starting this journey, I would like to briefly address a couple of current events, and then thank several people for the invaluable contributions that they have made to this book.

Recent Events

Economic Crisis. The economic crisis predicted in this book has taken hold more quickly than anticipated, but is largely playing out as outlined in the book. In particular, I wrote that the United States has experienced significant expansion of debt at all levels over the past decade, whether the consumer, investment banks or the US government. The book predicts that the debt bubble would be punctured and asset values would fall, and that the US government would react by printing more money. My view was that inflation would follow, as the government printed more and more dollars to stave off the inevitable decline in asset values. This is indeed happening. While I wrote that asset deflation was likely and logical, I saw *consumer* deflation as a more remote possibility, given that few countries with a fiat currency and large trade deficits ever suffer from it. However, *consumer* deflation is becoming an increasing risk in the *near-term.* That is, wealth is being destroyed faster than the government can print money to offset it, and consumers are simultaneously retrenching spending and consumption. The result is that consumer deflation is occurring in tandem with asset deflation.

Energy offers a case in point of short-term consumer deflation. With the global slowdown, energy consumption has plummeted and energy prices have subsided. Energy may well retreat to much lower levels—perhaps as low as $30 per barrel if the recession is deep and Asia cannot withstand the storm. Along with energy, consumer prices may start declining across the board as consumers retrench spending and producers grapple with overcapacity and falling prices. Thus, consumer prices may fall in tandem with asset prices, leading to an even deeper recession or worse.

However, at some point, asset values—in real terms—will stop falling. But, monetary expansion will not, as Western governments continue to print money to repay their increasing debt loads. When this occurs, inflation will emerge as the most pressing economic problem, and will be difficult to slay. Thus, I still believe—as outlined in the book—that inflation and a continued devaluation of the dollar are long-term trends that will be difficult to reverse, without a dramatic improvement in economic policy.

I have argued that the "easy money" policies of the US government (and other governments) have been the principal causes of asset inflation, and that it is foolish to stave off inevitable asset deflation with yet more "easy money" as we are currently doing. Only time and asset deflation will do the job, as painful as that may be. In particular, asset values will continue to fall until they revert back to their "fair value". More "easy money" cannot avert this; rather, it will merely fan the flames of *longer term* inflation.

Thus, US policymakers must think differently in addressing the current crisis. Rather than taking an *ad hoc* approach and throwing yet more "easy money" at the problem, they should understand the root causes of the current crisis (easy money) and develop a long-term strategy for the United States. In particularly, US policymakers should undertake a dramatic reform of monetary and fiscal policy and implement a series of policies to promote better investment, more transparency in government, better prioritization of spending and a reform of our tax and entitlement systems. If policymakers focus on an integrated plan to do so, the United States will emerge from this crisis better and stronger than before and retain its status as the world's leading economic power. If not, the US risks ceding its status as the world's economic superpower, much like Britain did a century ago.

Iraq. The surge in Iraq has succeeded far better than most people, including me, anticipated. Yet, the fundamental question is whether Iraq, as currently constituted, can survive after American troops leave. As noted in this book, Iraq was created by British policymakers in the early part of the 20th century and is comprised of three different cultural and ethnic groups—the Kurds, the Sunnis and the Shiites. In short, Iraq is an artificial country that has been held together over the past century by either a strongman (Saddam) or by a superpower (England during the early to mid 20th century; the United States today). Absent a long US military presence or a strongman, Iraq will likely follow the same course as Yugoslavia and ultimately splinter into a series of smaller countries that are more coherent from a cultural and religious standpoint. In particular, once the United States withdraws its troops, Iraq will see ethnic tensions resurface, and will likely fracture along ethnic, religious, and cultural lines. This will happen either peacefully or through violence. Given the tragic history of the region, my guess is that it will be the latter. The risk of violence and dissolution have increased with declining oil prices. Since the Kurdish north and Shiite south contain most of Iraq's oil reserves, the Kurds and the Shiites will likely assert more and more control over oil revenues in their regions, given that these revenues will be tighter in the future. These tensions may lead to more fighting and instability, and a messy dissolution of Iraq. If Iraq does not dissolve, I fear that it will fall under the sway of a theocratic regime (Shiite) closely aligned with Iran. This would be a terrible consequence to our ill-advised foray into Iraq.

Since the two likely outcomes are either a dissolution of Iraq or a theocratic regime, I still believe that Iraq should be partitioned. By partitioning the country, the United States could transition Iraq to its logical end while America still has the influence and troops in place to do it. This can be done peacefully. As with Yugoslavia, a series of countries that are more sensible from a cultural and religious standpoint will lead to greater *stability*. Otherwise, Iraq may suffer a bloody civil war after we leave, whether in the near or long term, or fall under a theocratic regime. Hundreds of thousands or even millions of people may be the worst for it, and this will create yet more instability in an already unstable region in the world.

A. Haag Sherman
October 2008

Acknowledgments

For their support in writing this book, I would like to thank the three most wonderful and beautiful girls in the world: my wife, Millette, and my daughters, Carson Alaina and Julia Grace. They have always given me their unqualified love . . . and patience. Their understanding has made this book possible. Regrettably, this book has taken away time I would have normally spent with them, and I am the poorer for it. I hope that dedicating *Shattering Orthodoxies* to them will in some small way make up for those lost hours.

I would also like to thank those who influenced or contributed to this book. Mark W. Yusko is a business partner, colleague, and one of the smartest investors in the world; he greatly influenced my thinking on China and energy. I am honored that he wrote the foreword. Andrew B. Linbeck, my very close friend and business partner, reviewed the text countless times and provided me with brilliant thoughts and analysis. George L. Ball, another colleague and friend, also provided his insight and wisdom on numerous occasions and made this book better. Jeremy L. Radcliffe, James Sivco, Bradley McDonald, and Michael Alguire also made contributions. Each of these gentlemen influenced parts of this book, while disagreeing with other parts. But, in each case, they made this book much better. For that I am grateful.

I hope *Shattering Orthodoxies* will make some small contribution to the debate that will rage as a result of the problems we face, and that America can emerge from this crisis stronger, freer, and better. That is not only my hope—it is my belief.

A. Haag Sherman

October 2008

Foreword

Orthodoxy, from the Greek *ortho* and *doxa*, means "having the right opinion." It can be defined as a belief or orientation that agrees with conventional standards, but in its most familiar form, *orthodoxy* has religious connotations. In the academic world, however, *orthodoxy* may be interpreted less favorably as conventional wisdom that is not justifiable, but rather is imposed on the general population by an authority such as a church or government. In the pages of *Shattering Orthodoxies* Haag Sherman takes this latter definition and expounds in elegant fashion on the dangers—caused by a set of widely held beliefs about our economic, political, and financial systems—that face America today. Doing the same thing over and over again with the expectation of a different result has been said to be the definition of insanity. By that definition, over the past decade our country has moved closer and closer to that undesirable state. We are facing an imminent crisis requiring immediate and dramatic action—in fact, a shattering of conventional thinking—to put us back on the right course. If we fail to follow the prescription for the future outlined in the following pages, we may forever be locked in the mindless cycle of orthodoxy illustrated by the following folktale.

A mother, daughter, grandmother, and the rest of their loved ones had gathered together at the daughter's home to celebrate Christmas. It was the first time the daughter was preparing the traditional holiday meal, and the mother attentively watched her daughter's every move in the kitchen. The daughter took the main course, a beautiful country ham, out of the refrigerator, and placed it on the worktable. She then chopped a third of the ham off of the end, and threw it in the garbage. The mother looked at her aghast and asked her why she had thrown away a third of the ham. The daughter replied, "Because you always did." Then she asked, "Why did you do that?" The mother, looking perplexed, said sheepishly, "Because Nana always did." So the two women rushed to the parlor to find Grandma rocking in her chair. They asked in unison, "Nana, why did you always cut a third of the ham off and throw it away before you put it in the oven?" Nana replied quite simply, "Because my pan was too small."

While this anecdote may seem trivial, its message clearly relates to the primary tenet of *Shattering Orthodoxies*: that accepting things because "we have always done them that way" can have significant long-term negative consequences. A little wasted food may not create a serious crisis, but the attitudes embedded in the story permeate American society on a number of levels; they are beginning to threaten our economic, political, and financial superiority on the global stage. If we do not address these threats, we are almost certainly headed for a crisis that could plunge us into a deep economic depression, eroding our standard of living for decades to come.

The word *crisis* evokes many emotions, most of them unpleasant. Place the word *national* in front of *crisis* and the level of discomfort rises dramatically. Haag Sherman does a superb job of moving the reader outside of his or her comfort zone to confront the looming national crisis. In our storied history, America has faced, and met, significant national crises on three occasions, but the coming crisis presents us with the unique challenge of simultaneously having to address a "perfect storm" of fundamental threats—economic, foreign relations, constitutional, and environmental.

Sherman's outstanding historical analysis of previous crises and his elegant road map for navigating the impending calamity provide a much needed wake-up call for Americans. Throughout the ages empires, from the Egyptian to the Roman to the British, have fallen because they did not heed warnings such as those contained in the following pages. We are fortunate that this book was written; it provides a comprehensive collection of information and ideas that most of us would never have the time to compile given our hectic daily lives. There is an old expression, "It's the bullet you don't see that kills you." With Sherman's help, at least we will be facing in the right direction when the trigger is pulled. With a little luck, we will have the courage to follow his plan and step out of the way of trouble just in the nick of time.

Shattering Orthodoxies chronicles how national crises in America have occurred on a roughly seventy-year cycle. In the lifespan of the average citizen there is usually a once-in-a-lifetime phenomenon each of us has to face. David Byrne, former lead singer of Talking Heads, in his song "Once in a Lifetime" poses a critical question: "And you may ask yourself—well . . . how did I get here?" Sherman takes us on a historical tour of the times, places, and events that led up to the previous crises, delivering a panoramic view of the policies and mistakes that contributed to those less than shining moments in our nation's history. Mark Twain once said that "history doesn't repeat, but it rhymes." Understanding the circumstances that led us to the brink in the past will help us understand why we now stand on the brink for fourth time. This information is critically important for identifying and acting upon a solution to prevent, or at least lessen, the impact of the impending disaster.

The Chinese symbol for *crisis* is actually made up of two symbols: *wei*, which means "danger," and *ji*, which means "opportunity." Sherman does an excellent job of identifying the myriad dangers facing America today—a rapidly aging population, a bankrupt entitlement system, a broken monetary policy, the lack of fiscal discipline, a nonexistent long-term energy plan, an environmentally unfriendly energy infrastructure, a disengaged foreign policy, an inefficient defense system, and an eroding constitutional governance legacy. While it has always been easy for commentators to identify problems, rarely do those same commentators offer realistic solutions for addressing those problems. The *ji* is the hard part: identifying opportunities where others see only the *wei*, or the danger.

Sherman methodically and intelligently maps out a workable plan, if not to avoid, then to mitigate the damage from the impending national crisis. He focuses on the opportunities available to keep America strong and viable. *Shattering Orthodoxies* offers solutions—restructuring Medicare, Medicaid, and Social Security to take care of the "entitlement generation" (the post–baby boomers); offering a simple, market-based formula for managing interest rates; as well as suggesting a rational plan for federal budgeting and fair taxation aimed at balancing those budgets.

Sherman provides commonsense solutions for energy independence and comments on the implications for foreign policy as we move toward a more proactive "diplomat" philosophy rather than a reactive "policeman" philosophy. With hard-hitting recommendations on the toughest topics, including defense spending, constitutional rights and freedoms, taxes and entitlements, Sherman proves to be as skilled a writer as he has been an investor, an attorney, and a scholar over much of the past three decades.

Reading *Shattering Orthodoxies* will prove to be somewhat disconcerting, as if the author had rushed to the closet and pulled out Dorian Gray's aging portrait to show America how she really looks. Unlike that story, there is time to change our ways. This book lays out the plan for successfully navigating the turbulent times ahead of us in the next decade.

As the song "Once in a Lifetime" continues, David Byrne sings, "And you may tell yourself . . . My God! What have I done?" *Shattering Orthodoxies* asks a similar question, but unlike the song, whose fadeout is "Same as it ever was, same as it ever was," this book offers practical policies and creative solutions to avert the dangers ahead, so that we may seize the opportunities that can carry America to a higher and better future.

MARK W. YUSKO
President and CIO,
Morgan Creek Capital Management, LLC

Introduction

In the 1800s, the sun never set on the British Empire, and the pound sterling was the world's reserve currency. Today, it is America and the dollar. Tomorrow, it may well be China and the yuan.

America's rise was not preordained, but the policies of the British Empire in the 1800s and early 1900s made it not only possible but inevitable. As late as 1900, Britain was the world's military and economic superpower—the largest creditor nation in the world. The next fifty years proved fatal to its global dominion. Two costly world wars and the economic strain of maintaining an empire caused Britain to borrow heavily from its largest emerging global competitor: the United States. By the mid-1950s, Great Britain was a debtor nation, no longer in control of its currency. The United States emerged as the largest creditor nation in the world, destined to dominate world affairs for the remainder of the century.

Currently, the United States finds itself in a position eerily reminiscent to that of Great Britain a century ago. Undoubtedly, the US is the world's superpower, both militarily and economically. Yet, like England before it, America is becoming increasingly indebted to its largest global competitor, China, and is fighting a costly war with no end in sight. America's economic and foreign policies are making China's rise as the world's next leading superpower not only possible, but increasingly likely.

This is not news to most Americans. Americans sense that the United States faces a series of challenges to its position as the world's lone superpower. The problems are easy to identify. They are economic: the risks associated with America's budget and trade deficits, its runaway entitlement programs, and its aging population. They include military threats from asymmetrical foes such as Al Qaeda and other terrorist groups, as well as energy and environmental problems. These challenges are easily spotted. They are even easier to demagogue, whether from the right or the left. Solutions, however, have been in short supply.

The purpose of this book is to address the most pressing issues confronting the United States—including economic, foreign policy, environmental, and energy issues—in one place.

Lack of Prioritization

My vantage point is not that of an academic, but that of a businessman. The task of any businessman is to assess opportunities and risks, and then allocate finite resources to seize opportunities and minimize critical risks. Prioritization and cost-benefit analysis are the hallmarks of a successful businessman, but have been largely ignored by the US government for decades.

Almost every aspect of American policy underscores the fact that America has failed to prioritize and allocate resources efficiently, as Americans prefer to "have it all." For example, Americans criticize the Europeans for boasting expansive entitlement programs and having a high tax burden. However, in many respects, Europeans are acting rationally and prioritizing. They want government services, so they have a high tax burden to pay for them.

Americans prefer low taxes, but also want expansive entitlement programs and a national defense that spans the globe. The result has been predictable. Rather than forcing politicians to choose among priorities—an expansive entitlement system and national defense versus low taxes—Americans want both and politicians have promised both, and paid for both by borrowing heavily from abroad.

America's business community, particularly Wall Street, has much the same problem. It rails against government involvement in the markets, until there is the prospect of a recession or a crisis. At that point, Wall Street bays for a government bail-out, whether through low interest rates (monetary inflation), fiscal stimulus (government spending), or a government bail-out (Bear Stearns).

In short, Americans must do a better job of establishing national priorities and developing reasonable, cost-effective solutions to achieve them. In this book, I will offer a business plan to address this nation's most pressing problems, without a dramatic increase in taxes or more government borrowings. The goal is to provide a foundation to preserve America's global leadership well into the twenty-first century, and leave our children and grandchildren with a better country and world as a result.

Nonpartisan Solutions

Conservatives will likely applaud my focus on free market principles, low taxes, and an effort to establish national priorities, until it hits at some of their sacred cows. These include a worldwide national defense, tax cuts financed by borrowings, an energy policy that does not appropriately cost the commodity, and an interventionist foreign policy. Liberals will embrace many themes as well, particularly my focus on the environment, ensuring health care and pension benefits for the neediest, and a less interventionist foreign policy. However, liberals may flinch at some of the recommended solutions—that is, the United States must undertake an ambitious nuclear power program to reduce greenhouse emissions and make decisions about the breadth of its entitlement programs.

Why Write This Book Now? The Cycle of National Crises

Why write this book, particularly now? For starters, I believe that America is on the verge of another national crisis that would loosely coincide, at least from a timing perspective, with its cycle of national crises. America seems to have a defining national crisis or crises about every seventy years. Based on this cycle, we are due for another.

In its history, the United States has had three major or defining crises: the transition from the Articles of Confederation to the Constitution (1787), the Civil War (1861–1865), and the Great Depression/World War II (1929–1945)[1]. In each case, the United States faced a threat either to its very existence or to its fundamental character or well-being. These threats ranged from economic to constitutional to national security. Of these crises, in only one instance did policymakers anticipate the problem and address it proactively. Fortunately, it may have been their response to the most significant of the three—the transition from the Articles of Confederation to the Constitution— that ensured the survival of the infant republic.

Not surprisingly, the Articles of Confederation crisis may have been the simplest to solve. After all, only one issue was at play: the best manner to govern the country, a constitutional issue. In the other cases, more than one threat existed and had to be addressed. The current situation is unique: America faces three fundamental historical threats—economic, foreign, and constitutional—at the same time. Further, this nation also faces a fourth threat—an energy crisis and potential environmental catastrophe as well.

Examining previous crises provides a sense of the seriousness of the obstacles confronted today. It also illustrates that the current problems, while significant, have historical precedents and can be addressed, with the proper foresight and determination.

The Transition from Articles of Confederation to Constitution (1787)

The crisis surrounding the Articles of Confederation was addressed in a proactive manner by our founders, who understood the risks con-

fronting the young republic as a result of a weak central government—
so weak that it could not bind together the states in a cohesive whole
to address internal and external threats.

Under the Articles of Confederation, the central government had
little authority, as most of the authority to govern resided in the individual statehouses. With frequent disputes among the states and the
ever-present foreign threats from France and England, the United
States faced a short future absent a radical overhaul of its government.
Fortunately, the founders recognized this and called a constitutional
convention in 1787 for the purpose of modifying the Articles of Confederation. The result, however, was far different than what was promised—an entirely new system of government.

As with the Articles of Confederation, the Constitution contemplated a federal government of limited powers; most of the powers remained in the hands of the states and people. Unlike the Articles of
Confederation, the states ceded enough powers to the federal government to provide for a more efficiently run central government, one
with sufficient power to bind together the disparate states and provide
some measure of stability and protection against foreign threats. Without the adoption of the Constitution, the United States might not have
survived the War of 1812 or the Civil War.

Civil War (seventy-four years later): 1861 to 1865

The Civil War represented America's second great challenge. Unlike
the Articles of Confederation crisis, policymakers failed to address the
problem until the nation was at war. This failure was understandable.
Slavery vexed America's greatest generation, that of the founders, just
as it did the generations leading to the Civil War. Further, the disputes
leading to the Civil War were broader than just slavery; they encom-
passed constitutional, moral, and economic issues.

While slavery was rightly front and center, the constitutional question was the right of a state to withdraw from the United States if it
so chose. With an eye to preserve slavery, Southern states believed that

each state, once a sovereign state, had the right to withdraw from the Union at any time. This theory held that the Union derived its power from the rights conferred to it by each of the sovereign states and people, and that that power could be withdrawn.

Quite obviously and rightly, the Northern states and President Abraham Lincoln disagreed, and the Civil War settled the issue once and for all. In the process, the federal government was strengthened, setting the stage for the abolition of slavery, the settlement of the rest of the continent and the emergence of the United States as a global superpower in the twentieth century.

Great Depression/World War II (sixty-four years later): 1929 to 1945

The Civil War and Articles of Confederation were American crises. The Great Depression, however, was altogether new. It represented a global crisis: the simultaneous collapse of the United States and other major Western economies. As with the Civil War, policymakers did not take actions to avert the ultimate crisis, and arguably the Great Depression was a result of the failures of policymakers across the world. American and global prosperity during the 1920s fueled a period of excess that resulted in a sense of complacency on the part of politicians and the people. So when a crisis did occur—the collapse of the American stock market in 1929—the reaction was violent and resulted in protectionist legislation that further contributed to the depression engulfing the world.

Further, as a result of the punitive measures exacted against Germany after World War I, totalitarian regimes emerged in Europe, resulting in World War II. The war ended the Great Depression, but also resulted in over 50 million deaths worldwide. Without question, this was the worst conflict in world history.

Fortunately, the United States emerged from World War II as the world's leading industrial and military power. More important, the United States established its preeminence among nations as the leader of the free world in combating Soviet totalitarianism.

The Fourth Crisis (2008–2018): Will the United States Become Western Europe?

Within the next decade, the United States faces several critical challenges that seem to be converging in a manner that *could* create a catastrophic crisis: the Fourth Crisis. The Fourth Crisis will be unlike any before it, given that it may well encompass issues of each of the previous three crises: economic, foreign policy/military, and constitutional. In addition, it may include an energy and environmental crisis as well.

Addressing the Issues: Structure of the Book

This book will attempt to address in an integrated and comprehensive manner the major challenges facing the United States. Since the issues are wide ranging, the book will, by necessity, be broken into sections.

The Fourth Crisis. The first section will outline the critical components of the crisis confronting the United States.

Immigration, Demographics, Entitlements. This section of the book will focus on the demographic challenges confronting the United States. A part of the solution is to find more workers to support the baby boomer generation in retirement through a more aggressive and liberal immigration policy, which will also be necessary to sustain economic growth to compete with the growing populations of China and, in particular, India. This section will also provide a plan to restructure Social Security and Medicare, combined with a more rational national policy for saving for retirement.

Monetary, Fiscal, and Tax Policy. This section of the book will outline the flaws in America's current monetary policy, as managed by the Federal Reserve. It will also provide a more rational basis for formulating budget and tax policy.

Energy and Environmental Policy. Energy and environmental policy are inextricably intertwined, and are also closely related to foreign policy. By weaning itself off foreign oil, America can reassess its Middle Eastern foreign policy and stop funding the dictators and autocrats who populate the region.

Foreign Policy. This section will outline a more rational and cogent policy to deal with all nations, including rogue nations, as well as focus on combating the threat of global terrorism and defining a plan to establish peace in the Middle East, much like the Marshall Plan in the aftermath of World War II.

Constitutional Theory. The book will also address the need to maintain and protect—and, in some cases, recapture—the constitutional legacy provided to us by our founders.

Challenges and Opportunities

The policies outlined in the book offer a brighter alternative to a potentially bleak near term. To be sure, there may be some short-term pain associated with the excesses of the past several years. However, with sound policies in place, America could have unparalleled opportunity in the decades to come. The last section focuses on synthesizing the various policies outlined in this book into a summary, as well as providing the reader with a sense of what can be.

PART I

AMERICA: 2008–2018
THE POWDER KEG

- Economic Challenges
- Energy Challenges
- Foreign Policy Challenges

Introduction

The United States of 2008–2018 will face challenges that are unlike any in history, which will culminate in the Fourth Crisis in American history. The Fourth Crisis may be triggered by any number of events or catalysts, ranging from a trade war with China, a large bank failure, an energy price shock, another war in the Middle East, or some other event. If America's economic foundation was strong, none of these, in and of themselves, would be significant enough to cause a great crisis. However, the US economy has been hollowed out by past policy decisions. These decisions have resulted in an explosion of debt at the national and consumer level, particularly over the past several years, and an erosion of our economic base.

The catalyst will be the spark that ignites the powder keg—the massive debt incurred by the federal government, businesses, and consumers over the past several years. The explosion will be profound and could dramatically impact Americans' standard of living for decades to come. In this section, I will outline the explosion of debt in the US economy at all levels, and the other risks that may provide the triggering event to a broad national economic crisis.

CHAPTER I

The Powder Keg: An Explosion of US Debt

Introduction

America's inept foreign policy, reliance on foreign oil, aging population, etc. would not be problematic in and of themselves if the underlying fundamentals of both the US government and the American consumer were strong. But they are not. This section will focus almost exclusively on two critical policy decisions over the past several years (and arguably decades) that have contributed to the explosion of debt. The first is the US budget deficit. The second is the ultra-easy monetary policy (artificially low interest rates) established by the Federal Reserve during the 2001–2006 time frame. These policy decisions, combined with the willingness of foreign savers to finance US consumption, created the perfect storm of speculation, asset inflation, and debt creation. This will be the powder keg that explodes due to either a gradually occurring economic crisis (e.g., the repricing of risk by investors, potentially including the Chinese) or an exogenous shock (bank failure, energy crisis, foreign policy crisis, etc.). These events, or catalysts, will be addressed in the latter part of this section.

The Powder Keg: Exploding US Government and Consumer Debt

Fiscal Policy Excesses

In fiscal years 1998 through 2001,[1] the United States government ran budget surpluses, with surpluses projected for years to come. American policymakers, perhaps unwittingly, were preparing for the impending retirement of the baby boom generation. This all changed under President George W. Bush.

In 2000, President Bush campaigned on tax cuts, and passed two in 2001 and 2003.[2] At the same time, he accelerated spending, including nondefense spending, at a rate unmatched by any president of the modern era.[3] Further, the Bush administration pushed the Prescription Drug Plan through a reluctant Congress, adding trillions in future obligations under this new, expansive entitlement program. Despite claims to the contrary by the federal government, the US budgetary picture is dire.

America's official budget deficit for 2007 was approximately $162 billion.[4] However, the US government incurred nearly $500 billion in additional debt during fiscal year 2007.[5] Why are these two figures so different? Shouldn't the United States' official deficit generally equal the amount of its borrowings during a given year? The answer would be yes, unless the US government was masking the true extent of the deficit through accounting gimmicks, à la Enron. Indeed, that is what is happening.

In its official budget deficit figures, the US government *includes* the net revenues from Social Security and Medicare, despite the fact that these net revenues are supposed to be held in trust to pay future benefits. This is just one of many accounting shenanigans. Comparing a company's stated profit or loss with its cash profit or loss is a standard manner to ferret out corporate fraud. If, over time, there is a substantial difference between the two, then the company is using financial chicanery to inflate its stated financial profit. Indeed, that is precisely what the federal government is doing and that is why the official budget deficit is so much smaller than the actual deficit, measured by our government's annual borrowings.

Worse yet, the budget deficits would be even higher if the US government had to account for its finances in the same manner as corporate America. In that case, the US government would have to accrue each year the future obligations under Social Security and Medicare—the equivalent of a public company accruing for future pension and health-care obligations. Given the magnitude of future obligations under these programs, the annual accruals would be staggering and send the budget deficit to well over $4 trillion for 2007—approximately 30 percent of gross domestic product (GDP).[6]

The following chart shows the "official" US budget deficit versus the increase in national debt and the GAAP deficit. The picture shows a dismal financial picture over the past five years, which is in direct contrast to the Bush administration's assertions that the budget picture is improving.

Put in this context, it is clear that the budget numbers provide a false sense that the budget deficits are declining. They were used, at

CHART 1-1

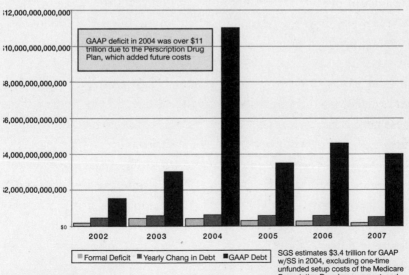

United States Government Deficit

GAAP deficit in 2004 was over $11 trillion due to the Perscription Drug Plan, which added future costs

Legend: ■ Formal Deficit ■ Yearly Chang in Debt ■ GAAP Debt

SGS estimates $3.4 trillion for GAAP w/SS in 2004, excluding one-time unfunded setup costs of the Medicare Prescription Drug Improvement, and Modernization Act of 2003.

Source: Shadowstats.com
US Department of Treasury; Shadowstats.com; Salient Partners

least in part, to justify the $150 billion stimulus package[7]—passed by Congress and signed by President Bush in 2008[8] to address a declining economy and the credit crisis. Unfortunately, if you look at the true budget deficit, we cannot afford this or any other stimulus package. Worse yet, the stimulus package will be ineffective in addressing the problems associated with the debt-fueled spending spree by consumers and the federal government over the past several years.

Monetary Policy: Cheap Money Encouraged
Americans to Borrow, Spend, and Speculate

Unfortunately, these exploding budget deficits were accompanied by extraordinarily loose monetary policy. In response to the 2000 recession and 9/11, then Federal Reserve chairman Alan Greenspan lowered short-term rates from 6.5 to 1 percent. In doing so, he held "real" short-term rates (nominal interest rates, less inflation) close to or below 0 percent for nearly four years, as illustrated by the following chart.

CHART 1-2

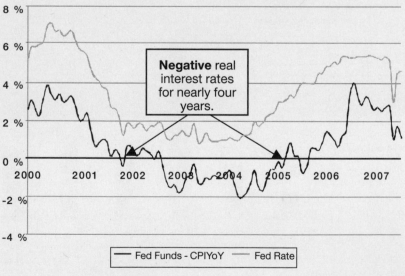

Fed Funds Rate - CPI Annual Change

Negative real interest rates for nearly four years.

Fed Funds - CPIYoY — Fed Rate

Source: Bloomberg; Salient Partners, L.P

The American consumer, seeing essentially "free" money (0 percent financing, courtesy of the Federal Reserve), acted rationally and started borrowing and spending liberally. Not surprisingly, the US trade deficit soared and the consumer savings rate plummeted, as consumers used cheap money to buy more consumer goods abroad.

CHART 1-3

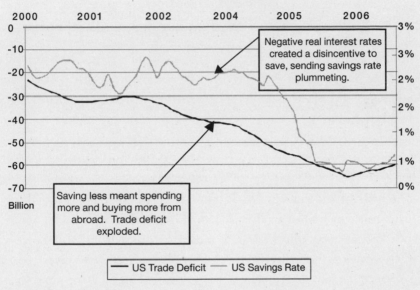

US Trade Deficit vs. US Savings Rate
(one year rolling avg.)

Negative real interest rates created a disincentive to save, sending savings rate plummeting.

Saving less meant spending more and buying more from abroad. Trade deficit exploded.

—— US Trade Deficit   —— US Savings Rate

Source: Bloomberg; Salient Partners

Artificially Low Interest Rates Caused Asset Inflation and Explosion of Debt

Armed with artificially cheap money, investors started speculating in asset classes of all stripes during the 2003–2006 time frame, pushing many asset prices ever higher. The following chart illustrates the direct, inverse correlation between ultra-cheap interest rates (Fed Funds) plotted inversely and compared with prices of a variety of asset classes.

CHART 1-4

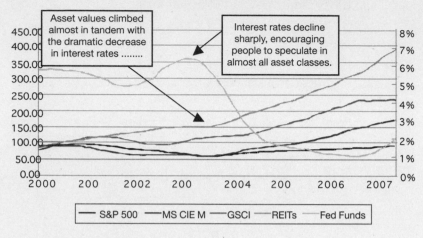

S&P 500, MSCI EM, GSCI, and REITs vs. Fed Funds
(inverted fed funds rate) (12 month rolling avg.)
(indices normalized at 12/31/1999) (18 month lag on Fed Funds Rate)

Asset values climbed almost in tandem with the dramatic decrease in interest rates ....

Interest rates decline sharply, encouraging people to speculate in almost all asset classes.

— S&P 500   — MS CIE M   —GSCI   —REITs   — Fed Funds

Source: Bloomberg; Salient Partners

Consumers Speculated with Cheap Money

The housing market was not immune from the speculation resulting from this easy money era. Indeed, consumers started borrowing *short-term money* (e.g., adjustable-rate mortgages, or ARMs) to finance a *long-term asset* (housing). Because of artificially low interest rates, consumers could buy ever more expensive houses based on the same level of income. This speculative borrowing inflated housing prices, as illustrated by the following chart:

In short, a borrower who made $100,000 in 2000, at a time when interest rates were at more normal levels, could buy a $350,000 home using a one-year ARM. The same borrower, just five years later, could buy a $625,000 home—an astounding 80 percent increase in the price of a home the consumer could buy. Nothing changed, except the cost of money.

Some older readers might recall the general rule of thumb when they bought their first house: you could afford a home that was about 2.7 to 3.5.[13] times your income level (i.e., a $100,000 wage earner could

CHART 1-5

	6.5% Fed Funds Rate (2000) [9]	1% Fed Funds Rate (2003) [10]
1-year ARM [a]	7.2% [9]	4.0% [10]
Income Level	$100,000	$100,000
Max Interest Costs [b]	$25,000	$25,000
Max Home Value [c]	$350,000	$625,000
Increase in Value		**+80%**

Source: Salient Partners

(a) One-year conventional adjustable rate mortgage, or ARM.

(b) Assumes that the loan is underwritten based on 25 percent of borrower's income being used to finance housing payments but no amortization of principal.

(c) The home value is calculated as the maximum interest costs divided by the interest rate on the ARM. (There is an implied "cushion" in this calculation, given that there would be a down payment involved, which has not been taken into account in this calculation.)

afford a $270,000 to $350,000 home). That rule held fairly constant for decades. That ratio changed significantly in the 2002–2006 time frame, skyrocketing to over 4.5 times income level (representing, again, an approximately 30 percent increase in value relative to current income levels).

Unfortunately, most things that are "too good to be true," whether they are very low interest rates or rapidly rising housing prices, usually come to an end. As the Federal Reserve began to raise interest rates to more appropriate levels (i.e., levels closer to historical norms), home buyers had to pay higher interest rates (or more normal interest rates) to buy a home. This has led to a dramatic change in housing prices. The following chart shows the increase in the price of housing that occurred from 2001 through 2005 as interest rates declined, followed by the dramatic sell-off in the housing market that accompanied the normalization of short-term rates.

Note: Interest rates are plotted *inversely*, and housing is plotted normally with an eighteen-month lag.

Not surprisingly, housing exploded during the period of ultra-low interest rates, since consumers could buy more expensive houses on

CHART 1-6

Housing Starts vs. Fed Funds Rate

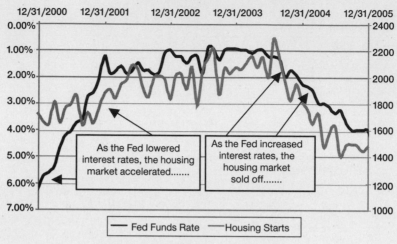

*Housing start data h recorded at t where t = th – 18 mo.

Source: Bloomberg; Salient Partners.

the same income levels. Since then, the housing market has declined almost in tandem (with an eighteen-month lag) with the increase in short-term rates. [Note: Some have hoped that the current round of easing by the Federal Reserve would support collapsing asset values. However, for reasons set forth later in this book, loose monetary policy will not bail the United States out of its mess this time around; it will only prove inflationary.]

Unfortunately, many consumers viewed the increase in housing prices as permanent, and borrowed heavily against their homes on this belief. Thus, household debt exploded, as consumers cashed equity out of their homes and borrowed money to buy consumer assets.

Today, the story is much different. With the collapse in the housing and financial markets, consumers are now feeling the double-edged pinch of declining asset values and higher debt loads, particularly due to ARMs being reset.

CHART 1-7

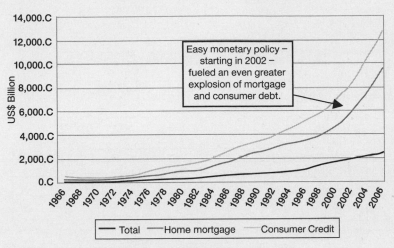

US Household Debt: 1966-2006

Easy monetary policy – starting in 2002 – fueled an even greater explosion of mortgage and consumer debt.

Source: http://www.globalpolicy.org/socecon/crisis/tradedeficit/tables/household.htm

Wall Street Joined the Consumer

Consumers were not the only ones who speculated and piled up debt during this era of easy money. In this low return environment, the financial engineers on Wall Street sought to enhance investors' returns through the creation of more and more complex financial products, including derivatives. A derivative is a financial instrument designed to provide an investor with exposure to a particular asset class. In many cases, derivatives provide enhanced exposure through the use of leverage, which magnifies both gains and losses. Investors increasingly used these instruments to generate higher returns in this low return era, leading to an explosion in the use of derivatives and leverage.

A prime example is an instrument called a credit default swap, or CDS. A CDS is an agreement where Party A (beneficiary) pays Party B (insurer) a fee for Party B to insure the debt of Party C (issuer of debt). Investors in Party C's debt view this insurance favorably—if Party C doesn't pay the debt, the insurer does. In this manner, insurance companies also guaranteed or insured debt for a fee. With this in-

CHART 1-8

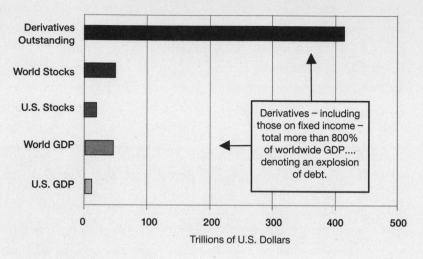

Derivatives Outstanding vs. Stocks & GDP – 2006
Sources: SGS, FRB, BEA, INF, BIS

Derivatives – including those on fixed income – total more than 800% of worldwide GDP.... denoting an explosion of debt.

Trillions of U.S. Dollars

Source: Shadowstats.com

surance in place, rating agencies increased the investment rating of many bonds from lower investment grades (say, a "junk" rating) to a higher grade of debt (e.g., investment grade). This insurance encouraged the creation of exotic debt instruments covering increasingly lower-quality debt (e.g., subprime home loans) and encouraged rampant speculation in fixed income. Without low interest rates and an abundance of liquidity, the abuses would have been much less.[14]

Derivatives outstanding now total more than worldwide GDP by a factor of *eight*. This embedded leverage represents a significant systematic risk. Should one of the big debt insurers or investment banks fail, tens of billions of dollars of debt would be downgraded and worth much less than before. And a crisis would turn into a catastrophe, with worldwide policymakers having little ability to control the resulting credit contagion.

Aging Demographics Compounds Problem

To paint a bleaker picture, the explosion of debt could not have come at a worse time—just before the impending retirement of the baby boomer generation. In sum, during an era when both the government and consumers should have saved for the impending retirement of this generation, US policymakers encouraged just the opposite by piling up huge budget deficits and holding interest rates too low for too long. With excess liquidity and low interest rates, the US government and American consumers incurred mountains of debt. Not to be outdone, Wall Street joined in. To make matters worse, an increasing portion of this debt was issued to foreign borrowers rather than US borrowers.

Going into Debt to China. Surging Trade Deficit

The United States' yawning budget deficits and rampant consumer spending has required it to increase its borrowings from abroad. It has had to borrow as much as $800 billion from abroad in a given year, nearly 7 percent of GDP, to maintain government and consumer spending at these levels.[15]

The Chinese, and other countries, have financed the United States' consumption to date. With a savings rate of over 40 percent[16], China has determined that keeping its currency artificially cheap relative to the US dollar represents one way to expand its trade with the United States and establish itself as a global economic powerhouse. With its massive savings, China has bought US dollar assets to keep its currency depressed against the dollar. In doing so, China makes its exports to the United States relatively inexpensive, giving it a significant trade advantage.

The chart on the next page shows the deterioration of America's trade position with China since the United States began running massive budget deficits and sporting ultra-low interest rates.

The following chart shows the rapid increase in foreign reserve holdings of the Chinese government since 2001.

CHART 1-9

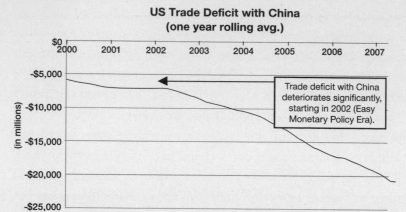

US Trade Deficit with China
(one year rolling avg.)

Trade deficit with China deteriorates significantly, starting in 2002 (Easy Monetary Policy Era).

Source: Bloomberg; Salient Partners

CHART 1-10

China Foreign Exchange Reserves

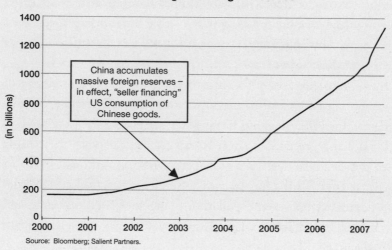

China accumulates massive foreign reserves – in effect, "seller financing" US consumption of Chinese goods.

Source: Bloomberg; Salient Partners.

In effect, China has been seller financing America's purchase of Chinese goods over the past several years, and now the United States is dependent on China, and others, to finance its excessive consumption.

If and when the Chinese and others stop buying dollar assets—or, worse yet, start selling US dollar assets—the dollar will fall precipitously, resulting in higher interest rates and inflation in the United States. That is why the Bush administration reacted strongly to an indication by the Chinese authorities of an intention to stop accumulating US dollar assets. The Chinese quickly backed off. But the reaction was proof positive of what many already know: the US government has lost control of the value of the US dollar, and the fate of the dollar now rests firmly in the hands of China.

Collapse of the US Dollar: Threat to US Dollar as World's Reserve Currency

Inflation, simply defined, is too many dollars chasing too few goods. The explosion of America's national and consumer debt has created more and more dollars. Further, lower interest rates due to easy monetary policy have made holding dollars less attractive for many foreign investors, as these investors have rotated out of dollars into higher-yielding currencies (i.e., currencies with higher short-term interest rates). With these inflationary policies, the dollar, not surprisingly, has declined precipitously over the past six years.

CHART 1-11

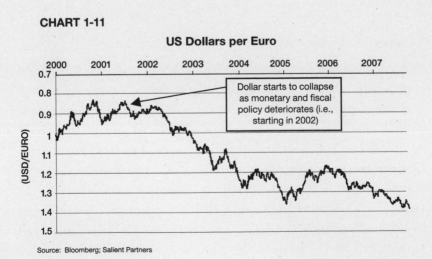

US Dollars per Euro

Dollar starts to collapse as monetary and fiscal policy deteriorates (i.e., starting in 2002)

Source: Bloomberg; Salient Partners

The collapse of the dollar will continue until the United States regains control of its finances. If dollar depreciation accelerates, the US dollar could see its status as the world's reserve currency supplanted by the euro or, more likely, the yuan, at some point in the future. Further, as noted below, inflation will approach levels not seen since the 1970s and early 1980s, another period of fiscal and monetary excess and dollar duress.

The Catalysts

A litany of lesser but significant evils surrounds the powder keg of excessive debt. Any one of these could prove to be the catalyst for the Fourth Crisis.

The Looming Energy and Food Crises

In addition to an economic crisis precipitated by America's fiscal and monetary policy, the United States also faces a significant economic threat due to an energy price shock. The energy and food markets are being driven by a weak US dollar and supply and demand imbalances, a situation that is likely to continue.

Commodities Driven Partially by a Weakening Dollar

A weak US dollar has been one of the propellants of the energy and commodity markets. Given the dollar's status as the world's reserve currency (for the moment), most international energy transactions are denominated in dollars. With the weakening dollar, energy prices have surged. The following chart shows energy prices in dollars versus euros over the past several years.

The US dollar was at parity with the euro in late 2002 (1 dollar = 1 euro). If the US dollar had held its value versus the euro over the past five and a half years, oil prices would be approximately $85 per barrel

CHART 1-12

US Crude Value

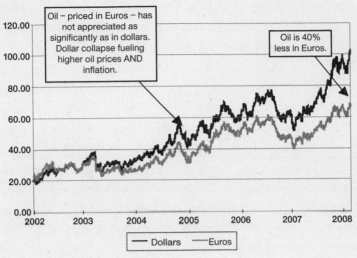

Oil – priced in Euros – has not appreciated as significantly as in dollars. Dollar collapse fueling higher oil prices AND inflation.

Oil is 40% less in Euros.

— Dollars — Euros

Source: Bloomberg; Salient Partners

(as of May 2008), instead of $135 per barrel. Arguably, the $50 difference is due to dollar depreciation, which illustrates the inflationary impact of a weakening dollar. That is, as the dollar weakens, imports become more expensive to US consumers. A weakening dollar drove, in part, energy prices and inflation during the 1970s, just as it will in the decade to come.

As significant, if the United States had a more sensible foreign policy, the world would likely have more excess production (Iraq is now just approaching prewar energy production) and a lower "terror" premium, points discussed in the foreign policy section below.

Supply-Demand Imbalances

Past energy crises resulted from supply disruptions. In particular, during 1973–1974, the Arabs halted the sale of oil to the West in response to the Yom Kippur war. Oil prices more than tripled. However, they quickly declined after the crisis ended, and the Arabs reopened supply. The same dynamic occurred in 1979–1980 during the Iranian Revolution and the early stages of the Iran-Iraq war. Oil production was disrupted, and oil prices surged. Prices soon retreated as production came back on line. Today's dynamic is much different.

Surging Demand. Contrary to the stories about price gouging, energy companies can barely keep up with global oil demand, particularly in China and India. The math of energy production now works against the world. Historically, energy companies have been able to produce enough energy to keep pace with demand and provide a "cushion." That is, there was enough "excess" production that could be tapped to stabilize the energy markets in the event of a modest supply disruption. However, "spare" capacity has been declining as demand increases in emerging Asia. America's Energy Information Agency (EIA) recently estimated that global surplus crude oil production was a little over 1 million barrels per day (over an 80 percent decline in excess supply since 2002). The EIA report notes that the "reduced level of spare production capacity significantly increases the risk to oil prices from a disruption to supply because as many as twenty different countries currently produce at least 1 million barrels per day, including countries such as Iran, Iraq, Nigeria, and Venezuela."[17]

This situation is not likely to improve, as energy consumption continues to increase. Energy consumption tends to increase as nations industrialize. After World War II, the United States and the West used increasing amounts of energy as their manufacturing base expanded and consumer demand grew. During that same time period, much of the world was stuck either behind the Iron Curtain (Soviet Union and Eastern Bloc) or Bamboo Curtain (China and parts of the Far East). As a result, consumption in these countries did not keep pace with that of the West. Over the past decade or so, this dynamic has changed. China and other emerging nations have started to industrialize.

As India and China continue to industrialize, they will increase energy consumption. Experts predict that Chinese oil consumption will triple from 2003 to 2030, surging from 5.6 million barrels per day (bpd) to over 15 million bpd.[18] China will have to find another Saudi Arabia to meet its energy needs by 2030. The question then becomes, where do we find another 10 million barrels of production per day for China alone and another 20 million barrels of production for the rest of the world?

Oil Production Cannot Keep Up with Demand. The short answer is: we probably won't over the long term.

Most of the West has been heavily explored, and major "finds" (fields producing more than 500,000 barrels per day) are a rare occurrence. In fact, only one major find has been discovered and produced in the last twenty-five years.[19]

More chilling, Matthew R. Simmons, a world renowned energy expert, and others claim that the world may very well have reached peak oil production and that oil production will start declining in the near future.[20]

Obviously, oil consumption cannot exceed oil supply over a long period of time. So if supply declines in the face of increased demand, energy prices will continue on an upward trend until enough demand is destroyed to bring the markets into balance. The impact on the price of oil could be profound, and we are seeing the early stages of this phenomenon. Energy prices quintupled since 2002 and nearly doubled from 2007 (average price of $72) to 2008 ($135 per barrel in May 2008). While the energy markets are volatile and price surges are often accompanied by sharp retreats, the trend line for energy prices is clear: onward and upward until enough demand is destroyed to bring the markets into balance and/or other energy sources are found to reduce the demand for oil.

Declining Production, Energy Reserves in Hostile Places. The energy picture becomes even murkier when taking into account the stability of energy supply. Most of the world's untapped reserves are either in areas controlled by state-owned oil companies, or in regions of the world that are not terribly stable or that are outright hostile to the United States, such as the Middle East and Africa.[21]

As the world becomes more reliant on these nations for energy, the risk of supply disruptions increases dramatically. The price shock from the 1973–1974 Arab oil embargo and the 1979 Iranian revolution resulted in surging oil prices, more than tripling in the case of the embargo.

If a similar supply disruption occurred today, the United States would see price increases from $135 per barrel (May 2007) to over $400 per barrel, resulting in $10 per gallon gasoline for drivers. Given current US foreign policy, the risk of a supply disruption is greater today than at any time in the previous twenty-five years.

The Looming Food Crisis

With US policymakers pushing, with subsidies and mandates, corn-based ethanol as an alternative to the importation of foreign oil, the United States is adding to the world's environmental woes and creating yet another crisis: a worldwide surge in food prices. In particular, corn-based ethanol is, by definition, energy inefficient. It takes more energy to create a gallon of ethanol than the energy it produces.[22] So using corn-based ethanol is actually adding to this country's energy and environmental problems, rather than addressing them.

Worse yet, as corn prices have increased, due, in part, to greater demand for corn for ethanol, farmers have been planting more corn in lieu of wheat.[23] By reducing the acreage devoted to wheat and other crops, wheat prices, as well as those of other agricultural commodities, have increased dramatically as well.

Since corn, soy, and wheat are used either directly as food or as feedstock, food prices have soared. After all, livestock eat grains, and increased grain prices logically lead to higher beef prices.[24] The same holds true with other products that use grains as an input: sodas, cereals, breads, beer, etc.

CHART 1-13

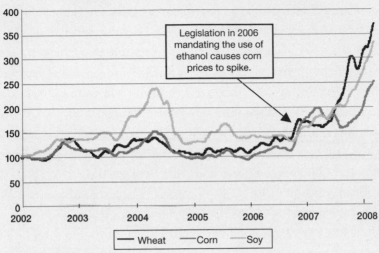

Agricultural Commodity Prices Since 2002
(30 day rolling avg) (Normalized on 1/1/2002)

Legislation in 2006 mandating the use of ethanol causes corn prices to spike.

Wheat — Corn — Soy

Source: Bloomberg; Salient Partners

This is clearly a problem for the United States, but it is more troubling for developing nations. Since grains are worldwide commodities, price spikes driven by US policy failures are causing worldwide food inflation. This is particularly painful for impoverished countries, whose citizens spend a higher percentage of their income on food. In these nations, food inflation results in malnourishment and even starvation, creating a volatile situation. China, India, and Persian Gulf states are clearly worried about inflation and the resulting unrest.

American Foreign Policy

Instability Has a Cost. American foreign policy has done little to reduce the risk of an energy supply disruption. If anything, American foreign policy has markedly enhanced this risk.

Since the invasion of Iraq, the Middle East, never a particularly stable region, has become even more volatile. Many believe this instability has added significantly to the price of oil since the invasion of Iraq in 2003, due in part to a loss of Iraqi production. Before the invasion, Iraq was producing about 2.6 million barrels per day.[25] By 2006, Iraq was barely producing 1 million barrels per day—a staggering decline of 1.6 million barrels per day—although production has recovered of late.[26] In addition, the increased instability in the region has increased the supply "disruption" premium.[27] The end result has been much higher energy prices.

Not only has the Iraqi war cost America thousands of lives and hundreds of billions of dollars in direct costs, the indirect costs to the American consumer have been enormous. By some estimates, the economic cost of the Iraqi invasion will approach $2 trillion.[28] In the case of higher oil prices, the benefits of this instability have, ironically,

CHART 1-14

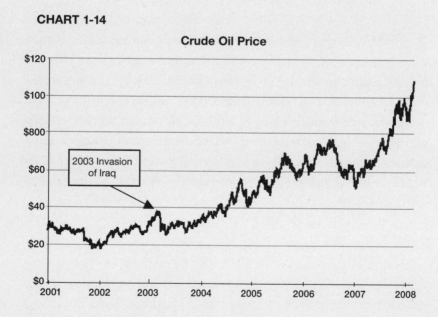

Source: Bloomberg; Salient Partners

flowed directly to the dictators and oppressive regimes that we castigate. In effect, Americans are financing these rogue regimes by paying higher energy prices that are to some extent of our own making, through incompetent foreign policy.

The same architects of this foreign policy are now focused on Iran. If America were to wage a war with Iran, the economic consequences would be even more profound. Iran would surely mine or blockade the Strait of Hormuz, through which about 20 percent of the world's oil travels, which would send prices soaring.[29,30]

America Is Losing Global Leadership. China and Europe Emerge as Alternatives. While precipitating more unrest in the Middle East, America is also seeing its world leadership erode, an ominous threat to its superpower status. In particular, America has led the world for the past sixty years based on its economic strength, military power, and moral clarity. Yet, on all three fronts, the United States is slipping.

As China becomes an increasingly important economic power, the balance of power in Asia is rapidly tilting toward China. Further, China is following a foreign policy that is very similar to the one espoused by our founders, particularly George Washington. Namely, China is establishing relationships with nations across the world and trading with all of them, regardless of form of government. So while the United States is bent on imposing sanctions on regimes with which it disagrees, China trades with them, securing vast quantities of natural resources for its booming economy. By trading, China spreads its influence throughout the developing world, largely at the expense of the United States.

At the other extreme, Europe has established itself as the leader on moral issues, in contrast to the United States and China. Europe largely opposed the war in Iraq, and has established leadership positions in areas largely eschewed by the United States, particularly the environment. On this front, there is a chasm between America and most of the industrialized world. Europe and, to a lesser extent, Japan have taken a leadership role in addressing the issue, with the America maintaining a rather ambivalent (at best) position on the matter. On Iraq, Europe's standing in the world largely grew as its position on the war proved prescient.

Given these differences, the North Atlantic Treaty Organization (NATO), long the bedrock of US-European national security, is also under pressure, as European states have resisted sending more troops into Afghanistan (because of Iraq, many believe). American policymakers have called for increased European support in Afghanistan, arguing that it represents a different conflict than Iraq. Unless American policymakers can thread this needle, the reluctance of Europeans to support America in Afghanistan may undermine NATO's impact on future conflicts.

The unraveling of America's influence could not come at a worse time. With a struggling economic base, America needs allies to shoulder the burden of policing a more dangerous world. Without them, America will continue to strain its military, spending far too much money on it. And the balance of power will continue to shift.

Unlike the last transition from one superpower to another (Britain to America), there are few shared ideals between today's aging superpower (America) and the upstart (China). Given this, the consequences of the transition may not be nearly as peaceful or beneficial as the last one. China's growing economic and military leadership—and America's inability to provide a persuasive counter—may give rise to the Sino century. With this transition, the ability of the world to take actions for the betterment of mankind (e.g., conserving the environment or acting against terrorist states) may be limited, and the lives of billions of people may be markedly worse as a result.

Constitutional Issues

It is unlikely that the degradation of the rights of the people and states found in the US Constitution will be a catalyst for the Fourth Crisis.

But a further degradation of these rights may well be one of the costliest casualties.

Over the past several decades, Americans have largely ignored the continued growth of the federal government, which has come largely at the expense of the states and the people. The explosion in the size of the federal government has sown many of the seeds—outsized entitlement programs and America's desire to police the world—of the impending crisis.

In yesteryear, most of these programs, and many of the foreign policy blunders of the past fifty years, would not have been undertaken, given that most would have been deemed unconstitutional.

A significant part of the plan outlined in this book will require a dramatic retrenchment of the federal government, which would devolve more power where it belongs—in the hands of the states and the people.

What Will the Fourth Crisis Look Like?

There is almost an infinite set of circumstances that could trigger the Fourth Crisis, but I believe that it will be driven by an economic dislocation due to the significant imbalances of the US government and consumer. Energy may well play a role in the crisis. The failure of a large financial institution might prove to be the catalyst. Most likely, it will be a gradual and building crisis, as asset values decline and credit contracts, as outlined later in this book.

In any significant crisis, the US economy and dollar are at risk, given America's need to borrow heavily from the rest of the world to fund its government and consumer spending.

If the crisis is extreme, the United States will see its global leadership position overtaken by China, Europe, or perhaps a combination of other nations, particularly given much of the world's hostility toward America's foreign policy of late.

Parallels to the Late 1960s and Early 1970s, But Worse

The trends today are reminiscent of those of the late 1960s and early 1970s, but the result may be much worse.

In 1964, another Texan, Lyndon B. Johnson, pushed a tax cut through Congress. In 1965, he took a budget that was close to balanced and, in conjunction with the tax cut, LBJ began financing the Vietnam War and his ambitious domestic agenda (called the Great Society) by dramatically increasing deficits (dubbed "guns and butter").[31] As US fiscal policy became unhinged, US monetary policy also eased. Fueled by easy money and oil price shocks, inflation became the norm throughout the 1970s and early 1980s. The similarities with today are striking as noted in chart 1-15, and the results are likely to be as well.

Inflation was not arrested until then Federal Reserve chairman Paul Volcker raised short-term rates to 20 percent in 1981.[32] This plunged the United States into a deep recession but laid the foundation for declining interest rates and inflation—and strong economic growth—throughout the 1980s and 1990s.

Looking forward, the challenges confronting Federal Reserve chairman Ben S. Bernanke and the next president are daunting.

CHART 1-15

Factor	Late 1960s and early 1970s	2000s
President	Texan [a]	Texan
War	Southeast Asia	Iraq
Tax Cut	1964	2001 and 2003
Deficit Spending	Yes	Yes
Monetary Policy	Easy [b]	Easy
Energy	Surged (Middle East supply disruptions) [c]	Surged (demand surges: emerging Asia)
Gold	Surged	Surged
Dollar	Collapsed in the 1970s	40% decline since 2002

Source: Salient Partners (May 2008)

(a) Laid the foundation for inflation, particularly in mid 1960s

(b) Monetary policy significantly eased during the Nixon administration.

(c) Energy prices surged in 1973–1974 (Arab oil embargo) and 1979–1980 (Iranian revolution; Iran-Iraq War)

What Happens Next?

1. Monetary Policy Will Be Ineffective and Inflationary

Current Federal Reserve Chairman Ben Bernanke now faces a "hemlock" economy, one that has a toxic mix of inflationary pressures and recessionary risks, including a deflating asset bubble. If he raises rates to combat inflation, he faces a potential recession and a further collapse in asset values; if he lowers them to stave off recession, he faces a further weakening of the dollar and inflation.

Taking his cue from his predecessor, Bernanke has lowered interest rates in an attempt to stave off a further collapse in asset values and a recession, and to prop up the ailing credit markets.

However, this move will prove self-defeating. Monetary policy will prove ineffective to avert collapsing asset values, particularly in the housing market, the debt market (the worst parts of the spectrum), and ultimately the stock market. The fundamental issue will not be the "cost of capital"—that is, interest rates, particularly short-term ones—but "access to capital" and the fundamentals of the credit market.

Most banks hold mortgages and related securities on their balance sheets. With the crash in the housing market, many of these banks have had to write off many of these loans. This has caused many banks to stop making as many loans and to tighten lending standards significantly, sending interest rates higher.[33] Indeed, the Federal Reserve has lowered rates to 2 percent (as of April 2008), yet the risk premium on mortgages has increased dramatically, giving consumers little benefit from the easing, as illustrated by the following chart.

CHART 1-16

The Myth of Lower Rates in 2008

	Jumbo 30-Year Mortgage (May 19, 2005)	Jumbo 30-Year Mortgage (April 3, 2008)
30-Year Treasury [a]	4.44%	4.39%
Spread	1.55%	3.13% ← Risk premium has doubled
Jumbo Mortgage Rate [a]	5.99%	7.52%

(a) Source: Salient Partners (May 2008)

The spread, or risk premium, being paid by consumers has nearly doubled since the housing market heyday, reflecting a contraction of credit and risk aversion on the part of the banks.

As noted, the one-two combination of a higher risk premium for mortgages and tightening credit standards means that the Federal Reserve's easy monetary policy will prove ineffective in propping up collapsing asset values—and it will prove inflationary.

The principal driver of inflation will be the collapse of the dollar that will accompany monetary easing. The United States runs a massive "current account" deficit, which is the trade deficit plus the investment by foreigners in the United States, less investments by the US made abroad. The current account deficit is enormous because America consumes much more than it produces, and has to receive massive infusions of capital from abroad to maintain its consumptive binge. Some of this investment is needed by the US government to finance its enormous deficit; some is needed by Americans, who have been borrowing significantly to, in part, continue consuming. So far, attracting foreign capital at relatively cheap interest rates has been easy, for a variety of reasons that will be explained later.

At some point, foreigners will tire of financing America's consumption at low rates, particularly when the dollar is losing value by the day. Over time, US long-term rates will ultimately have to increase and will have to increase dramatically to attract foreign capital and compensate foreign investors for holding a declining currency. (In the near term, US treasury rates may well decline, as the "credit crisis" causes investors to plow their money into "safe assets". Over the long term, market forces, including inflation, rather than fear will dictate interest rates on US treasury debt, a dynamic outlined later in this book).

Currently, foreign investors lose money every year by holding US treasuries. The yield—say, 3.8 percent (as of May 2008) on a ten-year US Treasury note—is being eclipsed by declines in the dollar (averaging about a 4 to 7 percent annual decline based on a trade weighted basket of currencies).[34] Further, the yield on a ten-year US Treasury note should generate a 2 percent "real" return, which would equate to an approximately 6 to 7 percent interest rate today.[35] To this, a foreign investor would add another few percentage points for a declining currency (currency risk), though the dollar would likely gain some stability through higher rates. This would mean long-term rates would surge to high single digits or low double digits.

Ultimately, US short-term rates will rise as well, potentially to very high levels, to combat inflation and protect the dollar. Higher financing costs, coupled with inflation, would send the United States into a period of stagnant growth or potentially worse.

2. US Federal Government

The US government will face a similar challenge: out of control entitlement programs, a huge structural deficit, and surging interest rates. The US government will likely take several actions: (a) dramatically cut benefits to beneficiaries under current entitlement programs, (b) dramatically raise taxes and/or (c) inflate the US government out of its debt crisis.

As with every crisis, it will be set off by a catalyst. In my view, any or all of the following are likely catalysts:

a. Monetization of US Housing Debt

The housing crisis is in its earliest stages. Those that borrowed using ARMs are now seeing their interest rates increase. Already stretched by higher gas prices and inflation, many borrowers do not have the resources to pay a higher mortgage payment. As a result, more and more homeowners are defaulting on their mortgages or trying to sell houses that they can no longer afford. Accordingly, there has been, and will continue to be, a greater stock of housing on the market. The increased housing inventory, along with higher mortgage interest rates, will continue to depress housing prices.

If the past is any indication, the US government will not have the discipline to allow the market to work through this mess. It will move aggressively to either guarantee or buy (through a government agency such as Freddie Mac or Fannie Mae) the mortgages of less creditworthy investors. This will temporarily support the housing market, but will have terrible consequences for the federal government.

When this happens, the US government will, in effect, have nationalized (or monetized) a portion of the US housing stock or mortgage market and added hundreds of billions of dollars to an already untenable debt load.

With this, foreign investors may well flee the dollar to an even greater extent than is currently happening, and the dollar will continue to collapse, sending inflation and long-term rates higher.

b. Fire Sale of Dollars by Foreigners

Currently, the US dollar still maintains its status as the world's reserve currency. However, it is weakening due to terrible US monetary and fiscal policy, thereby putting its status in jeopardy.

With the dollar as the world's reserve currency, some countries have tied their currencies to the US dollar to maintain currency stability (called a "peg"). The net effect is that these countries see their currencies go up and down vis-à-vis the dollar. With the dollar's steady and unrelenting decline, many of these countries, including Kuwait and the Ukraine,[36] have abandoned the dollar peg, preferring to either allow their currencies to float and/or pegging them to a broader array of currencies.

A dollar peg, however, has significant benefits for the United States. A dollar peg often requires the "pegging" country to accumulate dollars to manage its currency (if its currency strengthens against the dollar, the country often buys dollars and places them in foreign reserve to keep its currency depressed against the dollar). This creates additional demand for dollars than would otherwise exist, thereby keeping the dollar stronger than it would otherwise be.

China and Saudi Arabia are the two most significant countries with a dollar peg. (Although China relaxed its "hard" peg to the dollar in

2005, it still manages its currency to the dollar.) China has accumulated nearly $1 trillion in US dollar assets in foreign reserves, holdings it has accumulated to manage its currency, among other reasons.[37] Saudi Arabia has also accumulated hundreds of billions of dollars. Any significant movement away from the dollar by these countries would have the effect of reducing the demand for dollars, sending the dollar plummeting further and pushing up US interest rates and inflation.

In addition, oil sales across the world have been denominated in dollars for decades. However, with respect to Middle Eastern, Asian, and African oil producers, this makes little sense. First, many of these countries transact more business with Europe than the United States, and thus have a greater need for euros than dollars. Second, many of these countries already have significant exposure to the US dollar, so diversifying into other currencies makes sense. Finally, the Bush administration has made few friends in the region, and the thought of "tweaking" the United States by abandoning the dollar has noneconomic allure to many of these countries as well. In short, it is just a matter of time before this happens.

When these nations start using other currencies to a greater extent, the dollar will suffer a further fall. It is unlikely that China will make any dramatic moves before the Beijing Olympic Games in 2008. And it is also unlikely that China will take any action that will result in a dollar "panic," given that it holds nearly $1 trillion in dollar assets and is interested in protecting the value of those assets. But the migration away from the dollar will continue. The bleeding will either be slow and long term (probably the most likely case) or abrupt, as countries flee the dollar (while not the most likely case, this is certainly not out of the question).

c. Downgrade of US Treasury, or Put on "Watch"

The major rating agencies (e.g., Moody's and Standard & Poor's) have received considerable criticism for their shoddy work in rating mortgage-backed and subprime mortgage securities. Mindful of this criticism, these agencies might be much quicker to act on US treasuries.

US treasuries carry the highest credit rating in the world (AAA). The United States shares this rating with just twenty other countries.[38]

Based on the US government's balance sheet and huge unfunded liabilities, US treasuries should not be rated AAA by Moody's, and should be, at a minimum, put on "credit watch" by the rating agencies. After all, Japan's sovereign debt has a lower rating than US treasuries, even though Japan has better underlying fundamentals than does the United States.

Yes, it is true that the United States will never default on its debt. In fact, it is almost impossible for a nation issuing debt in its own currency to default on its debt. After all, it can just print more money to repay its debt. Of course, in doing so, a country will have devalued its currency and spurred inflation (i.e., inflated its way out of its obligations). This is, in effect, the equivalent of defaulting, since the investor holding US treasuries would receive repayment in a much lower valued currency.

Take the case of a European buying a ten-year Treasury note at the end of 2002. At that time, the euro traded at parity with the dollar (one dollar = one euro). By April 2008, the euro traded at nearly $1.60. Thus, if the European sold his or her Treasury note and converted the dollars back to euros, he or she would have lost nearly 40 percent of principal on his investment.

One might expect to lose a modest amount in currency devaluation (or make a modest gain in currency appreciation). However, a 40 percent loss is unacceptable for a "reserve" currency. And it is my view that even at this level the dollar is overvalued—particularly against many Asian and Middle Eastern currencies—and foreign holders of US treasuries will see the value of their dollar holdings decline further.

Due to the US's massive unfunded entitlement programs and the declining dollar, it is increasingly likely that one of the major credit rating agencies will downgrade US treasuries at some point in the near to medium term (within the next five years).[39]

A monetization of the housing debt or a sale of US dollar assets by the Chinese or other foreign investors might be the catalyst that results in a downgrade of US treasuries, or at a minimum, US treasuries being put on "watch" by rating agencies. Again, when this occurs, a dollar rout will likely follow.

d. Rampant Inflation

Inflation may well be a significant problem for the United States over the next several years. By creating more money supply and keeping rates artificially low, the US government is debasing the value of the dollar, making it increasingly worthless and boosting the price of almost all goods and services. Import prices, particularly commodities, are surging in value.

Wages have yet to see the impact of inflation, a key distinction from the 1970s. However, a significant reason for wage inflation in the 1970s was the "birth dearth" of the Great Depression[40] and the baby boomer generation, which meant the United States had fewer mature workers during the 1970s and more adolescents. This spurred competition for workers, and spurred wage inflation, leading to a decade and half of economic problems.

Worst Case Scenario

In the worst case scenario, the United States continues on its current path and does not address its ballooning entitlement programs and military footprint. Rather, it continues to address its problems with "quick fix" Band-Aids that bridge America from one crisis to the next. Since these "remedies" often involve more easy money, the US dollar collapses, sending interest rates and inflation soaring. US treasuries are downgraded, as investors flee US treasuries for investments that will provide a better store of value. Faced with massive entitlement programs and much higher interest costs, the US government retrenches significantly, particularly during a time of economic stress. The US military presence abroad is dramatically and radically reduced to cut costs.

The result will be a period of stagnant growth, with inflation, or a deep inflationary recession, or worse. What happens to the rest of the world is another matter. If the United States falls into something less than a deep recession, the rest of the world may escape with a milder one, and China may emerge as the next global power. In that case, China can use its massive trove of foreign reserves (albeit diminished in value as the dollar declines) to invest in its own country, and spur internal consumption. With its economic strength, the Chinese currency, the yuan, becomes the global medium of exchange, and nations gravitate toward China from a foreign policy perspective. The Sino century begins. If the United States falls into a deeper recession or worse, we have no idea what will befall the rest of the world, since the US is still such a large component of the worldwide economy.

Conclusion

The rest of this book will focus on detailing a series of policies that would have the effect of averting an economic and/or foreign policy calamity, and laying the foundation for yet another American century.

With only moderate sacrifice, America can transition from a nation with profound economic and foreign policy problems to one that will continue its global leadership position into the twenty-first century, to the benefit of Americans and other peoples across the world.

PART II

DEMOGRAPHIC CHALLENGES

- Immigration
- Social Security
- Replacing Pension System for Retirement
- Medicare

Introduction

America's population is aging, which presents a significant challenge for US policymakers. This section outlines the problems caused by an aging population, and provides a series of solutions that attempt to address these problems. These solutions include immigration reform, an overhaul of America's entitlement system (Social Security and Medicare), and a new pension system for private savings.

Problems:

1. America has not saved enough for the retirement of its baby boomer generation.
2. As the baby boomers retire, the United States will have to replace them in the workforce, and
3. Unless replaced, a declining middle-aged workforce (as a percentage of the overall population) will push wages upward as employers compete for a relatively smaller pool of mature workers. This will create an inflationary problem that rivals or exceeds that of the 1970s.

Imperatives:

- America must replace aging baby boomers to maintain economic strength, a low inflationary environment, and its competitive advantage versus its global competitors.
- America must dramatically reform Social Security and Medicare in preparation for the baby boomers' retirement, or these entitlement systems will bankrupt the United States.

CHAPTER 2

The Economics of Demographics

As the world worries about commodity shortages, the United States and other industrialized nations should focus on another increasingly scarce resource—human capital. Almost every industrialized country faces population declines in the decades to come, a problem without modern precedent.

Aging Industrialized Countries:
Wage Inflation and Retirement Benefits Will Soar

Japan's population is now shrinking; industrialized Europe is not far behind.[1] China, the world's most populous country, may be the first nation to age before it industrializes, largely due to its one-child policy.[2] This crisis has been largely ignored by policymakers and the public, yet the "birth dearth" may reach crisis proportions in the next forty years.[3] Among developed countries, only the United States has a growing population, due in large part to our liberal immigration policy.[4]

The implications of a flattening or even declining population are profound. For younger workers, it means that taxes will likely rise to pay entitlements to retirees. Elderly Americans, on the other hand, will likely see cutbacks in their benefits. Economic growth will slow as more people are either retired or semiretired, and as more capital is diverted away from investment activities and used to support an aging population. Wage pressures (inflation) will build, as the percentage of middle-aged workers declines and employers compete for a declining pool of mature workers. Wage inflation will be a worldwide problem, as nations fight over a tighter and tighter pool of labor.

America's Demographics: The Good New and the Bad News

America is projected to maintain a growing population, even as the baby boomer generation starts retiring in 2011. However, the impact of this generation, both good and bad, cannot be understated.

Demographic Bubble. Middle-aged workers tend to be more productive than younger ones; they are also prodigious spenders and have an overall beneficial impact to the economy. From the mid-1960s through the early 1980s, the percentage of middle-aged workers declined. This decline can be explained by two factors. First, there was a decline in births[5] during the Great Depression and World War II era, resulting in fewer middle-aged workers during the 1970s. Second, there was a dramatic increase in the number of births after World War II, which meant that America's population trended younger in general. These contrasting trends caused the percentage of middle-aged workers to decline during the 1970s, as illustrated by chart 2-1.

The trend reversed in the 1980s. By this time, the entire baby boomer generation had entered the workforce, and the percentage of middle-aged workers started climbing steadily. This trend continued throughout the 1980s and 1990s.

Economics of Demographics: Productivity, Stock Market, and Inflation. The economics of the relative "birth dearth" of the 1930s and early 1940s and the baby boomer generation have been significant. First, the relative shortage of middle-aged workers during the 1970s created a period of competition for workers, as employers vied for a declining (as

CHART 2-1

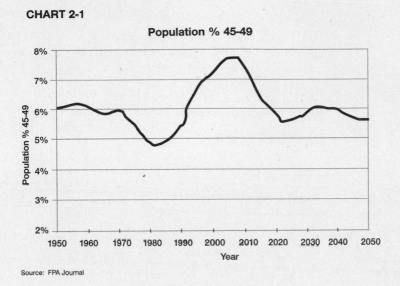

Population % 45-49

Source: FPA Journal

a percentage of the overall population) pool of mature workers. Accordingly, wage inflation surged during the mid-1960s through early 1980s and abated as the baby boomers started entering the workforce in full.[6] Further, America was also investing heavily in the baby boomer generation, an asset that would not start producing for this nation, en masse, until the 1980s.

These demographic trends had a significant impact on the equity markets. With a heavy investment in human capital (baby boomers) and inflation, the "real" returns from the US stock market were terrible from the mid 1960s through the early 1980s. As the baby boomers started maturing in the early 1980s, productivity started increasing and inflation declined, since more workers and greater productivity meant less wage inflation. The stock market started its meteoric rise as noted in chart 2-2, which would almost track the maturation of this generation.

As the baby boomer generation matured, America's demographics changed; there was a more plentiful workforce of mature workers. Not surprisingly, wage inflation subsided and the stock market started its relentless ascent, providing this country with its greatest productive

CHART 2-2

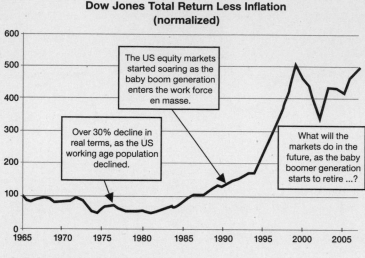

Dow Jones Total Return Less Inflation (normalized)

The US equity markets started soaring as the baby boom generation enters the work force en masse.

Over 30% decline in real terms, as the US working age population declined.

What will the markets do in the future, as the baby boomer generation starts to retire ...?

Source: Bloomberg; Salient Partners, L.P.

asset from the early 1980s through the present. There is almost a direct correlation with the demographic shifts that occurred over the past four decades and inflation, the US economy, and stock market.

And, as illustrated by the demographics chart, the demographic trends that assisted the economy and stock market during the 1980s through 2007 will start to reverse, with a vengeance, in 2011. This has potentially negative implications for the US stock markets and inflation, and on the baby boomer generation, which will have a significant amount of retirement savings in the market.

The Demographic Tide. The Reagan revolution, the Clinton era of prosperity, and Greenspan's genius might be attributable to the policies of each man. Or these men may have had the good fortune in formulating policy when America had an incredible asset, the baby boomer generation, at full productive capacity. But now the question is, what happens when this generation retires, particularly if the United States has not prepared for it? The answer is that America will have a much thinner margin of error than in the past, and each day that passes without tackling the impact of this demographic shift narrows the margin of error. The following chapters will focus on the four issues that must be addressed in conjunction with the impending retirement of the baby boomer generation: immigration policy, Social Security reform, and Medicare reform and a new system of retirement savings.

CHAPTER 3

Immigration: America's "Free Lunch"

A country that is aging has, whether consciously or not, underinvested in one or more generations and does not have enough younger workers to support a growing group of retirees. Unlike other "assets" (e.g., machinery), a country cannot build more workers in short order. The lead time is not months or even years; it is decades: twenty years, give or take. However, a nation can find more workers by "importing" them from other countries to fill in "demographic gaps," and the United States has done this better than almost any nation during the modern era. This chapter will explore the economics of immigration and outline a case for more liberal immigration policies, accompanied by tight border enforcement, as a potential solution to the demographic issues resulting from America's aging population.

The Immigration "Free Lunch"

Immigration represents an immediate transfer of wealth from other nations to the United States of at least $150,000 per adult immigrant, a free lunch if there ever was one. The following example illustrates the point.

Assume an unskilled worker from Mexico, aged eighteen. It takes a substantial investment to produce an unskilled worker. While the investment in formal education may not great, the basics of shelter, and other necessities do cost money. To get a comparable person in the United States to age eighteen would cost approximately $8,300 per year. This represents the basic cost of educating, feeding, and clothing a person. Thus, producing an eighteen-year-old worker in the United States would cost nearly $150,000.[1] This does not include the parents' investment to teach a child the very basics necessary to function in society, to work, and to raise a family. If you count this investment, the cost of a menial laborer "manufactured" in the United States would be more than double that cost, or over $400,000.[2]

If one assumes that over 1.5 million people immigrate to the United States each year (legally and illegally),[3] this represents a unilateral transfer of at least $225 billion per annum (low estimate) to over $600 billion per annum (high estimate). If one assumes that 300,000 of these immigrants are skilled and college educated, which should occur under a liberalized immigration policy,[4] the benefit to the United States is over $25 billion greater in each case.[5] When taking this into account, our current account deficit is reduced from a staggering 6 percent of GDP (2007) to a more manageable level of 3 to 4 percent of GDP (based on the low estimate).[6] Or, when taking into account the value of parenting, the current account deficit is nearly eliminated. Overall, this represents a transfer of wealth from the rest of the world to the United States of between $2 trillion to $5 trillion—a staggering number.[7]

When viewed in purely economic terms, immigration represents a phenomenal value for America. It offers the means to (a) narrow the United States' budget deficit by taxing all immigrants, including illegal immigrants, (b) reduce wage inflation, and (c) address America's demographic problems. In addition, a more liberal immigration policy will narrow the United States' current account deficit (discussed in a later chapter).

Narrowing Budget Deficit; Shoring Up Social Security and Medicare

If the United States adopted a policy that provided for the registration and taxation of all illegal immigrants, the impact on the US treasury would be immediate and significant. In particular, assuming that approximately 75 percent of this group included wage earners, the impact on the US Treasury (tax revenues, including Social Security and Medicare) would be added revenues of as much as $50 billion per annum.[8] The additional revenues would help shore up Medicare and Social Security, America's sagging entitlement programs.

Additional Benefits: Eliminating Unfair Cost Advantage

A more liberalized immigration plan would benefit American workers and immigrants alike. Currently, employers hiring illegal immigrants are able to pay them less than Americans because illegal immigrants have little bargaining power and often do not receive benefits. Even the barest benefits of an American worker are significant, even if you exclude private health care. These benefits include the minimum wage, Social Security, and Medicare. Social Security and Medicare taxes add approximately 15.3 percent to payroll costs.[9] This has effectively made American labor uncompetitive in many menial jobs, even if the US worker was willing to work for the same wages as the illegal immigrant. That is, if an American worker was willing to work for $10 on a construction site, that worker would cost at least 15 to 20 percent more after factoring in benefits, taxes, etc. than an illegal immigrant.

By liberalizing immigration policies but taxing immigrants, the United States would ensure a steady flow of labor. More importantly, these immigrants would not have an unfair pricing advantage vis-à-vis US labor. In this regard, US workers would benefit by competing on a level playing field with immigrants. Also, immigrants are currently being exploited by employers, who understand that illegal immigrants have little bargaining power (i.e., they cannot complain about work conditions or pay to the authorities). This enables employers to pay them less than minimum wage and to ignore labor laws. This creates labor conditions within the United States that are not consistent with American values or standards. This result is the exploitation of illegal immigrants.

The Plan: Controlled, Liberalized Immigration

While immigration does offer a "free lunch" from an economic perspective, it is difficult to deny that uncontrolled immigration also presents a national security problem. Thus, the United States must control its borders for national security reasons and should also ensure that immigrants pay the same taxes as Americans. Accordingly, the United States should have a controlled but highly liberalized immigration policy for both skilled and unskilled labor. This would entail building a fence or finding another means to control its border. At the same time, the United States should greatly liberalize immigration as it did, with great success, in the 1940s through 1960s.[10] The combination of the two will result in a more secure nation with a plentiful supply of tax-paying labor that will support an increasing number of retirees in the coming years.

Liberalized Immigration: The Precedent

The first phase of an immigration plan would provide for people to immigrate to the United States in a faster, more efficient manner. Anyone who does not have a criminal record and wants to immigrate to the United States would be allowed to do so under the terms of this immigration policy. This policy is not without an historical analogue, namely the *Bracero* ("helping arms") Program that started in the 1940s.

The history of the *Bracero* Program provides a useful illustration of how a controlled but liberalized immigration program allows the government to regulate immigration, cuts down on illegal immigration, and promotes economic activity during labor shortages. During World War II, a shortage of agricultural labor was caused by the disgraceful internment of Japanese citizens in detention camps because of public suspicion of espionage. In response, the Roosevelt administration negotiated the *Bracero* Agreement with the Mexican government. This agreement guaranteed temporary agricultural laborers (known as *braceros*) a minimum wage of thirty cents per hour and exemption from the draft. The program brought in 220,000 documented Mexican workers between 1942 and 1947.[11] Under pressure from agribusiness owners, the agreement was renewed after the war, and 300,000 legal *braceros* entered the United States annually until 1964, when the program was eliminated.[12] Liberalized immigration reduced apprehensions of illegal aliens by *95 percent* between 1953 and 1959. During that same period, legal immigration from Mexico doubled.[13]

The elimination of the *Bracero* Program in 1964 meant that many potential immigrants had to seek extralegal means in order to immigrate to the United States, causing a rise in the level of illegal immigration.[14] Between 1964 and 1976, the number of apprehensions of illegal aliens increased by 1,000 percent.[15] The success of the *Bracero* Program demonstrates that a combination of strict enforcement and liberalized immigration policies can stem the flow of *illegal* immigration (so long as there are harsh penalties for US employers who hire illegal aliens, a matter addressed later in this chapter) *and* provide a plentiful flow of immigrant labor to support American industry.

The Proposed Program

General. The proposed program would permit those who want to immigrate to the United States to pay a reasonable fee to cover processing costs to prove they are not a convicted felon. Their backgrounds would be verified through a criminal check in their country of origin. This would require the cooperation by the countries of origin. Accordingly, these countries would have to enter into agreements with the United States to provide the US with background information on the proposed immigrants. Since the liberalized immigration policy would be combined with strict border enforcement, few would enter the United States without undergoing this process.

The background check process would not be perfect. Without question, many foreign countries do not have sophisticated record-keeping systems, making verification difficult at best. However, the

United States should rely on whatever records are available that can be accessed relatively quickly, to at least provide some control over the immigration process. Under the immigration treaties, countries of origin would also agree to take back immigrants who commit crimes in the United States. Once a person is determined fit for immigration to the United States, they would be issued a Social Security card and pay taxes on any income earned in the US. *This would ensure that immigrants pay the same taxes as American citizens, putting US citizens and immigrants on the same level when competing for a job in this country.* In addition, each immigrant would be fingerprinted and provide a DNA sample. These would be entered in a national database, providing a means to track workers and to find and prosecute illegal immigrants who commit crimes.

Assimilating Immigrants in the United States

The estimated 13 million illegal immigrants already in the United States[16] would have to pay the same fee and submit to a background check, fingerprinting, and DNA test. There should be a timeline for them to go through the process, perhaps two to five years. If a person has not undergone this process within this time frame, they would be subject to deportation. Anyone employing them would be subject to significant and immediate criminal charges and penalties, including jail time. This policy would dramatically reduce the incentive to hire illegal immigrants.

By enabling illegal immigrants to become legal, the United States could also address another complaint made by some opponents of immigration: namely, that immigrants are not assimilating and pose a threat to the culture of the United States. This criticism is largely being lodged against the illegal immigrants from Mexico and Central America. However, in some respects, this criticism is misplaced. Most of these immigrants share the same religious faith as most Americans, a key distinction from immigration patterns in some Western European nations. And most immigrants are hard working and law abiding.

However, there is some legitimacy to the argument that these immigrants are not assimilating as they should. This problem could be better addressed by allowing these immigrants to come into the mainstream of American life. The best way for this to happen is to allow them to become legal residents, and then to provide a powerful incentive to learn English, American traditions, and culture—American citizenship. By making it relatively easy to become a legal resident of the United States, illegal immigrants will no longer have to live in the shadows, away from mainstream America. This, along with more stringent citizenship requirements (discussed later in this chapter), should prove beneficial to assimilation.

Securing the Border

The next, and seemingly incongruous, step in this liberalized immigration regime is a tightly controlled border. This step would ensure that illegal immigration is almost entirely eradicated. After all, if the United States has an extremely liberal immigration policy, then only criminals or suspected criminals would seek to immigrate to the United States illegally. The security fence should be a double fence or an electronic one along the nation's southern border, with sophisticated sensors to ensure that illegal immigration flows are greatly reduced. With less incentive to immigrate to the United States illegally, the flow of illegal immigrants would be dramatically reduced, which should make it easier to police the border.

As noted in a subsequent chapter on the US military, our military would man the fence to enforce the borders. In this regard, the military would resume its traditional role of securing American borders. In addition, the US military should fly aerial reconnaissance to further enforce the border. A fence would not eliminate all illegal immigration. But along with a liberalized immigration policy and strict enforcement of immigration laws, a border fence would greatly reduce the flow of illegal immigration. It would also have the benefit of halting the flow of contraband, particularly illegal drugs, into the United States.

Ensuring Security

Immigrants from countries on the international watch list would require additional processing. This would include a number of countries from the Middle East and even Africa. To ensure that such persons do not try to immigrate through Mexico, the United States would require proof of Mexican citizenship and perhaps even a language test for passage into the US. Finally, all immigrants coming to the United States would have to submit to fingerprinting and also provide DNA for a national database for tracking purposes.

Issuance of Work Visas

For those who immigrate to the Unites States legally, the United States would issue temporary work visas. Visas would automatically renew every two years if the worker had not been convicted of a felony and had held a job within six months of the expiration of the visa and paid taxes over this period of time. This would ensure that the guest workers had behaved themselves, been gainfully employed and generally been productive members of society during their stay. Providing proof of employment should be relatively easy: a pay stub that could be matched against the government database reflecting payment of Social Security taxes would suffice.

To the extent that an immigrant did not renew his or her card, he or she would be subject to deportation. Further, any employer who employed a worker with an expired work visa would be subject to extremely strict fines and jail time. To eliminate visa fraud, visas would have a computer chip and/or identification number that could be submitted via telephone or computer and matched against the worker.

Harsh Fines Against Those Who Harbor
or Employ Illegal Immigrants

Each employer of an immigrant would be required to submit the chip
or ID number via phone or computer before hiring a worker, along
with filing a W-8 (tax reporting). This process would ensure that the
immigrant being hired was in this country legally and that his or her
work visa was still valid. Any employer who did not go through this
process, or employed an illegal immigrant, could be subject to harsh
fines, penalties, and even jail time. Further, a landlord would be required to check the status of an immigrant before leasing a residence
or apartment to him or her. Landlords should only be allowed to enter
into one-year leases with legal immigrants. Renewals should entail the
same process and place the onus on the landlord to check the tenant's
visa to ensure that the immigrant is still legal.

By making it easy to legally immigrate to the United States, there
would be no incentive to be here illegally. Accordingly, both employers and landlords who aid and abet those in the United States illegally
should pay stiff fines and face jail time. Along with a much tighter
border, this would be the quid pro quo of liberalized immigration.

Gaining United States Citizenship

While immigration should be liberalized, the United States should
have a stringent system for gaining US citizenship. The process should
require seven years of legal residency, payment of all due taxes over
that time, and sponsorship by two US citizens (who have no felony
convictions). Immigrants would be tested on their English language
skills and our system of government.

The US Constitution requires that any child born in the United
States automatically becomes a US citizen. This creates a significant
problem. Many illegal immigrants have children while residing in the
United States and this results in a situation where the US government can deport the father and/or mother of a child who is an Amer-

ican citizen. This leaves the child in a terrible situation. He or she is a US citizen but must follow his or her parents home when they are deported. This problem would be further exacerbated if the United States had a liberal immigration policy. Thus, the United States should pass a constitutional amendment providing that a child cannot become a US citizen simply by being born in America. Instead, a child can only become a US citizen if one of the parents is also a US citizen. This solves an incongruous and largely unfair situation where both parents are illegal yet their child is legal by virtue of being born in the United States.[17]

As for social programs, immigrants would not be entitled to participate in Social Security or Medicare unless they became US citizens. This would encourage immigrants to undertake the citizenship process. Once they became citizens, the immigrants would get credit for all amounts paid into Social Security and Medicare from inception (i.e., even before they were citizens).

The Time to Act Is Now

America has taken for granted the benefits from free and steady flow of overseas talent. However, this trend may not continue forever. In particular, the rest of the world is starting to realize the profound benefits of immigration. This recognition could usher in an era of fierce competition for labor, both skilled and unskilled. Over time, countries may start paying incentives to immigrants, undercutting the economics of immigration significantly. Facing the prospects of a shrinking population, Germany is now developing a more friendly immigration policy to lure immigrants. Regrettably, the United States is now tightening immigration standards making it more difficult to immigrate. These new, tighter procedures are coming at precisely the wrong time. The United States is graying and, as noted above, immigration offers a means to infuse the country with more young workers.

In addition, the US economy and collapsing dollar have made the

Unites Stated a less attractive place for immigration. Many immigrants' countries of origin are developing at a rapid pace and offering opportunities unheard of a decade ago. This development will make it more enticing for immigrants to stay home instead of immigrating to the United States. Given these factors, America needs to maintain its competitive advantage on immigration and make the door to this nation wider than ever.

CHAPTER 4

Social Security

The United States' aging population is also putting pressure on America's entitlement system, particularly Social Security and Medicare. Between these two programs, the net present value of future liabilities total $40 trillion.[1] To put this in perspective, the current shortfall is greater than all of the stocks, bonds, and cash held by US citizens and equates to as much as $133,000[2] for each man, woman, and child in the United States.[3] Given these huge unfunded liabilities, the central question is how to address the shortfalls in Social Security and Medicare in a cost-effective, sensible manner. That is the topic of the following two chapters. The first chapter deals with Social Security because it generally gets more press than Medicare. It is also the simplest problem to solve and, thus, a good place to start.

Social Security: "Pay As You Go" System

Currently, the Social Security system takes in more revenues than are paid out. The excess revenues are put in a "trust fund," which invests in US treasuries. In theory, the trust fund has enough assets (approximately $2.2 trillion)[4] to cover retirees well into the future. The trust fund, however, is invested in US treasuries. So, in effect, the government borrows the money from the trust fund to finance current operations and issues IOUs back to the trust fund. Worse yet, the government's budget numbers include net Social Security taxes in its overall revenues, providing a false sense of the government's finances, a point already discussed. Despite the obvious breach of fiduciary duty issues that accompany a trustee (the government) using trust assets for its own benefit, the Social Security system has been transformed from a "funded" pension system to a "pay as you go" (or "pay go," for short) system.

A "pay go" system requires that the system raise enough revenues from current workers to cover the benefits being paid to retirees. Indeed, Social Security has taken in more revenues than it has paid out since the inception of the program in 1935.[5] For the past thirty to forty years, however, the baby boomer generation has been paying into the system[6] but is set to start retiring en masse over the next twenty years. This demographic shift will cause significant stress on the system. The following chart shows the Social Security shortfalls over the next twenty years.

CHART 4-1

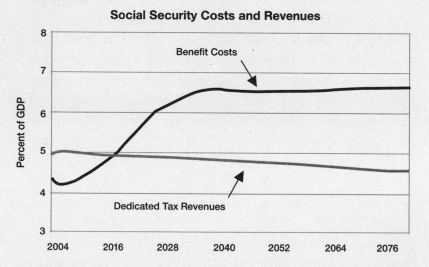

Social Security Costs and Revenues

Source: Congressional Budget Office, Centrists. Org (2004 Trustees Report)[7]

The trend lines are dismal for two very simple reasons. First, the baby boomer generation is starting to draw on Social Security, and not enough younger workers exist to support this generation of retirees. Second, Americans are living longer and being paid higher benefits.

Tying Immigration into Social Security

In a "pay go" system, the entire system is based on ensuring that the United States has enough younger workers to support the current group of retirees. However, as the baby boomer generation starts to retire, the ratio of workers to retirees is steadily declining. Currently, we have 3.3 workers for every retiree. By 2030, the ratio will fall to 2 workers for every retiree.[8] As the ratio of workers to retirees shrinks, policymakers will have to consider some unpleasant alternatives, such as raising taxes and/or cutting benefits.

Given these dismal choices, US policymakers should consider a third option: finding more young workers to support the current set of retirees through a more liberal immigration policy. With 13 million illegal immigrants,[9] the United States has a large population that can be taxed for the benefit of its current group of retirees. So policymakers in Washington should carefully consider America's immigration policies not only to promote economic growth (addressed above) but as a necessary move to bolster the flagging Social Security system. In this regard, a liberal immigration policy is almost an imperative in the United States' "pay go" Social Security system. By legalizing all of the illegal immigrants in the United States and having them pay payroll taxes, the US would generate nearly $1 trillion or more in payroll tax revenues in the future, representing 10 to 20 percent of the projected shortfall.

Changing the Character of the System

The next step is to be honest about the character of the system. The politicians in Washington do not consider the Social Security system a national pension plan. If they did, the revenues from the system would be put in a trust and invested in a broadly diversified portfolio, consistent with other pension plans.[10] Instead, the Social Security Trust Fund is invested in US treasuries. Again, the US government is writing IOUs to itself to pay future benefits.

Rather than continuing this charade, the government should redefine Social Security as a national *insurance* program for those who did not save enough for retirement. In this regard, Social Security would be means tested (i.e., checking the financial situation of each individual applicant), providing better benefits for those most in need and less for those who saved appropriately. Since the overall benefits would be modest, there would be little incentive for future retirees to shirk saving for retirement and rely solely on Social Security. Further, a more sensible plan for promoting saving for retirement, outlined below, would complement a reconfigured Social Security system.

Changing the Benefits Under Social Security

By changing the character of the system, future retirees would understand that the Social Security system is no longer a full-blown pension plan, but a plan where the worker would receive varying benefits based on other sources of income in retirement. The quid pro quo for future workers would be twofold. First, the Social Security system would continue and be available for future generations. Without these drastic changes and the taxation of immigrants, the system will be bankrupt and benefit no one. Second, taxes would not have to increase dramatically, if at all, to preserve the system.

To be sure, the affluent will see their benefits eliminated entirely, an outcome that they might find unfair. However, the alternative might be even less palatable. The wealthy would have to pay substantially higher taxes to fully fund the current system. Or, if the government continues to borrow at current levels, the wealthy will live in a country that is basically bankrupt and face potentially devastating devaluations in the dollar and inflation. Both of these outcomes would be more detrimental to the wealthy than foregoing Social Security benefits. The poor would, ideally, see very little change in benefits going forward.

The specific changes in Social Security are outlined below:

1. *Limited Benefits. Means Testing.* Benefits should be tied to retirement income levels. The higher a retiree's income level, the lower their benefits from Social Security. In addition, the defined contribution system—401(k) plans, IRA plans, etc.—would be changed to address the need for higher personal savings in the future, as outlined in a following chapter.

2. *Index Age to Average Lifespan.* Shortly after Social Security was introduced, life expectancy at birth was approximately sixty-four years.[11] So the average worker paid into Social Security, but given the life expectancy of that era, did not draw much in benefits.[12] As life expectancy has increased, the retirement age has not been increased proportionately. Accordingly, now the average worker's lifespan is seventy-four years.[13] So, American taxpayers are paying greater benefits because the percentage of workers reaching retirement is greater and, after reaching retirement, they are living longer and receiving benefits for a longer period of time. The best manner to address this issue is to "index" the retirement age to the average lifespan of an American worker. By way of example, the age at which a person would qualify for Social Security benefits would be equal to some percentage of the average American's life span. If the average lifespan is seventy years for those born in 1960 and the new retirement age for them is sixty-seven, the retirement age for someone born in 2000 with a life expectancy of seventy-seven years would be higher, say seventy years or more.[14] The new retirement age would be set every ten years based on the average life expectancy for the applicable generation of Americans. Thus, the new retirement age would go up every decade, but most likely only incrementally.

3. *Index Benefits to Inflation, Not Wages.* Benefits are currently linked to wage increases rather than inflation. Wage increases generally track a combination of inflation *and* worker productivity increases. While it is entirely appropriate for retirees to maintain their purchasing power by indexing benefits to inflation, it is not fair to further increase their benefits due to worker productivity increases. Productivity increases are due to greater worker efficiency and/or capital investment by employers. Thus, productivity increases should be shared by workers and employers and should not inure to the benefit of retirees.

4. *Enable Workers to Save More Tax-Deferred Income.* US workers should be able to save more tax-deferred income, provided they enroll in a new retirement savings regime discussed below. This new regime would be a cross between the old-line pension plans, with professional management overseeing large asset pools, and the current 401(k) plans. This would give rise to the "ownership" society touted by President Bush, without the government intervening in the investment process.

This plan would have the following benefits:

Halt Redistribution of Wealth from Future Generations to the Current One. Currently, Social Security represents a vast transfer of wealth from younger generations to older generations. On the whole, today's retirees are getting higher benefits than what they paid into the system. America is borrowing heavily to pay these benefits. This means that future generations will pay for these benefits in the form of higher taxes and/or reduced benefits to retire this debt.

Maintain Social Security for Those Most in Need: The Poor. Social Security should represent a compact between the US government and its citizens. If a person worked and paid taxes over the course of his or her lifetime, the government should provide them with at least a modest retirement through a social safety net. If the person ended up doing well and saved plenty for retirement, benefits would be reduced, if not eliminated entirely. This would allow benefits to flow to those most in need.

Maintain System for Poor Without Draconian Tax Increases. This is the quid pro quo for wealthier retirees. That is, if the current level of benefits is maintained for *all* retirees, the tax burden will have to increase dramatically. If that happens, the burden will likely fall on the wealthy and the tax increase could be quite large. By targeting benefits to the poor, the overall tax burden can be maintained at current levels or perhaps even reduced, a benefit to the wealthy.

Lower Overall Costs of System (Target 4 percent of GDP). Social Security should not consume more than its current level of approximately 4 percent of GDP.[15] However, without dramatic changes, Social Security will consume 6.2 percent of GDP by 2030.[16] Through means testing, age indexing, and expanding the worker pool through immigration, the United States can maintain its spending on Social Security at 4 percent of GDP and avoid punitive tax increases on the wealthy.

Many of these elements are found in other plans, including President Bush's proposed plan to reform Social Security.[17] Given the controversy surrounding President Bush's personal retirement accounts (PRAs), many of the commonsense proposals that came out of the White House were ignored. By eliminating PRAs but improving the 401(k) system as outlined below, most aspects of Bush's plan could be preserved and Social Security placed on firm footing for generations to come, without dramatically increasing taxes.

CHAPTER 5

Saving for Retirement. Pension Reform

In conjunction with reforming Social Security, the United States should refine the manner in which most Americans are now saving for retirement. Over the past twenty years, Americans have seen the demise of the defined benefit plans (DB plans), or traditional pension plans. Under a DB plan, an employer contributes into a retirement plan on behalf of its employees. The plan, in turn, is managed by the employer or its designee. Assuming a minimum number of years of service, workers are guaranteed an annual payment or lump-sum payment upon retirement. However, the employer is obligated to make up any shortfall between the benefits promised and the retirement assets on hand.

Unfortunately, many of America's global competitors do not provide similar benefits. Facing an increasingly fierce global marketplace, US corporations are loath to continue these plans and put themselves at a cost disadvantage versus foreign corporations. DB plans are thus being replaced with defined contribution plans (DC plans), which include 401(k) plans. Under these plans, employees make contributions from pretax wages (subject to a maximum contribution). Contributions to these plans are not taxed until withdrawn by the employee, starting at age fifty-nine and a half. DC Plans allow employees to save for retirement in a tax-advantaged manner. However, the onus to manage the assets and the risk of any retirement shortfalls fall squarely on the employee rather than the employer.

DC plans present several problems for workers. First, many workers do not have the skill to manage their assets like pension plans of old. Accordingly, over time the returns generated from the average 401(k) plan fall behind those of pension plans—by nearly 1 percent per annum during the 1985–2001 period, excluding fees and expenses.[1] While this may not seem like a lot, this equates to about a 20 percent difference in retirement assets over a thirty-year period (assuming an 8 percent annual return). Second, fees and expenses paid by participants in 401(k) plans are usually much higher than those paid by the typical pension plan. Given their much larger size, pension plans have the buying power to reduce management fees and administrative costs, whereas most 401(k) accounts—the average one being $60,000—do not.[2] Accordingly, the proposed reform would require corporations to pool employee assets in a common retirement pool like the pension plans of old. However, the risk of loss would be shifted from the employer to the employee, as with current 401(k) plans. By pooling assets and having professional management of the overall pool, the participants would generally pay lower fees and have better management and, most likely, better returns over time. The following chart shows the benefits of a commonly managed pool of assets vis-à-vis a self-managed 401(k) plan for most Americans.

This assumes a 3.5 percent savings rate (approximately the historical average over the past several decades) and is based on a $40,000 an-

CHART 5-1

	Pension Plan Returns	401(k) Plan
Average Return	10.7%	9.7%[2]
Annual Contribution (starting age 30 to 60)	$1,500	$1,500
Retirement Assets	$309,000	$254,000

nual income. Chart 5-1 shows how a modest amount of annual savings can amount to a tremendous amount of money over time. As important, it shows the benefit of pooling assets and managing employee assets in a manner consistent with pension plans.

Encouraging Savings Accounts

The two biggest challenges of this plan are: (a) enticing employers to sponsor these hybrid plans and (b) encouraging employees and employers to contribute to them.

Encouraging Employer Sponsored Plans or Participation

Corporations could be encouraged to sponsor these plans through a limitation of liability and tax benefits. First, there should be a limitation of liability if the employer either sponsors such a hybrid plan or directs employees to a plan sponsored by another party. In general, the limitation of liability would be based on some degree of due diligence and a reasonable person standard. Absent willful misconduct, employers would not incur liability for either setting up a plan or directing employees to one sponsored by a financial institution. The first hallmark of a reasonable plan would be keeping overall fees at the plan level consistent with those of a similarly sized pension plan. The second hallmark would be common management across the pool of assets, which would provide employees with the buying power and professional asset management consistent with those of large pension plans. The goal would be to deliver the investment returns generated by traditional pension plans, at the same costs, without placing the investment risk on the employers.

Second, assuming that corporations still pay taxes (i.e., my plan to eliminate corporate taxes is not adopted, as discussed in a later chapter), the federal government should provide a dollar-for-dollar tax offset, or rebate, to corporations that sponsor a plan for the first $1,000 contributed to the plan by the employer on behalf of the employee. That is, if the employer elected to participate and contributed $1,000 for an employee, the employer would get a dollar-for-dollar tax credit. Currently, employers are only able to take a *tax deduction* for such a contribution. Thus, as opposed to a dollar-for-dollar tax credit, a tax deduction yields, at most, a 35 percent tax benefit, or $350 on a $1,000 contribution.

Based on 100 million workers, the total cost of the plan to the US Treasury would be approximately $80 billion per annum (assuming an effective tax rate of 20 percent)—a sizable amount. However, the benefits would be incalculable. The nation would be diversifying away from Social Security for retirement benefits and would potentially offer a much more comfortable and secure retirement for many Americans. Given that this plan would promote savings and investment, the loss in tax revenue might be partially offset by greater economic growth. Further, since the new Social Security plan would be means tested, a rational national savings plan—one that was more effective at promoting wise savings and investment—would result in lower outlays for Social Security over time. Accordingly, while the cost of the program might be higher in the near term because of the tax credits, the program might be cost neutral or even accretive to the federal government over time.

Employee Participation

Employee participation in these plans should be high. After all, an employee would receive $1,000 per annum at no cost to either the employee or the employer (since the employer would get a dollar-for-dollar tax credit from the government). To further encourage participation, the government should provide for automatic enrollment of employees in the hybrid plan unless the employee specifically opts out. A "default" setting of this nature was recently enacted by Congress and resulted in a higher participation rate in 401(k) plans. Chart 5-2 outlines the benefit of the annual $1,000 contribution over forty years, assuming an 8% and 10% annual rate of return.

Beyond the $1,000 annual contribution made by the employer, an employee would be entitled to make additional contributions in a tax advantage manner, consistent with 401(k) plans of today. That is, any amount above $1,000 contributed to the plan would be tax deferred for the participants (i.e., if the participants directed a portion of their salary to the plan, they would not pay taxes on that portion of their salary until it was withdrawn in the future). The employee would have withdrawal rights on the money he or she contributes, with restrictions consistent with those of today (e.g., withdrawal penalties). However, the employee would not have a right to withdraw amounts contributed on his or her behalf by the employer (the first $1,000, basically). This would promote the growth of an employee's asset base.

In sum, the plan would have the effect of producing personal savings accounts, as promoted by President Bush, without undermining Social Security as a safety net. Further, this plan promotes wiser, more cost-effective savings in exchange for the tax benefits being offered to employers and employees alike by the US government. It is certainly reasonable for the US government to request wiser savings practices on the part of employees as the quid pro quo for favorable tax treatment. Finally, this plan recognizes that corporate America is shifting away from DB plans, because the risk of investment loss with these plans falls squarely on the shoulders of the employers. The proposed plan places those investment risks on the employee. Yet the plan also posi-

CHART 5-2

	$1,000 Contribution (10% return)	$1,000 Contribution (8% return)
Average Return	10%	8%
Annual Contribution (starting age 20 to 60)	$1,000	$1,000
Retirement Assets	$482,737	$278,172

tions the employee to enjoy more success by providing him or her with investment attributes that have greatly benefited pension plans: economies of scale, commonality of management, and lower costs. Given that, this plan provides the best opportunity to create a more viable retirement system for Americans, with as little government interference as possible.

CHAPTER 6

Medicare

The Medicare shortfall dwarfs that of Social Security and presents the greatest challenge to the future financial health of the United States. The projected shortfall for Medicare is $34 trillion, or about $113,000 for every American citizen.[1] By 2050, Medicare will consume about 20 percent of GDP, about the amount the US government spends on its *entire* budget today. To pay for this increase, American taxpayers would face an 80 percent tax increase.[2]

The Current System

Given these metrics, it is not surprising that the United States spends more on health care than any other nation in the world. In some respects, this spending is not in vain. The United States has arguably the most advanced health care system in the world. Yet, surprisingly, the US health care system ranks low among developed nations and barely in the top quartile among all nations in terms of overall effectiveness. And with the continued explosive growth in medical costs, the United States must review its health care system and attempt to devise a better system for the allocation and rationing of medical services. The first step is to analyze the two main ways that health care services are delivered in the United States: the managed care system and Medicare.

Managed Care vs. Traditional Insurance

The managed care system came into vogue in the 1980s as a means to slow the growth of medical inflation.[3] Managed care plans, in the form of health maintenance organizations (HMOs) provide participants with subsidized doctor visits and drugs, with the cost being borne largely by the insurance companies. The hope is that people will focus on preventive care and thereby reduce medical costs over time. These plans have supplanted traditional insurance plans, which required participants to pay for all medical costs until a deductible was exhausted. After that, the insurance company paid for all costs associated with the medical care of the participant.

Several flaws have been exposed with regard to managed care plans vis-à-vis traditional plans. First, since the cost of doctors' visits and medicine are subsidized, participants have little incentive to ration health care costs. Medical care usage has expanded since that time, causing the cost of these plans to explode. Second, the paperwork associated with doctors' reimbursement by insurance companies (and Medicare) is staggering. In some cases, paperwork costs are greater than the cost of the office visit itself, adding to the overall price of offering plans to consumers. Third, insurance companies, since there is no free market, set the rates for a variety of office visits, procedures, operations, etc. Accordingly, not only do doctors have to fill out a significant amount of paperwork to get reimbursed, the amount reimbursed is sometimes much less than an open market would provide. This has resulted in declining compensation for doctors, and many have left the field in frustration.[4]

To put this in perspective, from 1970 to 2005, the out-of-pocket costs for medical care have dropped from 40 to 15 percent. This means that consumers pay very little of their medical costs directly. Given that, consumers have little incentive to ration medical care. In fact, they are incentivised to do just the opposite. Namely, there is an incentive to use medical services more frequently, and that is what has occurred. A recent study by PriceWatherhouse Coopers, the international accounting and consulting firm, indicated that most of the annual increase in medical care costs are due to increased *utilization* rates by consumers.[5]

None of these flaws were as prevalent in traditional insurance plans. In a traditional plan, consumers had insurance for "catastrophic" health care emergencies. These plans had relatively high deductibles but covered emergencies above the cost of the deductible. Accordingly, a considerable portion of health care costs were borne by consumers until they chewed through the deductible. So for most minor health emergencies, the consumer paid for the medical care directly—no insurance company was involved until the deductible was exhausted. Doctors did not have to fill out paperwork to be reimbursed, and rates were set by the supply-and-demand characteristics of the local marketplace, not insurance companies.

Since the costs of compliance were lower, less "friction" occurred on dollars being spent by consumers. In other words, less of the money changing hands went to pay administrative costs, and more money stayed in the consumers' and doctors' pockets. (Consumers paid lower insurance premiums; doctors could charge market rates and did not have to deal with high administrative costs). Further, supply-and-demand conditions in the local marketplace dictated how much doctors were paid; the best doctors were paid more. However, doctors' fees were ultimately constrained by market forces—that is, competition. Insurance kicked in once the consumer spent an amount equal to his or her deductible. Typically this came into play only in major medical emergencies, the types of situations insurance was supposed to cover in the first place. With regard to major medical emergencies or undertakings, procedures were typically more costly. Therefore, any red tape or paperwork associated with the emergency would generally pass a rudimentary cost-benefit analysis. It makes sense to have the insurance company involved, with all the associated paperwork, in the event of a $10,000 heart surgery as opposed to a $50 office visit.

Revamping the Current System

The Medicare system should be revamped to be a catastrophic health-care insurance program for the poor. The change would require two steps. First, the system should only cover medical emergencies above a certain dollar amount, say, $15,000. This would serve as a "deductible" for Medicare. People would be required to carry a minimum health care insurance policy with a private carrier to cover the deductible. The federal government would mandate that the states establish a regime to provide all citizens—especially poorer ones—access to such policies. States would thus require their citizens to carry small health policies, similar to the minimum liability car insurance required by many states. This policy would pay the Medicare deductible on behalf of poorer citizens. Second, only the poor would be eligible for the catastrophic coverage provided by Medicare. Wealthier Americans would either have to carry insurance above the minimum policy levels or pay for their medical care out of their own resources.

Analogous to Minimum Motorist Insurance. The minimum policies under proposed plan would be much like the minimum motorist insurance regime found in some states. In these states, motorists are required to carry a minimum amount of automobile insurance to cover accidents with other motorists. The amount of required insurance is typically low enough to be affordable to the poor, and it is purchased from private insurance carriers to keep the government out of the matter.

By way of example, Texas requires a motorist to carry $15,000 worth of insurance to cover damage done to another driver's car in an accident.[6] This level of insurance covers the vast majority of accidents. The Texas law has resulted in more motorists carrying minimum liability insurance and in more accidents being covered by insurance.

Applying the Regime to Health Care. The same should hold for health insurance. The federal government should require states to establish minimal health insurance regimes for their citizens. The system would require individuals to carry such insurance in order to get a driver's license. The state regime would then dovetail into the federal safety net of Medicare. Tennessee is currently experimenting with minimum health-care insurance in this manner, although it does not dovetail with Medicare or provide for a deductible (two key differences).

Minimum Insurance: Tennessee Example. Tennessee's plan is premised on the idea that the amount of minimum insurance should be low enough that it is not cost prohibitive, but high enough to cover most medical incidents. The CoverTN plan,[7] provides $15,000 of insurance ($25,000 for families) and covers the vast majority of medical incidents and/or emergencies in a given year. In addition, doctor visits and drugs are covered as well, with a modest co-pay. The cost for a healthy person (nonsmoker) of average weight is $37 per month, with the remainder covered by the state and the person's employer. The CoverTN plan does not have a deductible.

The proposed plan should provide for a modest deductible for the reasons set forth above, to better allocate and ration medical care. The deductible should be set at $500 ($1,000 for families). At this level, consumers would be forced to pay for many doctor's visits, drugs, and minor medical procedures out of pocket, thereby promoting greater efficiency in the use of medical services. This amount would be about the same as an automobile deductible for most consumers.[8]

Based on a middle-aged wage earner in good health, the total cost of such a policy would be about the same as the CoverTN plan (about $1,200 to $1,500 per year).[9] Assuming a similar split between the state, employer, and worker, the worker would pay less than $40 per month, an amount well within the reach of most employers or employees.[10] Even assuming a $500 deductible, the total cost would represent about 7.5 percent of the gross wages for a minimum-wage earner. For these and other lower wage earners, the state could have pools or aid programs to assist in paying premiums and/or the deductible, as is the case in Tennessee.

"Buying Up": Taxing Greater Insurance Benefits

Consumers could, of course, buy more comprehensive plans than the law required, much like many consumers in Texas now buy more comprehensive automobile insurance than the law requires. However, the tax law needs to be changed, as President Bush has suggested, to ensure that the federal government is not subsidizing higher wage earners in this regard.

Currently, the federal government gives a tax break for companies that offer insurance to employees (the companies can deduct the cost of health care), but the insurance is not considered compensation to the individual, as most other perquisites are.[11] Thus, if a company provides $3,000 in insurance coverage to a highly paid executive, it deducts the $3,000 in insurance costs but the executive does not recognize any compensation from the $3,000 in benefits he receives. The federal treasury loses out on a little over $1,000 in taxes (assuming the highest marginal rate).[12]

Since this insurance is tax advantaged, the executive has an incentive to buy as much insurance as possible. This creates an inflated market for health care services, where people have an incentive to overbuy insurance coverage because of the tax subsidy. In response, the federal government should allow a company to deduct any costs associated with providing insurance to employees, but that an employee must recognize as taxable the income for any benefits received *above* the minimum liability insurance coverage mandated by law. In our earlier example, assuming that the minimum policy cost $1,000 and the executive chose a more expensive plan ($3,000), the executive would recognize $2,000 in compensation, which would be taxable. In this regard, the federal government would continue to create an incentive to buy insurance, but the incentive would be capped out at the minimum liability insurance level. This would create a more efficient marketplace for the allocation of medical services.

Medicare: Excess Coverage

Which finally brings the discussion to Medicare. As with Social Security, Medicare would be a catastrophic regime covering the poor after the $15,000 policies ($25,000 for families) were exhausted. Accordingly, Medicare would be a means-tested welfare program designed to provide poorer Americans with a minimal level of catastrophic medical care. The Medicare system would be supported by tax dollars and Congress would establish an annual budget for Medicare that targets a particular percentage of GDP. For example, Congress might establish a target of 5 percent of GDP. Based on the amount devoted to the medical insurance regime, the government would have to determine the level of benefits that could be provided. This exercise would require difficult decisions on the part of US policymakers. However, given means testing and that most medical emergencies would be covered by the $15,000 policies, the scope of coverage for poorer Americans could be fairly expansive.

Under this system, the costs of Medicare would be significantly reduced, as would the scope of coverage. This would require many affluent Americans to maintain insurance or save for medical emergencies for their senior years. It would also require better allocation of medical services. Both of these steps are necessary to preserve the financial viability of the Medicare system and provide services where they are most needed—to the poor.

PART III

Economic Policy

- The Collapse of the Dollar
- Fiscal Policy
- Accountability, Reporting, and Budgeting
- Tax Policy
- Monetary Policy
- The New Federal Reserve
- Addressing the Current Account Deficit

Introduction

The previous section outlined the ramifications of the aging of the baby boomer generation, and proposed several changes to America's immigration policy, entitlement system, and retirement savings regime. However, these changes are merely the first step in a complete reorganization of America's economic policies. The United States must also address its budget deficits and easy monetary policy, which have caused chronic imbalances in its own economy and across the world. These policies have put extreme pressure on the US dollar, threatening its status as the world's reserve currency within the lifetime of many readers of this book. Losing this status would have catastrophic consequences to America's economic standing and the American standard of living.

This section will outline the collapse of the US dollar—in effect, this nation's stock price—and the impact on America if the US dollar continues its relentless decline. The remainder of the section focuses on significant changes to America's fiscal and monetary policy that will assist the nation in recovering its financial footing.

Problems:

1. America has enormous budget deficits that are being masked by the federal government's dubious accounting gimmicks.

2. America has not established budget priorities and has run large deficits because it is unwilling to curtail spending and/or raise taxes to pay for it.

3. The Federal Reserve, which runs America's monetary policy, has created bubbles by reducing short-term rates to abnormally low levels and holding them there for too long.

4. Due to these policies, America's trade and "current account" position has deteriorated. By pumping money into the economy through deficit spending, the US government must borrow heavily from abroad to finance itself. Further, by keeping interest rates abnormally low, the Federal Reserve has promoted spending, rather than saving, causing America's trade deficit to spiral out of control and creating a paucity of savings as the baby boomer generation enters retirement.

5. As a result of these policies, the US dollar, in effect the verdict of foreigners on US economic policy and prospects, has plummeted over the past six years.

Imperatives:

- The US government must provide its citizens with a clear understanding of the budget picture so that they are informed of the true financial health of the nation.
- The US government should establish a general level of taxation acceptable to the American people during peacetime and, based on those revenues, prioritize spending.
- The US government should reform and dramatically simplify the tax system to raise revenues in a manner that does not distort economic activity.
- The Federal Reserve should not have the power to create bubbles (or recessions) through raising or lowering short-term rates to abnormally high or low levels.

CHAPTER 7

The Collapse of the Dollar

Over time, a nation's currency reflects its economic strength and financial stability. In some respects, a nation's currency is much like a company's stock price. Just as a low stock price reflects poorly on a company's current and future prospects, a currency's decline, if prolonged, reflects poorly on a nation's fiscal position and economic prospects. A nation's currency is influenced by its fiscal policy, monetary policy, economic growth and prospects, and current account situation (whether a nation is running a trade deficit or surplus and whether it can finance its own consumption and spending). In other words, a country running large and persistent budget and current account deficits, accompanied by easy monetary policy, will likely see its currency decline in value. In this regard, the last several years have been disastrous for the US dollar, caused by the dramatic change in America's fiscal policies (going from surplus to deficit), its ballooning current account deficit, and exceedingly easy monetary policies. Since 2002, the dollar has declined by approximately 40 percent against the euro and approximately 30 percent against a trade-weighted basket of currencies.

Impact of a Declining Dollar

A declining dollar has a significant impact on the financial well-being of Americans. It means, among other things, that US citizens have to pay more for imported goods. This is illustrated by chart 7-1, which shows the price of oil in both euros and dollars over the past six years.

As noted in the chart, the price of oil in dollars has risen at a much greater pace than the price of oil in euros over the past six years, because the dollar has declined in value relative to the euro during this time. If the dollar had maintained parity with the euro, oil would be approximately $85 per barrel as of May 2008, rather than $135. So as much as $50 of the increase in the price of oil over the past six years has been a result of dollar depreciation. The decline in the dollar—versus the euro, for example—means that US consumers are paying higher oil prices than their European counterparts, creating inflationary pressures in the US economy. In addition, since the United States imports substantially more goods and services than it exports, it will pay higher prices for these goods and services, which is not only inflationary but

CHART 7-1

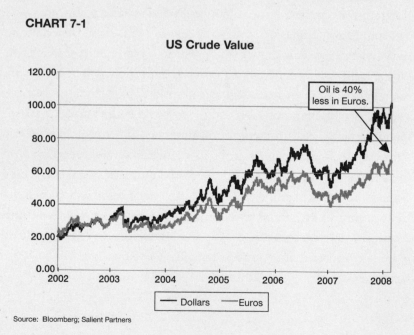

US Crude Value

Oil is 40% less in Euros.

Dollars — Euros

Source: Bloomberg; Salient Partners

also creates a drag on the US economy. Unfortunately, trends in US fiscal and monetary policy have made the decline of the dollar almost a certainty over the next several years vis-à-vis Asian and Middle Eastern currencies.

Loss of Status as the World's Reserve Currency

In addition to fueling inflation, a declining dollar also jeopardizes its standing as the world's reserve currency. Since World War II, the US dollar has functioned as the world's reserve currency (the currency of choice in international or cross-border transactions). A currency achieves this elite status because of the nation's economic strength and sound fiscal and monetary policies. Given these factors, investors have faith that the currency will not decrease in value.

As the world's reserve currency, the US dollar has a favorable place in international commerce, fueling demand for dollars that support its value. For example, it is often used by many developing countries that are issuing debt (they issue their debt in dollars[1] rather than in their own currency), for the sale of petroleum products by OPEC, and everyday transactions involving international commerce. Furthermore, to create currency stability, some nations "peg," or tie the value of their currency to the US dollar.[2]

All these factors create a demand for dollars by investors that is greater than the currency's underlying fundamentals dictate. This demand provides greater support and strength to the reserve currency than it might otherwise have based on fundamentals. In the case of the dollar, US citizens therefore have "buying power" that far outstrips the dollar's intrinsic value. And this makes imports cheaper and enhances Americans' standard of living. However, I likened a nation's currency to a company's stock price. A company with a high stock price must continue to perform to maintain it. Similarly, a nation with a reserve currency must maintain strong economic growth and sound government policies to maintain its currency's status. Countries with high budgets, current accounts, and trade deficits tend to fare poorly in this regard. The United Kingdom provides a sobering lesson on this front.

The British pound served as the world's reserve currency through the early part of the twentieth century until two world wars sapped the nation of its economic strength. The dollar started taking the place of the beleaguered British pound as the British government became increasingly indebted to the United States and lost economic strength. By the early 1950s, the pound had lost its status as the world's reserve currency. Britain was so indebted to the US that it had ceded at least some control over its foreign policy to America, as illustrated by the Suez Crisis. During this crisis, Egypt nationalized the Suez Canal, then a possession of Britain. Britain intervened to regain control of the canal. The Eisenhower administration, which ultimately opposed this intervention, told the British that the United States would begin selling British pounds unless the British ceased activities against the Egyptians. British pounds had been accumulated by the US government as a result of loans made to Britain during the two world wars.[3] Britain bowed to US demands. But it was an important lesson for the British. Britain no longer controlled its own currency. Just as Britain was held hostage by the United States, America now finds itself with the prospect of foreigners controlling the fate of the US dollar going forward.

Foreign Support of Dollar and US Treasuries

For the past several years, the dollar has managed to maintain more of its value than the financial condition of the United States would dictate. Despite an explosion of debt over the past six years, foreigners still line up to buy US treasuries for two reasons. First, few people know or understand the magnitude of the US government's future obligations because of our dubious accounting practices. Second, because it can always print more money to repay its debts, it is impossible for the US government to default on its debt. With that said, US Treasury bond holders can see the value of their holdings decline significantly due to currency depreciation. Indeed, that is precisely what is occurring.

Take the following example: If a European bought a ten-year US treasury bond in 2002 with the intent of holding it to maturity, the investor would have lost money on the investment. The yield of the instrument, about 5 percent when issued in 2002, has been entirely offset by currency losses averaging about 6 percent per annum.

Over time, this is not tenable. The US dollar cannot continue to depreciate without offering investors a premium for investing in US Treasuries. The premium will come in the form of higher interest rates. To this point, foreign investors have been content on holding low yielding US treasuries for two reasons: (a) the view that US treasuries are a safe haven ("riskless" investments) and (b) to further other objectives. For example, China's massive holdings in US treasuries and other instruments were bought, at least in part, to keep China's currency artificially weak against the dollar in order to drive exports. However, at some point, foreign investors will tire of losing money. When that occurs, the US dollar will come under further selling pressures, sending interest rates higher—potentially much higher.

China, Japan, and Middle East. The magnitude of dollar holdings by foreigners is best illustrated by China, Japan, and the Middle East. China has amassed over $1.4 trillion in foreign reserves, with about 70 percent invested in US dollar–denominated assets. Japan has accumulated over $900 billion in US dollar holdings.[4] The accumulation of US assets over the past few years has been astounding and has provided significant support for the dollar. However, even China's prodigious appetite for US dollar assets has waned. In August 2007, China and other investors started fleeing from the dollar—with nearly $163 billion in net dollar sales, according to the US Treasury.[5] While a paltry amount in the grand scheme of things, it may well be a portent of things to come.

Middle Eastern nations and private citizens also have significant holdings of US dollar assets, about $3.5 trillion. Several of these nations, including Saudi Arabia, tie or "peg" the value of their currencies to the US dollar. Accordingly, these countries have to maintain interest rates at the same level as the United States. To do so, they occasionally intervene and purchase or sell dollars to maintain the value of their currency relative to the dollar. Specifically, if their currency threatens to strengthen against the dollar, these nations use their currency to buy dollars to depress the value of their currency against the dollar. This provides key support for the value of the dollar. If it becomes apparent that the United States is not maintaining any degree of financial discipline and the dollar continues to weaken, these countries will start to abandon their peg against the dollar, or else risk considerable inflation in their markets and continued losses in their dollar reserves. Over the past few years, several countries have "depegged" their currencies from the dollar, including Kuwait, Uzbekistan and China.[6] It is likely that several Middle Eastern nations will follow suit in the years to come.

Oil Transactions. Oil sales are largely conducted in dollars despite the fact that most Middle Eastern nations conduct much of their business with Europe and need euros to transact business. With approximately 35 million barrels per day of OPEC[7] and Russian[8] energy transactions, the total notional value of energy transactions in dollars is approximately $32 billion per day (assuming $90 per barrel oil). Iraq, prior to the US invasion in 2003, started moving away from the dollar in its oil sales; Iran is now moving in the same direction. This move is logical, given the decline in the dollar and the fact that many Middle Eastern countries transact more business in Europe. The United Sates should expect more and more Middle Eastern countries to partially transition to the euro for transacting oil sales. The dollar will suffer as a result.

What Should We Expect?

Absent a dramatic change in US policies, Americans should expect the unthinkable: a downgrade in the credit rating of US government debt. The catalyst will be a continued deterioration of the US budget deficit and the US dollar, causing foreign investors to flee the dollar. At that time, interest rates on US treasuries will spike, further undermining the financial health of the US government. One of the few bright spots over the past several years has been the artificially low interest rates on US government debt. These low rates have kept our interest payments lower and our budget deficits more manageable. As interest rates spike, this "free lunch" will end, leading to much higher budget deficits. While these higher rates may finally stabilize the dollar, US stock and bond prices will collapse (bond prices move inversely with interest rates).[9]

America has two paths in front of it. It can cede its economic superpower status, much like Britain did a century ago, by continuing its current policies. In the end, America will continue devaluing its currency through ultra-loose fiscal and monetary policy, leaving Chinese and American savers with increasingly worthless dollars. Or the United States can get its financial house in order by dramatically improving its fiscal, monetary, and trade policies. This is the focus of the following chapters.

CHAPTER 8

Fiscal Policy

Like most industrialized countries, America runs a budget deficit. However, the US government has failed to convey the magnitude of these deficits to the American people. In particular, the US government does not provide the public with a clear picture of finances, consistent with what it requires of American public companies. So, most Americans do not have an understanding of the scope of America's budgetary problems. If they did, perhaps Americans would take steps to hold US policymakers accountable at election time.

Americans Need to Consider Themselves as Shareholders in America

Despite recent problems, American public companies are the most accountable in the world. The US government requires each public company to provide its shareholders with a clear picture of its financial condition. If senior management fails to do so, it faces civil penalties or jail time. Accordingly, the vast majority of executives take these responsibilities seriously and provide investors with sound information.

We should use these standards as a useful analogue to reform the reporting requirements of the US government. In effect, the US government and its leaders need to start treating the American public as shareholders in America and provide them with clear and accurate reporting on the nation's finances. After all, like a shareholder, an American citizen has a valuable asset to protect: his citizenship. This asset ensures a standard of living that is the envy of the world. For example, even an American living in poverty has a standard of living that puts him among the wealthiest 20 percent of the world's population. Indeed, the average US worker earns more than *twenty times more* than the average Chinese worker. Pivoting to industrialized nations, the average American earns 40 percent more than the average French citizen.

Like a shareholder, an American citizen has a vote in how the affairs of the country are managed and should therefore have a keen understanding of the state of affairs of the nation. Given this, it is critical for Americans to have a solid understanding of their nation's finances. Yet, they do not. While Congress requires public companies to provide investors with consistent, reliable financial information, it does not impose the same burden on itself. Accordingly, the information that an American receives regarding the finances of the US government is woefully inadequate for him to make a reasoned judgment at the voting booth. The remainder of this chapter will focus on these two issues: how Americans have been misled about the nation's finances and how to fix the problem.

Fool's Gold: How America Has Been Misled about Its Economic Condition

President Bush's economic policies offer an illustration of how Americans have been misled about this nation's finances. President Bush's policies have been defended on the grounds that they have generated economic growth and led to lower budget deficits. However, a closer examination of the record indicates that both assertions are well off the mark.

Distorted Sense of Economic Growth

President Bush's economic policies have not led to sustainable growth. Rather, they have relied on deficit spending to stimulate economic growth, much like FDR's New Deal policies. President Bush pushed a tax cut through Congress in 2001 and then another in 2003. To be sure, Americans had more money in their pockets. However, tax revenues collapsed, particularly as a percentage of GDP. At the same time, the US government accelerated spending of all stripes. This included not only defense spending; it also included discretionary spending and the biggest expansion of America's entitlement system—the Prescription Drug Plan—since LBJ's Great Society era. America's budget deficits exploded.

With a massive amount of fiscal and monetary stimulus, the US economy grew from 2002 through 2006. But how much of this growth was real and how much was the result of deficit spending? In other words, if a consumer accumulates wealth but uses debt to do so, the growth in his asset base is entirely offset by increased debt. When analyzing it in this manner, the economic growth over the past few years becomes less impressive. Indeed, once the increase in government debt is subtracted from economic growth, the resultant economic growth, after taking into account increased debt, was negative during this time frame. Chart 8-2 shows economic growth from 1998 (when we were running budget surpluses) through 2008 (after years of deficits), plotted as the gray line. The black line represents economic growth *less* the annual increase in government debt. Whenever the black line is positive, economic growth is greater than the increase in national debt and economic wealth is being created. When the black line falls below zero, the US government is borrowing more than the increase in economic growth, which indicates that economic growth is being generated through deficit spending. This has been the case from 2001 through 2008.

So, America's economic growth over the past several has been financed by a dramatic increase in government borrowing. Cast in this manner, few people would confuse this with an economic miracle or a sign of economic prosperity due to the Bush tax cuts. Rather, it is

CHART 8-2

GDP Growth vs GDP Growth Less Federal Debt Growth (One Year Rolling Avg.)

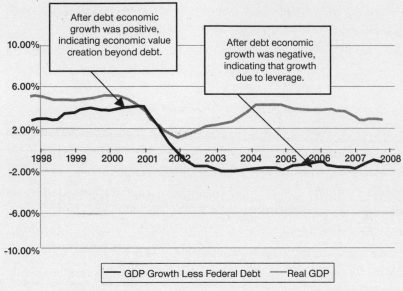

Source: Salient Partners; Bloomberg

much more like the New Deal era, where economic growth resulted from a dramatic increase in government spending (also called Keynesian economics).

These economic policies are very similar to the "prosperity" felt by a consumer who uses his credit cards to buy goods he cannot afford. The consumer may feel better because he owns a lot of consumer products. But he is not wealthier. Rather, his accumulation of goods has been entirely offset by the debt incurred to buy them. Indeed, the consumer is actually worse off than before since the value of the consumer goods will depreciate yet the consumer will still have to pay off the debt at some point. The same holds true with the US government. The growth in debt and spending has been used to fight a war and for social programs, rather than for infrastructure or other tangible assets. At the end of this debt-fueled spending spree, America will have very little to show for it except a bunch of IOUs to foreign governments. Future generations will have to pay for today's "economic prosperity" in the form of higher taxes and/or a lower standard of living. So it could be argued that President Bush's tax cuts are really a tax deferral—a bill that will be paid by future generations, most likely in the form of higher taxes, a materially weaker dollar, and a lower standard of living.

Budget Deficit Reality

As previously noted, the financial statements and budget deficits presented by Congress and the president give an overly optimistic picture of this nation's finances. In fact, the financial picture painted by the president and Congress is more misleading than that provided to investors by corporate malfeasants at Enron, Worldcom, and Adelphia. Without going into exhaustive detail, the following illustrates how muddled and misleading our nation's books are.

Social Security and Medicare. In fiscal year 1969, LBJ and a Democratic Congress started including Social Security and Medicare net revenues in the government's "unified budget" to mask the ballooning deficits from Vietnam and the Great Society social programs. Previously, Medicare and Social Security had been accounted for separately. The net revenues from these programs were ostensibly being paid by workers into a trust for their future retirement and/or health-care benefits. Since these programs have historically run surpluses, this change had the effect of significantly decreasing the annual budget deficits since that time. In 2006 alone, the Social Security surplus was $120 billion, which decreased the budget deficit by about 30 percent.

Further, US corporations use "accrual" accounting to convey the financial impact of current promises of future obligations. For example, if General Motors makes health care or pension promises to current workers, it must make an estimate of these future obligations. This estimate is recorded in General Motors' financial statement as a current cost. In addition, General Motors makes an annual payment to its pension plan and health care plan to cover these future costs. However, when the president and Congress discuss budget figures, they do not take into account the pension and health care promises to Americans under Social Security and Medicare. By excluding these figures, the president and Congress provide a far too rosy picture of America's finances.

Iraq, Afghanistan. The conflicts in theses and other countries cost the United States over $150 billion per annum. The Bush administration excluded these costs from past budget estimates because they are deemed temporary and difficult to estimate.

Standard of US Government vs. Standard for Corporate America

The Good: The Stated Deficit. To gain a true appreciation of this financial chicanery, the following table shows the official deficit figures provided by the Bush administration and Congress.

The picture provides some comfort. After peaking in 2004, the budget deficits have been declining steadily. Indeed, the budget deficit in 2007 (approximately $160 billion), represents a "mere" 1.5 percent of

CHART 8-3

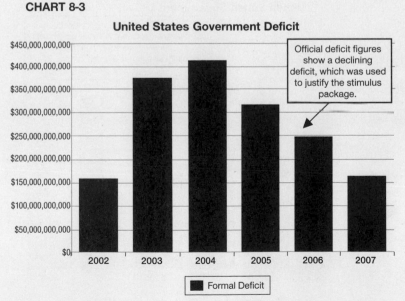

Source: US Department of Treasury; Shadowstats.com; Salient Partners

GDP, well below the average of the last thirty years. However, these numbers do not withstand even modest scrutiny. The real budgetary picture is not improving, but deteriorating rapidly.

The Bad: Annual Increase in National Debt. A standard way to determine financial malfeasance is to compare a company's stated profits with how much cash it is earning or losing. Over time, a company's cash flow should bear some relationship to its stated profitability. If not, then something is probably amiss. The same holds true for the US government. Its stated budget deficit should, over time, be close to its "cash deficit." The cash deficit is the amount the US government has to borrow each year to finance its operations. Logically, the amount it borrows should be roughly equal to its stated budget deficit. However, the US government's cash deficit unmasks the duplicity of the stated numbers. The cash deficit takes into account the cost of the war in Iraq, the cleanup costs associated with Hurricane Katrina, and the other financial gimmicks used by the government. Chart 8-4 provides the US

CHART 8-4

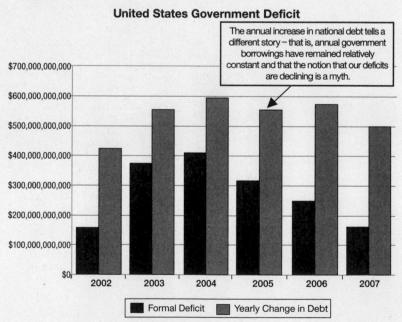

United States Government Deficit

The annual increase in national debt tells a different story – that is, annual government borrowings have remained relatively constant and that the notion that our deficits are declining is a myth.

Source: US Department of Treasury; Shadowstats.com; Salient Partners

government's cash deficit (the annual increase in national debt) and compares it to the stated budget deficit.

From 2002 through 2007, the federal government has borrowed far more than its "stated" deficit, indicating that its true budget deficit is much, much greater than what it is telling the people.

The Ugly: GAAP Deficits. However, even the cash deficits paint an overly optimistic picture of America's finances. They do not show the annual increase in the federal government's future health care and pension obligations. As noted in the General Motors example, corporate America has to "accrue" for these obligations every year. This approach sharply contrasts with the accounting approach taken by the US government. The US government does not accrue for the future costs of either Medicare or Social Security. If it did make this accrual, the budget deficits would explode. The table below shows the

CHART 8-5

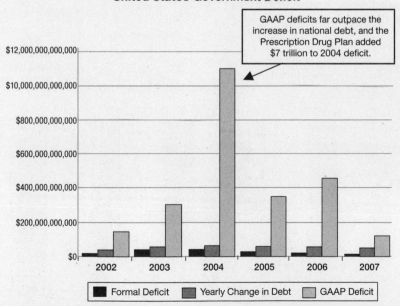

United States Government Deficit

GAAP deficits far outpace the increase in national debt, and the Prescription Drug Plan added $7 trillion to 2004 deficit.

Source: US Department of Treasury; Shadowstats.com; Salient Partners

SGS estimates $3.4 trillion for GAAP w/ SS in 2004, excluding one-time unfunded setup costs of the Medicare Prescription Drug Improvement, and Modernization Act of 2003.

true magnitude of America's budget deficit, by comparing the stated deficit (green bar) with the cash deficit (red bar) and the GAAP deficit (blue bar).

Acutely aware of this dismal picture, David Walker, former comptroller general of the United States (the nation's chief accountant), has said that the biggest threat to the United States is not terrorism, but our own financial irresponsibility. In particular, Walker said that "we're spending more money than we make . . . we're charging it to a credit card . . . and expecting our grandchildren to pay for it. And that's absolutely outrageous."[1]

Trend Lines

The US budget represents the "income statement" of the federal government and reflects its revenues (taxes), expenses, and its resultant surplus or deficit. As the previous chart shows, the US budget picture is a dismal one. Not surprisingly, the nation's financial condition, or its net worth, is also dismal, as evidenced by the following chart.

CHART 8-6

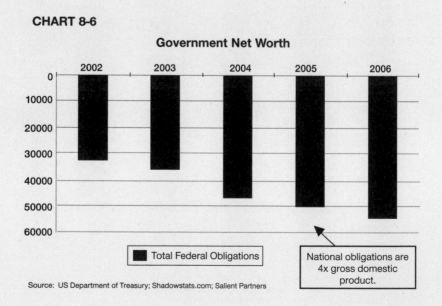

Government Net Worth

Total Federal Obligations

National obligations are 4x gross domestic product.

Source: US Department of Treasury; Shadowstats.com; Salient Partners

The trend lines point to a sharply deteriorating financial position (i.e., net worth) over the past five years. The current "negative net worth" of the US government is $55 trillion or about four times the economic output of the United States. More significantly, it is about eighteen times the US government's annual tax revenues, which would be the source to repay these obligations.

What Can We Do?

In short, the US government is insolvent and its insolvency is growing worse by the year. Since the US government cannot go bankrupt, this means that it will either raise taxes significantly and/or cut benefits dramatically. Or, worse yet, the US government will merely print more money and repay its obligations in increasingly worthless dollars, creating explosive inflation. Most Americans know that the US government has made promises that it will not likely keep, but they have no idea of the true magnitude of the situation. If the public did, voters might well demand a greater degree of accountability from US policymakers and the financial condition of this nation might well improve.

A useful analogue, again, is to treat the US government like a public company. First, the United States should provide its citizens with clear and accurate reporting. Like executives of public companies, politicians should be held accountable for misleading the public. Second, the US government should overhaul its tax system to make it simpler and enable the government to raise taxes without distorting economic activity. Third, the US government should determine how much it should spend (as a percentage of GDP) and establish budget priorities. These three concepts—clear accounting, a pro-growth system of taxation, and spending priorities—are addressed in the following chapters.

CHAPTER 9

Accountability, Reporting, and Budgeting

"We might hope to see the finances of the Union as clear and intelligible as a merchant's books, so that every member of Congress and every man of any mind in the Union should be able to comprehend them, to investigate abuses, and consequently to control them."

—President Thomas Jefferson
to his Treasury secretary, Albert Gallatin (1802)

Thomas Jefferson realized that a well-functioning democracy required the government to provide its citizens—or stakeholders—with a clear understanding of the nation's finances. Accordingly, the first step in getting America's financial house in order is to provide the public with a "clear and intelligible" understanding of the nation's finances. Once that is done, the American people will, hopefully, start holding politicians accountable for irresponsible economic policies and demand a change in how this nation is managed.

Accountability and Reporting

Require Congress and the President to Publish Accurate Financial Statements. The US government should provide an accurate report of the nation's finances to every American citizen, using the same accounting principles and reporting standards imposed on corporate America.[1] This report should be provided directly to the American people on an annual basis. The report should be compiled and published by the Federal Reserve, which is independent of the federal government and not as subject to influence by it. (Please note a change in the role of the Federal Reserve, outlined later in the book). No other budgetary figures should be used by politicians. The annual report should show not only current budget deficits; it should also show future deficits, assuming that current policies remain in effect. The forecast should extend for at least ten years.

By publishing and distributing accurate financial information, much of the responsibility for the financial health of the United States will shift to the people. The people will have to decide whether they support fiscal policies that are sensible and sound, which will result in a better country for future generations. If not, then so be it. But at least they will be making a well-informed and reasoned decision and understand the impact on this nation's finances and on future generations.

Hold Politicians to the Same Standard as Corporate CEOs. Congress and the president should also be subject to the same laws as the CEO of a public company, who is subject to civil and criminal penalties if he provides the public with false and misleading statements regarding his public company. Even a simple statement, such as touting a company's financial prospects, can subject a CEO to liability.

Government representatives are even more critical than those of individual companies, since every American is a stakeholder in America's future. By that standard, it should be a crime for a politician to provide false or misleading financial information to the American people, just as it is for the CEOs of public companies. Unfortunately, if that were the case, almost every politician in Washington would be in prison with the corporate malfeasants of Worldcom, Enron, and Adelphia.

Need for Constitutional Amendment. Attempts have been made to hold Congress to the same laws applied to the people. In almost every case, Congress exempted themselves from these laws. The only way to ultimately hold Congress and the president accountable is to amend the Constitution and require them to publish accurate financial statements. Such an amendment might take the following form:

Truth in Accounting (Twenty-seventh Amendment). Every United States citizen shall be provided, on not less than an annual basis, financial statements covering the United States government. Such financial statements shall reflect the true, accurate, and complete statement of operations and fiscal condition of the federal government, after applying generally accepted accounting principles applicable to public companies regulated by the Securities and Exchange Commission (or any successor entity) as the same may be adopted from time to time by the Association of Independent Certified Public Accountants (or any successor entity), with appropriate modifications to take into account differences between for-profit companies and the federal government; provided, however, that notwithstanding the foregoing, in no event shall such modifications be implemented to distort, obfuscate, or otherwise deceive the American public as to the true financial condition and statement of operations of the federal government; and provided further, that such financial statements shall assume obligations and promises under current law and shall not exclude such obligations based on the fact that Congress and the President can change such law in the future. Congress shall be responsible for sending such financial statements to every US citizen. Neither the President or his agents nor Congress or its agents shall publish (or in writing or orally) budget forecasts, projections, or other information, except for the foregoing financial statements without subjecting themselves to criminal prosecution under federal securities laws applicable to the officers and directors of public companies (in the case of everyone except the President). In the case of the President, a violation of this constitutional amendment shall be considered a "High Crime and Misdemeanor," subjecting the President to removal from office pursuant to Article II, Section 4 of the US Constitution.[2]

In addition to adopting more transparent accounting, the US government should have a more sensible tax system to raise revenues and a budgetary process that allocates tax revenues in a manner consistent with the nation's priorities.

CHAPTER 10

Tax Policy

This chapter will outline a simpler, more effective manner to raise revenues for the federal government and a budgeting process to allocate those dollars. The starting point of any tax policy is to determine the level of revenues to be raised. For fiscal year 2008, the federal government is projected to spend over $3 trillion, well over 20 percent of the GDP. Give or take, this rate of spending has remained constant for the past three decades. For the purposes of this chapter, both the federal government's tax revenue target and spending target is assumed to be 20 percent of GDP. Such a target would require the government to raise more revenues, which would mean higher overall taxes. In addition, the government would have to cut overall spending, thereby attacking the budget deficit from both the revenue and spending sides simultaneously.

Changing the Tax System

In revamping the current tax system, US policymakers should consider the following:

1. Fairness (largely subjective)
2. Ease of administration and compliance (more objective)

3. Ability to raise sufficient revenues to finance government (objective)

4. Avoid impeding capital formation or distortion of economic activity (more subjective)

The current system may be fair (depending on who you ask), but it is complicated, does not raise sufficient revenues to fund the government, and distorts economic activity. In this regard, it flunks three of the four tests outlined above. The current tax system is comprised of a tax on personal income, capital appreciation and dividends, corporate profits, and estate taxes, among others.

Current Personal Income Tax Regime

The US government generates most of its tax revenues from a tax on personal income. The US personal income tax regime is generally considered to be a progressive one. That is, the higher a person's earnings, the more (as a percentage of income) he or she pays in taxes. Citizens below the poverty line usually do not pay federal income tax. As a person's income increases, he or she pays an increasing amount of tax, ranging from 10 to 35 percent (the highest marginal tax rate). On its face, this system appears graduated and progressive: the more you make, the higher your tax rate. However, upon deeper inspection, the system is not as progressive as it appears. Charts 10-1 and 10-2 provide a comparison of average taxpayers at two different income levels, assuming that each wage earner takes the same deductions. Both examples assume a married couple with two minor children. The first family is headed by a wage earner making $80,000 per year, an average middle income family. The second assumes a family making $500,000 per annum, which is in the top 1 percent of wage earners.

Chart 10-1 underscores that the current tax regime is progressive. The middle-class family pays substantially lower taxes than the more affluent family. However, an individual's tax burden is not comprised solely of an income tax. An individual also pays payroll taxes, which

CHART 10-1

Family of Four Comparison*

	$80,000**	$500,000***
Family of Four: One Wage Earner, Salaried Employee	$80,000	$500,000
Deductions	$23,500	$100,000
Adjusted Gross Income (taxable income)	$56,500	$400,000
Taxes Due	$7,720	$134,000[1]
Percentage of Income	9.6%	26.8%

* Tax rates and deductions are from the 2006 Internal Revenue Service tax tables and regulations.

** Assumes there is one wage earner, a spouse, and two minor children. Assumes that the family takes the personal exemptions (deductions for each dependent) and the standard deduction (general deduction the IRS permits for a family if the family does not have itemized deductions).

*** Assumes the family has a $1,000,000 mortgage with a 6 percent interest rate, or $60,000 in mortgage interest. Assumes the family pays approximately 8 percent of its adjusted gross income. (estimated to be approximately $400,000) in state and local taxes, including property taxes. Assumes no further deductions.

CHART 10-2

Family of Four Comparison (Including payroll taxes)*

	$80,000**	$500,000***
Federal Income Taxes		
Family of Four: One Wage Earner, Salaried Employee	$80,000	$500,000
Deductions	$23,500	$100,000
Adjusted Gross Income (taxable Income)	$56,500	$400,000
Taxes Due	$7,720	134,000 [2]
Percentage of Income	9.6%	26.8%
Federal Payroll Taxes****	$12,240	$23,057
Percentage of Income	15.2%	4.6%
Total Federal Taxes	24.8%	31.4%

* Tax rates and deductions are from the 2006 Internal Revenue Service tax tables and regulations.

** Assumes there is one wage earner, a spouse, and two minor children. Assumes the family takes the personal exemptions (deductions for each dependent) and the standard deduction (general deduction the IRS permits for a family if the family does not have itemized deductions).

*** Assumes the family has a $1,000,000 mortgage with a 6 percent interest rate, or $60,000 in mortgage interest. Assumes the family pays approximately 8 percent of its adjusted gross income (estimated to be approximately $400,000) in state and local taxes, including property taxes. Assumes no other deductions.

**** Includes Social Security, including the employer's matching contribution, and Medicare taxes.

fund Social Security and Medicare. These taxes fall disproportionately on middle- and lower-income taxpayers. When Social Security, Medicare, and itemized deductions are taken into account, a middle-income wage earner's tax rate starts approaching that of a higher-income taxpayer. To illustrate the *overall* tax burden that falls on each family, chart 10-2 includes the amount of payroll taxes each family pays.

As you can see, by including payroll taxes, the picture looks quite different. Indeed, the middle-income family pays nearly the same percentage of its income in taxes as the higher-income family. Thus, our tax system is not terribly progressive and has a high degree of complexity, which often benefits the wealthy.

Complexity, Costs, and Cheating (Current Tax System)

Complexity. As any taxpayer knows, the US tax system is complex and difficult to navigate. According to an IRS study, Americans paid approximately $18.8 billion per annum in tax preparation costs in 2000 alone.[3] The same study indicated that Americans spent approximately 3.2 billion hours in tax preparation time, which equates to between $86 billion and $118 billion in total economic costs (assuming that each taxpayer's time is worth $25 per hour).[4] Another study estimated the overall compliance costs at a staggering $240 billion per annum.[5]

Depending on the study, compliance costs represent between 7 and 20 percent of overall individual tax revenues collected by the federal government.[6] These costs are a net drain on the economy since they do not produce overall societal wealth. They also divert highly skilled individuals—tax accountants and lawyers—from more productive societal endeavors. If the overall compliance costs are between $100 billion and $240 billion per annum, the complexity of the current system shaves about 0.7 and 1.8 percent off the United States' GDP per annum.[7] That may not seem like a lot, but it is roughly the difference between our economic growth and that of Europe. If we captured that incremental growth, it would pay the entire shortfall in Social Security over the next fifty years, with no cuts in benefits or higher taxes.

Lost Revenues Due to Cheating. The tax system's complexity also provides a tremendous opportunity to cheat. The IRS has estimated that tax evasion and cheating cost the US Treasury over $350 billion per annum.[8] By eliminating all loopholes and deductions, the United States would close one of the wider avenues used by tax cheats: the use of bogus or inflated deductions.

Distortion of Economic Activity. Economic Growth. The complexity of the tax code also distorts economic activity. For example, by providing a deduction for a certain type of expense, Congress is effectively subsidizing and encouraging that activity over another. The mortgage interest deduction provides a case in point. Through this deduction, the US government encourages Americans to buy more expensive and bigger homes and provides a subsidy to the US housing industry and homeowners. It could be argued that this capital might create greater national wealth if invested in factories, technology, or other assets rather than in bigger houses. Given the distortions created by the current tax system, US policymakers should dramatically simplify the tax code and allow people to invest or spend their capital based on free market principles, without government interference or incentives. The components of the new tax regime would be similar to the current one: a tax on income, a modest tax on capital, and an estate tax. But there would be key changes. For example, corporate taxes would be eliminated altogether and the income tax regime would be greatly simplified.

Components of New Tax System

Income Tax

The new system would retain the individual income tax, but there would be very few deductions and only three tax rates. This system would be simpler, easier to administer, and would not distort economic activity.

Deductions. The income tax regime should only have deductions for the following:

1. *Dependents.* Encourages larger families and investment in "human capital." Given our demographic problems, the US government should provide assistance to families with children. Further, the deduction would be relatively easy to calculate.

2. *Mortgage Interest Deduction.* The mortgage interest deduction encourages home ownership and, as noted above, represents a subsidy to homeowners and the housing industry. The current deduction has a relatively high cap: all interest paid on a mortgage of up to $1 million is tax deductible, while the average home price is much lower (approximately $250,000). The high threshold encourages Americans to buy more expensive houses. Accordingly, the mortgage interest deduction should be reduced to the average home price in the United States (e.g., $250,000). The reduction of the mortgage interest deduction should be phased in gradually over time to provide the housing market— already under tremendous pressure—time to adjust.

3. *Qualified Retirement Savings Accounts.* The current system provides workers with a deduction for amounts contributed to a qualified retirement account. This deduction would also be included in the proposed tax system because it encourages people to save for retirement. It should be noted that this is really just a tax deferral, since the savings would be taxed when withdrawn.

The overall framework of this system is simple and fair and does not distort economic activity. By limiting the deductions to just a handful of items, the typical tax return would be short—one page— and compliance costs would be dramatically reduced.

Some will no doubt criticize the elimination of many popular tax deductions. These include deductions for excess medical costs, state and local taxes, and charitable contributions. However, the threshold for excess medical costs currently is very high, and very few qualify for it. With the proposed medical insurance plan (see above), the necessity for a tax deduction for these costs would be greatly reduced, since catastrophic costs would be covered by private insurance and/or Medicare.

Also, taxpayers should not receive a deduction for state and local taxes, given that this equates to a subsidy by citizens of lower-tax states in favor of citizens in higher-tax states.

As for charitable deductions, the government should not subsidize charities by providing citizens with a tax break for contributions. While this may influence giving, studies indicate that the impact may not be as great as some might fear. In particular, research indicates that charitable contributions are much more sensitive to the overall health of the economy than tax incentives. If the tax system was simpler and overall taxes were lower, the US would have a healthier economy and individuals would have more discretionary income to spend, invest, or give away.[9] Charities, no doubt, would benefit, along with the rest of the country.

Progressive System. To further promote fairness, the system should be progressive or graduated. That is, the tax rates on income should increase as income levels increase. This recognizes a couple of important facts. First, less affluent families pay a greater percentage of their income for basic necessities such as food, energy, and shelter and therefore have less money to spare. This is the fairness issue (test number one). Second, wealthy individuals will benefit from lower taxes on capital, as discussed below. The progressive system of taxation should cap the highest marginal rate at 40 percent, which would only be slightly higher than it is today (35 percent). Historically, the highest marginal rate has been much, much higher—ranging from 70 percent before the Reagan tax cuts and 90 percent during the Kennedy administration (before the famous Kennedy-Johnson tax cut of 1964).[10] Studies (and common sense) indicate that punitive tax rates distort economic incentives. As tax rates increase, the wealthy work less. So tax rates should be high enough to raise sufficient revenues to finance the government's operations, but not so high that they discourage people from working. Forty percent seems to be the highest marginal rate that accomplishes this dual goal.

Conclusion. The proposed income tax system should be simpler and much more progressive. With the elimination of many of the deductions, higher-income families will pay more in taxes. However, the wealthy and middle class will benefit from a reduction in compliance costs (as much as $2,500 in compliance costs for wealthy families), greater economic growth from a simpler system, a more reasonable estate tax, and lower taxes on capital gains and dividends.

Estate Tax

The federal estate tax has stirred controversy for the past two hundred years. Though inheritance taxes financed both the Civil War and Spanish-American War, they were quickly repealed. The first permanent federal estate tax was enacted in 1916. Over the years, the estate tax has been modified to provide an exemption for estates below a certain level (currently, $2 million). Estates worth less than this amount can pass from one generation to the next without an estate tax.[11] Accordingly, the vast majority of estates to pass hands without the payment of estate taxes.

While the US estate tax has been the subject of considerable debate, it comprises a relatively small portion of the overall tax revenues, typically less than 2 percent.[12] Today, Republicans have rightly attacked the estate tax as unfair because it taxes dollars twice. That is, a person's earnings are generally taxed during his lifetime. Then, at death, they are

CHART 10-3

Taxes Paid Over Past 30 Years on Earnings Saved	$1.3 million
Taxes Paid on Investment Income	$1.3 million
Total Taxes Paid	**$2.6 million**
Estate Tax Paid	$1.5 million
Total Taxes to Federal Government on Savings and Estate	$4.1 million
Amount Left to Nephew	$4.5 million

taxed again. There is much logic to this argument, as illustrated by the following example.

Example 1. Uncle Robert, a highly paid professional, wants to leave his estate to his nephew. Uncle Robert lives frugally and saves $100,000 per year over thirty years. He invests in the bond market and earns a little more than 6 percent per annum on his bond portfolio. At the time of his death, Uncle Robert has amassed an estate worth approximately $6 million. Based on today's tax laws, chart 10-3 provides an illustration of the federal income taxes and estate taxes paid by Uncle Robert.

In this example, Uncle Robert has paid over $4 million in taxes on his savings and estate taxes, while leaving just $4.5 million to his nephew—an effective tax rate of nearly 50 percent. Accordingly, many people go through elaborate and perfectly legal tax planning to mitigate the impact of estate taxes. In many cases, these schemes would not have been implemented but for the high estate tax burden. On this basis, many Republicans have called for a complete repeal of the estate tax. This would mean that Uncle Robert's estate would pass to his nephew free of estate tax. After all, Uncle Robert has already paid substantial taxes on the dollars included in his estate. There is much logic in this position. However, the logic falls down if Uncle Robert accumulates his wealth differently.

CHART 10-4

	Highly Paid Professional	Business Owner
Taxes Paid Over Past 30 Years on Earnings Saved	$1.3 million	None
Taxes Paid on Investment Income	$1.3 million	None
Total Taxes Paid	**$2.6 million**	**None**
Estate Tax	None	None
Total Taxes Paid to Federal Government	$2.6 million	None

Example 2. Assume for a moment that Uncle Robert inherits (tax free) $10,000 from his grandmother and starts a business Over the next thirty years, his business prospers, and at the time of his death, it is worth $6 million. If there was no estate tax, Uncle Robert, the successful entrepreneur, would avoid paying taxes on his business all together, a somewhat unfair outcome when compared to the taxes paid by a high wage earner (the first example). See chart 10-4.

Under a tax system with no estate tax, Uncle Robert leaves this valuable asset to his nephew without paying any tax on the asset at all, since the increase in value is in the form of capital appreciation that has not been realized and taxed in his lifetime. When compared to the situation of a highly paid professional who has paid taxes his whole life and accumulated the same degree of wealth, this hardly seems fair.

Additionally, this tax regime might also have the effect of distorting decision-making by Uncle Robert. For example, Uncle Robert may be offered a significant amount of money for his business as he nears retirement. However, he knows that he can pass the business to his nephew, a poor businessman, without tax consequences. In this case, Uncle Robert might decide to avoid paying capital gains taxes and leave the business to his nephew. The potential consequence might be that the nephew destroys the value of the business over time through inept management.

Different Estate Tax Approach: Assumed Sale at Death. There is a better and fairer approach. The estate tax should be calculated assuming that the decedent (Uncle Robert) "sells" his estate to his heir(s) at fair market value at his death. The estate would then pay capital gains the difference between the fair market value and the estate's tax basis. In that case, Uncle Robert's estate would be permitted to deduct any tax basis he had in the asset at the time of death. In doing so, the estate would not be double-taxed.

In the first example, Uncle Robert, the frugal executive, would have a $6 million tax basis in his bond portfolio, because he had paid taxes on investment income over time. Thus, the nephew would inherit the entire estate *without additional estate tax*. After all, Uncle Robert already paid taxes on the accumulated earnings.

In the second example, where Uncle Robert built a $6 million business on a $10,000 investment, his estate would pay approximately $900,000 in *capital gains* taxes ($5.99 million gain taxed at 15 percent, the current long-term capital gains tax rate). But it is important to note that this gain is being taxed only once. More important, Uncle Robert would be agnostic about whether to leave the business to his nephew or to sell it during his lifetime and leave the proceeds to his nephew. The tax code would not influence him one way or the other.

This system would be fair because gains would only be taxed once and it would not be difficult to administer. Taxpayers are already required to maintain records relating to their capital assets (in order to calculate capital gains when these assets are sold). This would make accounting for such assets at death fairly easy.

Revenue Center. The estate tax should be a revenue center and generate at least 2 percent of overall tax revenues. If appropriately structured, the estate tax should not skew economic activity. It would also be fair because estates under this tax system would not be subject to double taxation. And if the exemption was greatly reduced, it should generate a reasonable revenue stream for the federal government.

Capital Gains

Efficient economies allow capital (human or financial) to flow to its highest and best use without significant friction or impediments. For example, US labor laws generally allow employers to fire workers without significant restrictions or red tape. This is in sharp contrast with Europe. France, Germany, and even Japan all have laws that are highly protective of workers. By allowing human capital to flow to its best and highest use, the United States has generated economic growth far in excess of its European counterparts. The same premise holds true for the allocation of financial capital. Tax policy can have a profound impact on capital formation and the free flow of financial capital. On this front, the United States has an opportunity to promote greater economic growth by reforming its tax regime covering capital gains, dividends, and corporate taxes.

Capital Gains Rates. An investor generates a capital gain when he or she buys an asset and then sells it for a profit at a later date. The profit, or gain, from the sale is considered a "capital gain." Historically, capital gains have been taxed at a lower rate than income.

The principal issue with a capital gains tax is that it impedes the free flow of capital. If the capital gains tax rate is too high, an investor may defer an asset sale or not sell the asset at all. In this regard, both the investor and the government lose. The investor cannot take the gain and redeploy the proceeds to a more profitable endeavor. The government does not generate tax revenues from the embedded gain. Thus, the capital gains tax rate must be high enough to generate revenues for the government without being so high that it discourages the sale of an asset by an investor.

A simple example illustrates this point. Assume that Bill Jones started a business from scratch and it is now worth $100,000. Bill now has a $100,000 unrealized gain in his business. He is trying to decide whether to sell his business and invest in another business. In a tax-neutral world, he will sell his business for $100,000 and invest in the second business if the second business has better prospects. That is, if Bill believes that his current business will grow at 10 percent per year and the second will grow at 12 percent per year, he will sell his current company and invest in the second one. From a societal standpoint, this is a decision that we want Bill to make. After all, by investing in the second business, Bill may create jobs and greater societal wealth. But this example is set in a tax-free world. If there is a capital gains tax, Bill's decision becomes more complicated. And the higher the capital gains tax rate, the higher a return that Bill Jones will have to generate on the second investment to offset the tax impact, as illustrated by chart 10-5.

In a high capital gains environment, Bill Jones has to generate 40 percent higher returns on the second business to justify selling his cur-

CHART 10-5

	No Capital Gains Tax	15% Capital Gains Tax	28% Capital Gains Tax (pre−1986)
Value of Business	$100,000	$100,000	$100,000
Taxes Paid on Sale	$0	$15,000	$28,000
Net Proceeds	$100,000	$85,000	$72,000
Break-Even Return for Second Investment (assuming Bill's current business generates a 10% return)	10.1%	11.9%	14%

CHART 10-6

	Lower Tax Rate	Higher Tax Rate
Asset Cost	$100,000	$100,000
Embedded Gain	$20,000	$20,000
Capital Gains Tax	15%	28%
Capital Velocity / Avg. Hold Period	2 years (assumed)	4 years (assumed)
Annualized Tax Revenues	$1,500	$1,400
Conclusion: With greater velocity of capital, a lower tax regime can generate more tax revenues than a higher tax rate environment. Further, by a more efficient allocation of capital, a lower tax rate environment can generate stronger economic growth over time.		

rent business. Accordingly, investors will forego otherwise attractive opportunities because they do not generate significant enough returns to overcome the tax burden. Obviously, if more attractive investments are bypassed, economic growth will not be as robust as in a lower capital gains environment.

Revenue Neutral. In addition to promoting economic growth, a lower capital gains tax may well be revenue neutral, or may actually generate higher tax revenues. Capital gains tax revenues are a function of (a) the tax rate, (b) gains on capital, and (c) the turnover in the capital base. A lower capital gains rate should promote a faster turnover in the capital base because investors can move capital from one investment to another without a significant tax burden. In addition, by allowing capital to flow to its best and highest use, a low capital gains rate should spur economic growth. Thus, even at a lower rate, the government might generate more taxes than with a higher tax rate, as illustrated by chart 10-6.

Indeed, after the 2003 capital gains tax cut, capital gains tax revenues surged by nearly 50 percent.[13] Thus, despite the lower rate, the turnover of the capital base generated ever higher tax revenues for the US treasury.

Unlike long-term capital gains rate, short-term capital gains should be taxed at a much higher rate, which is the case in our current system. Our system provides that short-term capital gains are taxed at the taxpayer's highest rate on income. So instead of paying 15 percent capital gains rate (the long-term capital gains rate), a taxpayer in the highest marginal tax rate bracket would pay 35 percent. The higher short term capital gains rate encourages longer-term investments and discourages short-term trading. *Conclusion: Long-term capital gain tax rates should remain at 15% or lower. Short-term rates should be the same as the highest marginal rate, for the reason indicated.*

Dividends

The taxation of dividends presents a trickier issue because the policy considerations are more complicated. At the moment, the tax regime surrounding dividends is terrible (but better than it used to be). The current dividend tax skews a corporation's incentive to use debt financing vis-à-vis equity financing. In particular, if a corporation issues debt to an investor, the investor is paid interest income, which is taxable to the investor at ordinary rates. And the corporation gets a tax deduction for the interest paid to the investor. Therefore, the interest amounts paid and received on corporate debt offset one another from a tax perspective, as illustrated in chart 10-7.

If a corporation issues equity and pays a dividend, the corporation does not get a tax deduction for the dividend paid, but the investor is

CHART 10-7 – Taxation of Interest on Debt

	Corporation	Investor
Corporate Earnings	$1,000,000	
Interest Paid/Received	$100,000 paid	$100,000 received
Tax Implications	$100,000 deduction	$100,000 taxable income
The tax deduction and the taxable income exactly offset each other.		

CHART 10-8 – Taxation of Dividends

	Corporation	Investor
Earnings	$1,000,000	
Dividend Paid/Received	$100,000 paid	$100,000 received
Tax Implications	No deduction	$100,000 taxable income (currently taxed at 15%; likely to go back to 35% or higher)
An additional $15,000 goes to the government in this example ($35,000 under the old law, assuming the highest marginal rate).		

taxed on the dividend. The result is an additional tax imposed by the government on equity vis-à-vis debt as illustrated in chart 10-8.

Further, if a corporation pays a dividend to its shareholders, the corporation's earnings are taxed twice, which substantially drives up the tax rate on those earnings.

Even at today's "low" dividends tax rate of 15 percent, the double taxation increases the effective tax rate on dividends to nearly 50 percent. And, obviously, if we go back to the old dividend tax rate, the double taxation becomes even more punitive, approaching nearly 60 percent as illustrated in chart 10-9.

Excessive Use of Debt Financing. Because of the impact of double taxation, a dividend tax encourages the use of debt versus equity. In particular, a corporation that uses debt financing has a significant tax advantage over one that uses equity financing, as illustrated in chart 10-10.

Thus, the tax code creates an incentive to use debt financing over equity financing. The tax code should make the two forms of financ-

CHART 10-9

	Tax Rate (15% Dividend Tax)	Tax Rate (35% Tax Rate, Old Tax Law)
Earnings	$1,000,000	$1,000,000
Corporate Tax Paid (35%)	($350,000)	($350,000)
Net Income	$650,000	$650,000
Dividends Paid	$650,000	$650,000
Dividend Taxes Paid by Investor	$97,500	$227,500
Net Left for Investor	$552,500	$422,500
Effective Tax Rate on Dividends	47.5%	57.5%

CHART 10-10

	Equity Financing	Debt Financing
Earnings	$1,000,000	$1,000,000
Dividends/Interest Paid	($500,000)	($500,000)
After-Tax Earnings	$1,000,000 (Dividends are not tax deductible by corporation.)	$500,000 (Interest payments are tax deductible.)
Corporate Taxes Due (35% tax rate)	($350,000)	($175,000)
Remaining Cash	$150,000	$325,000

ing equitable from a tax perspective and allow the market and market participants to determine the best manner to finance a particular business from a risk-reward perspective.

Reduction in Payment of Dividends. Over the past few decades, corporations have cut back on the amount of their earnings they repay to investors in the form of dividends. Dividend yields (the earnings distributed to shareholders, divided by share price) have declined significantly over the past forty-five years. In 1960, the dividend yield was approximately 3.4 percent. It remained above 3 percent for much of the next thirty years, falling below 3 percent only once.[14] Since 1991, however, the dividend yield has stayed below 3 percent. Since 1996, the dividend yield has actually been less than 2 percent.[15] Given the America's aging population, corporations should be encouraged to return capital to shareholders in the form of dividends, not discouraged.[16]

Conclusion. Dividends should only be taxed once. If the earnings are taxed at the corporate level, then a dividend should not be taxed when received by the shareholder. Not only does this skew the incentive to issue debt verses equity, it also ignores the demographic shift that is under way in the United States. As the baby boomers retire, they will need more yield for spending needs. By eliminating the double taxation of dividends, the tax code will put equity financing on even footing with debt financing and encourage corporations to pay dividends to their shareholders.

Corporate Taxes

The reduction or elimination of corporate taxes represents the greatest opportunity for the United States to enhance its global competitiveness through tax reform. The rationale behind the reduction or elimination of corporate taxes is twofold. First, corporations do not pay taxes. Tax costs are merely passed on to consumers in the form of higher prices. Since the poor spend more of their income on goods and services than the wealthy, corporate taxes tend to be regressive because they fall disproportionately on the poor.

Second, US corporate taxes are among the highest in the developed world.[17] This creates a competitive disadvantage for US corporations vis-à-vis its foreign competitors. Chart 10-11 illustrates how a US corporation is placed at a competitive disadvantage versus a foreign corporation in a lower rate tax jurisdiction. The chart assumes that both corporations generate the same profit and profit margin, and compares the US corporation with a company from a country with a lower corporate tax. The final column assumes that the US corporate income tax is eliminated entirely and outlines the pricing advantage that this provides to the US corporation.

As noted in the table, the US corporate tax rate takes a significant bite of a US corporation's profits, leaving it with a lower after-tax mar-

CHART 10-11

Tax Effect	US Corporation Paying Highest Current Rate	Foreign Corporation with Lower Tax Rate	US Corporation (Assuming No Taxes)
Revenues	1,000,000,000	1,000,000,000	1,000,000,000
Expenses	700,000,000	700,000,000	700,000,000
Operating Income	300,000,000	300,000,000	300,000,000
Tax Rate	35%	20%	0%
Net Income	195,000,000	240,000,000	300,000,000
Pricing Advantage		20% over US corporation paying highest current rate	20% over low tax jurisdiction

gin than many of its global competitors. The lower margin means that the US corporation has a lower margin for error, and has less pricing power than its foreign counterpart. However, by lowering the tax rate, the United States could go on the offensive.

Incentive to Conduct Business in America. With the higher US tax rate, American corporations are at a competitive disadvantage vis-à-vis lower tax markets in the global marketplace. This is during a time of rapidly deteriorating trade balances and job losses (some to overseas markets). Since corporate owners will try to maintain their return on equity expectations, corporations will allocate capital to lower tax countries, which will benefit workers in those countries. Or they will push down the wages of domestic workers to compensate for taxes.[18]

Job Creation in America. By keeping corporate taxes lower or eliminating them altogether, American workers will see an increase in wages, corporate owners will see modestly higher profits, and American consumers will see lower prices. Obviously, some of these gains will be offset by higher taxes elsewhere.

Making Up Lost Revenues. Corporate taxes generated about $370 billion in revenues in fiscal year 2007, or about 15 percent our total tax revenues.[19] The lost tax revenues would be offset in one of two manners. First, corporate earnings could be "passed" to the shareholders and taxed at the shareholder level. In this case, there would not be a significant shortfall in tax revenues. Second, if corporate earnings were not passed to shareholders, the shortfall would have to be made up through higher taxes elsewhere. Assuming that a significant portion of the tax reduction is passed on to workers in the form of higher wages, the federal government would pick up a large part of the corporate tax loss through higher individual taxes. To the extent that a portion is passed on to investors in the form of higher dividends, individual investors will pay taxes on their dividends (assuming that they are not taxed first at the corporate level). Between these two, the loss of corporate tax revenues should be significantly offset. The remaining differential would be partially offset through greater corporate opportunity and activity. Any remaining tax gap would be picked up through higher tax rates on individual income and a carbon-based tax (along with spending cuts).

Conclusion. In eliminating the corporate tax, America would have a significant competitive advantage over corporations from other nations, who would be subject to higher taxes. By this cost advantage, US corporations would create more opportunities to conduct business in the United States.

Shifting Budget Priorities. Shoring Up the Nation's Balance Sheet

With a more rationale tax regime, the United States can turn its attention to budgeting and allocating the dollars raised to address national priorities and to significantly reduce the budget deficit. The United States should establish an overall budget target of 20 percent of GDP, then create targets for each category of spending. Chart 10-12 provides for major areas of change in the federal budget based on the recommendations in this book.

Some of these goals, particularly the reduction of our defense budget (discussed in a subsequent chapter), may take several years to achieve, but the process should start immediately. Unless it does, the market will start forcing America to live within its means, which would

CHART 10-12

Budget Item	Current Cost	Recommended Cost (Target as % of GDP)	(Savings)/ Additional Costs	Comment
2007 Budget Deficit (Cash)			$500 billion	
Social Security	$500 billion (4% of GDP)	$400 billion (3% of GDP today; 4% maximum as the baby boomers retire en masse)	($100 billion)	Savings will result from reducing or eliminating benefits for the wealthy, indexing benefits to inflation rather than wage growth, etc. Over time, these savings will be offset by a greater number of retirees.
Medicare	$400 billion (3.1% of GDP)	$350 billion (2.5% of GDP); 4% maximum as the baby boomers retire en masse)	($50 billion)	See above.
Defense	$700 billion (5% of GDP)	$450 billion (3.5% of GDP)	($250 billion)	Reduction of troops abroad; redeploy a portion to defending the border.
Energy Import Tax		$100 billion	($100 billion)	A $20 tax on imported oil from nations not bordering the US.
Increased Taxes from Immigrants		$70 billion	($70 billion)	By legalizing illegal immigrants (but not making them citizens), the US can start collecting tax. Revenues.
Lost Revenues from Retirement Savings		$70 billion	$70 billion	The cost of a dollar-for-dollar tax credit on the first $1,000 contributed to a qualified employee retirement account.
Dividend and Capital Gains			$30 billion	Dividend tax would be eliminated.
Corporate Taxes	$370 billion	$0	$370 billion	Corporate taxes would be eliminated.
Personal Taxes	$1.8 trillion (13% of GDP)	$2.1 trillion (15% of GDP)	($300 billion)	Personal taxes would increase due to the elimination of deductions, a pass-through of corporate earnings and an increase in marginal rates among higher income workers. The quid pro quo would be the elimination of corporate taxes and maintenance of low capital gains and dividend taxes.
Adjusted Deficit (Cash)			<$100 billion	
Percentage of GDP			<1%	

CHART 10-13

Balance Sheet Item	US Government (Current)	Proposed	Comments
National Debt Owed to Outside Investors	$5.1 trillion	$5.1 trillion	We have to pay the national debt owed to third parties.
National Debt Owed on Social Security/Medicare	$3.9 trillion	-0-	Confirming the system as a "pay go" system, which would eliminate the IOUs in the Social Security and Medicare trust funds.
Obligations to Federal Workers/Veterans; Other Obligations	$4.8 trillion	$4.8 trillion	The US cannot welsh on its obligations to veterans or government employees; however, federal employees should have the same savings system as the rest of America (revised 401k).
Future Obligations of Social Security and Medicare	$40.9 trillion	-0-	Confirming the system as "pay go" and eliminating the charade that these are "funded" would eliminate Social Security ($6.8 trillion) and Medicare ($34.1 trillion) liabilities.
Other Obligations	$0.9 trillion	$0.9 trillion	
Adjusted Negative Net Worth	$55.7 trillion	$10 trillion	The current case means the US government is bankrupt; the second case indicates the US government is solvent.
% of GDP	400% of GDP (junk bond status)	<80% of GDP	The US goes from junk bond status levels of debt back to investment grade, with a clean balance sheet.

occur if foreigners started selling US treasuries, driving interest rates upward. In that event, the nation would be forced to make dramatic cuts in entitlements and defense spending at a time not of our choosing, quite possibly during a period of economic crisis. If that occurred, the pain and dislocation associated with the budget cuts will be profound and the economic hardship painful.

Nation's Balance Sheet: Reducing Long-Term Entitlements. The second phase is changing the composition of both Social Security and Medicare to social insurance programs, rather than entitlements. The US government should restructure these programs (as suggested in earlier chapters) to be the social safety nets for Americans. Once done, the nation's balance sheet cleans up nicely as illustrated in chart 10-13.[19]

The national debt (as a percentage of GDP) can be further reduced over time, even if America continues to run a modest budget deficit. By way of example, if America runs a deficit of 1 percent or less of GDP for ten years and has economic growth of 3 percent of GDP over the same time frame, it will reduce its national debt from circa 80 percent of GDP to less than 60 percent of GDP, a very manageable figure.

Conclusion. The recommended changes should not come as a surprise to most Americans. Most Americans understand that the US government cannot continue living outside its means indefinitely. At some point, America will be forced to restructure its finances and develop a more sensible means to raise tax revenues and prioritize spending. Although some may fear the pain associated with these decisions, opportunities abound for America if it can tackle these problems in the near term.

For example, through a more sensible tax regime, America can raise tax revenues in a more efficacious manner and gain a competitive advantage over its global competitors. By establishing targets for overall spending and each budget item, the United States can spend its money more wisely and avoid needless debt that has crippled so many past superpowers. Many of these recommendations can be implemented without inflicting significant pain on the American people, but the longer US policymakers wait, the more painful the medicine will be.

CHAPTER 11

Monetary Policy

Most Americans (and economists) accept the simple premise that central planning does not work. Few examples of successful central planning exist. Yet the failures are many, ranging from the old Soviet Union's long series of failed five-year plans to the disastrous economies of Cuba and North Korea, each a product of extensive central planning. Americans frown upon the extensive government regulation of the economies of Western Europe, particularly France, Germany, and Italy. They see ineffective economies that grow at a slower rate and result in an overall lower standard of living than that of the United States. If most Americans view central planning as a flawed concept, why would the United States permit the Federal Reserve control the price of one of the most important components of the economy: short-term interest rates? Yet, that is precisely what the Federal Reserve does. The purpose of this chapter is to challenge the notion a group of central planners should set short-term interest rates by (a) presenting multiple examples of how this has failed and (b) suggesting a better framework for setting short-term rates and providing market stability during times of crisis.

US Monetary Policy

Monetary policy and fiscal policy represent the twin pillars of US economic policy. Monetary policy focuses largely on the nation's money supply and credit, which in turn influences interest rates (directly) and overall economic activity (indirectly).

Focus of Monetary Policy

The goal of monetary policy is to maintain economic growth and full employment while minimizing the risk of inflation (or deflation), not an easy task for central planners. Inflation is has been called a "monetary phenomenon" by Milton Friedman, a respected economist. Indeed, inflation is generally defined as too much money chasing too few goods and services. This occurs when the money supply grows faster than real economic output. Inflation also tends to be exacerbated by "inflationary expectations." That is, when people expect inflation in the future, they tend to purchase things now in order to avoid paying higher prices later. Further, they demand higher wages to offset higher prices. This fuels higher prices.

Deflation, obviously, is just the opposite: a dwindling money supply chasing too many goods, which has the obvious effect of depressing prices. The money supply declines because people take money out of circulation by saving more. This occurs when prices are falling. Believing that prices will continue to fall, people hold on to their money expecting to purchase goods in the future at a lower price. Deflation periodically occurred in the United States when it was on the gold standard and the money supply was more or less fixed. More recently, it has occurred in Japan, from the early 1990s to the present. As prices fell, the Japanese saved more and more, causing further declines in prices.[1] This phenomenon was referred to by John Maynard Keynes as the "liquidity trap," which some believe caused the deflationary spiral of the Great Depression and also the deep and prolonged deflationary recession in Japan.[2]

Brief History of US Monetary Policy

For most of America's existence, deflation was a bigger problem than inflation. Deflation was a haunting specter because the United States' currency was backed by precious metals for much of its history. Under the gold standard, the United States was required to convert its currency into gold upon the request of the bearer of dollars, Thus, the money supply was limited to the amount of gold held by the US treasury or banking system. So during periods of excess production, there was too little money chasing too many goods and services, and prices fell. In that case, people would horde money with the expectation that prices would fall further, often a self-fulfilling prophecy.

This occurred during the post–Civil War period, as output started rising during the Industrial Revolution. Falling prices gave rise to William Jennings Bryan's famous "Cross of Gold" speech, in which he decried the gold standard. He believed that a limited money supply favored Eastern bankers, who could drive down the price of goods and crops by restricting the money supply. Bryan argued for an expansion of the money supply by permitting dollars (reserve notes) to be backed not only by gold but also by silver, which would have the effect of increasing the money supply and allowing prices to increase. The last great episode of deflation in the United States occurred during the Great Depression. Since then, deflation has given way to inflation as the principal problem facing US policymakers.

With the abandonment of the gold standard, the US transitioned to a "fiat" money regime. Fiat money is not backed by gold or any other tangible asset; rather, it is backed by the "full faith and credit" of its government. With that change, the US money supply was no longer constrained by the amount of gold held by the US Treasury and banking system. Rather, it was only constrained by US fiscal and monetary policy. At this point, the Federal Reserve took on even greater importance.

The Federal Reserve

Today, US monetary policy is controlled by the Federal Reserve Board, a quasi-governmental body. The Federal Reserve largely controls monetary policy by setting the short-term interest rates that banks use to make loans to one another (called the Fed Funds rate). To a lesser extent, it establishes capital requirements for banks and conducts open market activities. The Federal Reserve is led by its chairman, who is nominated by the president and confirmed by Congress. The chairman heads a board of governors and the Federal Open Market Committee (FOMC), which sets US monetary policy.

The FOMC is comprised of twelve members of the Federal Reserve, including the chairman.[3,4] While the chairman only has one vote (for setting interest rates) on the FOMC, his power is enormous. Through his public comments, the chairman can move the financial markets dramatically. Because of this, the chairman is supposed to operate outside the orbit of political pressures and whims. Alan Greenspan served in this role for over eighteen years. Today, Ben S. Bernanke is the chairman of the Federal Reserve.

Like its chairman, the FOMC's power is also enormous. In establishing the Fed Funds rate, the FOMC has a great deal of control over short-term interest rates. The lower the Fed Funds rate, the lower the rates on consumer and business loans because these rates are often tied to the Fed Funds rate. The FOMC establishes short-term rates based on inflationary and employment expectations, among other things. If it anticipates inflationary pressures, the FOMC will raise short-term rates to take money out of the economy (people will save more or spend less). This has the effect of slowing economic activity and dampening inflation. If it believes the economy is slowing, the FOMC will lower interest rates to increase the money supply (people will spend more) and simulate economic activity.

The FOMC does not, however, set long-term rates. These are set by the market based on supply and demand characteristics. After taking into account all available information, millions of market participants establish a price for long-term treasuries, which has the effect of establishing the interest rate for these securities. So, in contrast to short-term rates (or Fed Funds rate), long-term interest rates are set by the market, just like almost every other commodity.

Monetary Policy from 1966 to 1981

During the mid to late 1960s and early 1970s, money supply was expanding rapidly. During the mid-to-late 1960s, President Johnson began running large deficits to finance the Vietnam War and the "War on Poverty." By the early 1970s, Federal Reserve chairman Arthur Burns was running a relatively "loose" monetary policy. Easy monetary and fiscal policy culminated in a run on the US dollar by foreigners. These foreign investors and governments feared that the dollar would continue to decline in value and tendered their dollars to the US government for repayment in gold. Unable or unwilling to honor these requests, President Nixon abandoned the gold standard in 1971. At this point, the ability of the Federal Reserve and federal government to expand the money supply was endless.

The result was predictable. Once off the gold standard, the dollar collapsed, prompting a panic by trading partners who saw the value of their dollar holdings decline markedly. Appeals to Washington went largely unheeded, with then Secretary of the Treasury John Connally famously saying, "The dollar may be our currency, but it is your problem."[5] For the next ten years, inflation was the norm—a dark era for US monetary and fiscal policy. Congress began running large peacetime budget deficits, unusual for the United States up to that point. The Federal Reserve kept short-term *real* interest rates (interest rates, less inflation) relatively low. With low real short-term rates, people were encouraged to borrow and spend, since capital was artificially cheap. Too much money was chasing too few goods and inflation soared. This trend accelerated as inflationary expectations became engrained—people wanted to purchase today, fearing that prices would increase tomorrow.

Inflation was not subdued until Federal Reserve chairman Paul Volcker increased short-term interest rates to 20 percent in 1981.[6] This resulted in a sharp decrease in the money supply—as people saved more and spent less. With the contraction of the money supply, the United States went into a deep recession in 1981–1982, the worst since the Great Depression. But as bitter as the medicine was, it resulted in a dramatic reduction of inflation and inflationary expectations. In addition, at that juncture the first portion of the baby boom generation was transitioning into middle age and started having a profound impact on productivity and economic growth. Due to a combination of strong demographics (and production) and low inflationary expectations, the next twenty years were punctuated by low interest rates and inflation, as the relationship between the money supply and goods and services remained relatively in balance.

Monetary Policy under Alan Greenspan

Paul Volcker had to make difficult decisions in order to address the inflationary spiral, a problem created in part by his predecessors. Ben S. Bernanke, the current chairman of the Federal Reserve, faces a similar situation. To avoid these problems in the future, US policymakers should understand how decisions were made in the past, particularly during the Greenspan era. Armed with this insight, policymakers can correct some of the fundamental flaws in the current Federal Reserve system.

The FOMC makes interest rate decisions based on economic data gathered by various branches of the government, including the Federal Reserve itself. The quality of these decisions is dictated by: (a) the quality of the economic information provided by the federal government and (b) the decision-making capabilities of the Federal Reserve. Decisions made by the FOMC are tempered and shaped by the views and biases of men and women on the FOMC, particularly the Federal Reserve chairman. Although the Fed chairman has only one vote of twelve on the FOMC, he has considerable power in the public marketplace. Every utterance is scrutinized by the markets to get a sense of whether the FOMC is going to raise or lower short-term interest rates, or leave them alone.

Greenspan enjoyed considerable adulation by the markets for navigating the economy for eighteen years, seemingly steering it adroitly through the shoals and rocks. During that time, he made public comments about the markets—good and bad—that often had a profound impact on the markets themselves. In particular, Greenspan was famous for keeping his own counsel on the direction of rates. While he studied reams of data to set short-term rates, he seemed to enjoy substituting a healthy dose of subjectivity into his analysis. He guarded his reputation for economic prescience, typically by making statements that were vague and difficult to quantify. With financial professionals clinging to his every word, he gained a reputation as the principal architect of the economic expansion that occurred on his watch. By the latter part of his tenure, however, Greenspan's focus on his legacy and his actions created at least three bubbles.

The Greenspan Bubbles

From 1999 to 2005, Greenspan contributed to or created three asset bubbles, either through his comments or as the direct result of Federal Reserve monetary policy:

Equity Bubble of Late 1990s

After criticizing the equity market participants in December 1996 for displaying "irrational exuberance" (a phrase first used by noted Yale professor Robert Shiller), the US stock market tumbled by 3.5 percent over the next several trading days before resuming its heady march upward.[7]

The equity markets continued upward in relatively unabated fashion for the next two years, until Greenspan capitulated in 1998. In particular, Greenspan said that market valuations appeared to be supported by the technology revolution and the productivity growth associated with it.[8] Based on the blessing from Greenspan, the markets surged a bit more before plummeting back to earth starting in April 2000. With these comments, Greenspan gave his seal of approval and provided one last push to the great speculative "Internet bubble" of 1998–2000. Investors who took Greenspan's words to heart and invested in the US equity markets lost about 40 percent of their investment over the following two years.

The Fixed-Income Bubble of 2003

Sensing the risk of a deflating stock market bubble (which he had helped create), Greenspan began lowering interest rates aggressively in early 2001, to create a "soft landing." Yet the stock market kept falling. In March 2003, Greenspan sounded the alarm about deflation, creating yet another bubble.[9] This time, however, it was in the fixed-income markets. With Greenspan's comments, fixed-income instruments of all stripes, particularly high-quality ones, surged in value, since fixed income tends to hold its value during deflationary times.

Largely a product of Greenspan's creation, this deflationary scare wreaked havoc with pension plans. Pension plans have to value their future liabilities based on long-term interest rates. When rates fall, a pension plan's future obligations increase in value. That is, with low interest rates, it takes a larger fixed income investment to generate enough income to meet future obligations. So companies with pension plans had to find more cash to put into these plans to fund future liabilities, at the same time as stock prices were tumbling.

As it turned out, Greenspan's comments, particularly for US pension plans, could not have been more poorly timed for pension plans, or more wrong. Inflation, as it turns out, is the beast that will have to

CHART 11-1

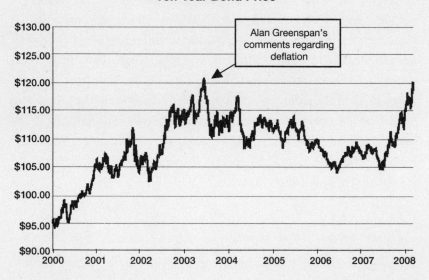

Ten Year Bond Price

Source: Bloomberg; Salient Partners, L.P.

be slain by US policymakers, a simple fact that most American families understand quite well.

The Housing and Financial Asset Bubble

The biggest bubble created by Greenspan is the housing bubble, caused by artificially low interest rates between 2002 through 2006 time frame. Greenspan helped create the housing bubble—and a litany of other dislocations—by holding short-term rates too low for far too long. In particular, he held "real" rates (interest rates after inflation) at or below o percent for nearly four years as illustrated in chart 11-2.

By holding real interest rates negative for a prolonged period of time, the Federal Reserve caused profound dislocations in the marketplace, which the United States is only now addressing.

Plummeting Savings Rate. Explosion of Trade Deficit. Artificially low rates encouraged Americans to consume rather than save. After all, financing costs were very low for almost all consumer products, whether

CHART 11-2

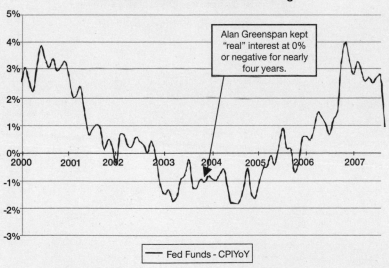

Fed Funds Rate - CPI Annual Change

Source: Bloomberg; Salient Partners

cars, flat-screen TVs, washer-dryers, etc. And low interest rates provided very little incentive to save. As a result, our national savings rate
declined markedly—to the lowest levels since the Great Depression.
And because the Chinese kept their currency artificially depressed
against the dollar (discussed earlier), America's plunging savings rate
was accompanied by a rapidly expanding trade deficit, which began
shortly after our monetary policy began to ease. Chart 11-3 illustrates
these two points.

In effect, the US and Chinese governments were encouraging
Americans to spend and not save. The US government did so by holding interest rates very low and the Chinese government by loaning the
US government and consumer hundreds of billions of dollars at these
low rates. The Chinese government was in effect seller-financing Chinese consumer goods to American consumers. Baby boomers were encouraged to spend at the exact time they should have been saving. At
the same time, the federal government started running large deficits.
This borrowing spree occurred at a time when both consumers and the

CHART 11-3

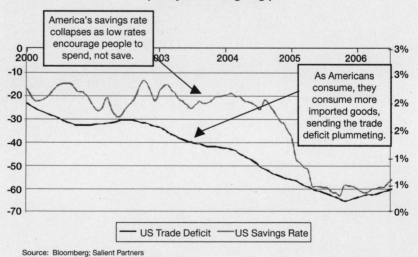

US Trade Deficit vs. US Savings Rate
(one year rolling avg.)

America's savings rate collapses as low rates encourage people to spend, not save.

As Americans consume, they consume more imported goods, sending the trade deficit plummeting.

US Trade Deficit ——— US Savings Rate

Source: Bloomberg; Salient Partners

federal government should have been preparing for the retirement of the baby boomer generation by reducing debt.

Housing Bubble. In addition, with short-term rates at historical lows, consumers started speculating and using cheap capital to finance "hard" assets, particularly real estate. With interest rates so low, consumers could afford more expensive houses, especially if they used adjustable-rate mortgages (ARMs) based on short-term rates. So consumers started bidding up housing prices and using ARMs to buy homes.

The speculation in real estate would not have occurred had money been priced appropriately during this period; the surge in housing prices corresponded almost perfectly with the dramatic reduction in short-term rates.

Pressure on US Dollar. The subprime debacle may prove minor when compared to the dislocation that will occur when the Chinese finally realize it is no longer in their interest to buy US assets. This will occur because of the collapse of the US dollar due to the loose monetary and fiscal policy of the past several years. If the dollar continues its fall, long-term interest rates in the United States will have to increase to attract capital to finance US deficits. Both the US equity and fixed income markets would plummet. Further, the dollar's collapse would at some point threaten the dollar's primacy as the world's lone reserve currency. As was the case in the late 1960s and early 1970s, poor fiscal and monetary policy would fuel a collapse in the dollar and a surge in gold prices, inflation, and interest rates.

Other Evidence of the Folly of Setting Short-Term Rates: The Inverted Yield Curve

Much of this chapter has been devoted to criticizing Greenspan's performance as Federal Reserve chairman. In some respects, the criticism is fair. Greenspan has been lauded and unduly credited with managing the economic boom of the late 1980s through early 2000s, when the credit should go to the baby boomer generation. This generation

provided the productivity growth and manpower that fueled an economic boom and overcame dubious policy decisions. However, in one
important respect, the criticism lodged at Greenspan is not fair. The
whole concept of central planning is flawed. So it is unfair to criticize
a man for trying to do what is inherently impossible, something that
is better suited for the market.

This point is illustrated by a phenomenon that is at least partly[10] the
product of Federal Reserve policy of setting short-term interest rates:
the inverted yield curve. A yield curve is a chart that shows interest
rates on the x-axis and the duration of a bond on the y-axis. Under
normal circumstances, the yield curve is upwardly sloped (normal yield
curve). A normal yield curve indicates that it costs more (higher interest rates) to borrow money for a longer period of time than a shorter
one. This is largely due to the risks associated with making long-term
loans. These risks include (a) interest rate risks (the risk that interest
rates will rise in the future, making your bond worth less) and (b) the
greater risk of default associated with longer-term loans. The following chart illustrates a normalized yield curve.

CHART 11-4

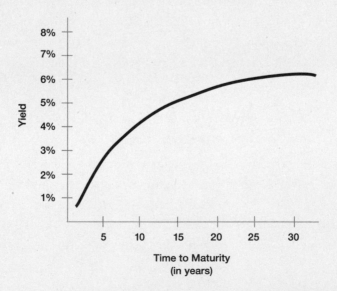

"Normal" Yield Curve

An inverted yield curve, on the other hand, occurs when short-term rates are higher than long-term rates. This generally means that the fixed-income market believes there will be economic weakness, which will prompt the Federal Reserve to cut rates. In this environment, market participants buy longer-term bonds as a hedge against both economic weakness and declining interest rates. As market participants buy long-term bonds, they become more valuable; long-term interest rates decline and the yield curve inverts.

The general rule is that an inverted yield curve is a presage of a recession, since it typically occurs when the fixed-income markets believes that economic weakness lies ahead.[11] Indeed, an inverted yield curve has preceded each of the last six recessions (although an inverted yield curve in 1998 was not followed by recession).[12]

An interesting question is whether the inverted yield curve is *predictive* of a recession or a *causal* factor of a recession. Either case undercuts the notion that the Federal Reserve should be setting short-term rates. By holding short-term rates too high for too long, the Federal Reserve might make money too expensive, causing the econ-

CHART 11-5

"Inverted" Yield Curve

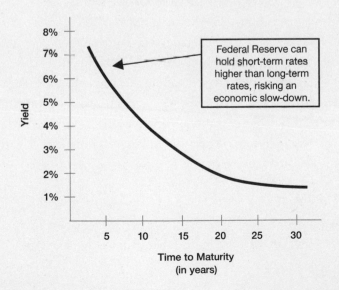

Federal Reserve can hold short-term rates higher than long-term rates, risking an economic slow-down.

omy to slow and slide into recession.[13] Thus, it might be argued that Federal Reserve policy *causes* (or helps cause) the recession. In this case, the inverted yield curve is merely the market's reaction to Federal Reserve policy that has contributed to economic deterioration. The second notion, concerns the market's *predictive* ability. This theory posits that the market has a greater understanding of future economic conditions and is "ahead of the Fed" regarding the direction of the economy. That is, the Federal Reserve should take note of the market and cut rates to stave off economic recession. If the market dictated *both* long- and short-term rates, it would be much rarer for the market to experience an inverted yield curve.[14]

Whenever the market became concerned about longer-term growth, both short- and long-term rates would likely fall in tandem (although they might fall by varying degrees). The market's self-corrective mechanism would moderate the recession. That is, as the market became more concerned about recession, both short-term and long-term rates would decline. This would make borrowing costs cheaper for borrowers and either lessen the impact of a recession or avoid it altogether. However, if the Federal Reserve intervenes and does not lower rates quickly enough, a recession becomes more likely and may be deeper. Some believe that the Federal Reserve's reluctance to cut rates caused an inverted yield curve and the 1991 recession, which likely cost President George H. W. Bush the 1992 election.

On the other hand, if the Federal Reserve holds rates too low for too long, then inflation will crop up. Inflation accompanied artificially low rates in the 1970s[15] and today. If the market sets rates, market participants would demand higher interest rates (both long-term and short-term) to offset higher inflation. This would cause rates to increase, which would have the effect of choking off inflation.

What Can Be Done?

As illustrated by the numerous policy failures outlined above, the market is better suited to set short-term rates than the bureaucrats at the

Federal Reserve. Alan Greenspan's tenure has been a case study on this front. By all measures, Greenspan is remarkably smart, well educated, and wise. However, his desire to avoid a recession at the end of his tenure resulted in his keeping short-term rates at artificially low levels for far too long. The housing bubble and overall asset inflation have been the direct and logical results of his low interest rate policies. An artificially low savings rate and skyrocketing trade deficit are also direct results of Greenspan's monetary policies and, to a lesser extent, Bush's fiscal policies. The wreckage from this profligacy could be quite ugly.

Unfortunately, there is little that current Federal Reserve chairman Ben S. Bernanke can do at this point. If he lowers rates, the dollar will collapse further, fueling consumer and commodity inflation. If he increases rates, the fixed income and equity markets will suffer accordingly in the future, we have to acknowledge that central planners such as Paul Volcker are the exception rather than the norm. And despite the good intentions of central planners such as Alan Greenspan, it is unrealistic to expect them to be more effective than the market in setting short-term rates. Thus, a new monetary regime should be established to ensure greater price stability in the future.

CHAPTER 12

The New Federal Reserve

The United States has followed two paths in the regulation of the money supply: the gold standard and the current policy of permitting the Federal Reserve to establish short-term rates. Some have argued that America should return to the gold standard, which would largely take the central planners out of monetary policy. Proponents argue that basing a currency's value on a historical and true "store of value" (i.e., a precious metal) is the only way to eliminate the government's ability to devalue currency and ultimately foster inflation (which has the corresponding effect of reducing the value of its future obligations). There is some truth to this argument. But the gold standard has its flaws and had a fairly spotty record for much of this country's history. By sharply limiting the money supply to the stock of gold held by the federal government (plus silver in circulation), the United States risks deflation, a significant problem for this nation until the post–World War II era.

In addition, the gold standard limits potential economic growth to the supply of gold in the market, a point made eloquently by William Jennings Bryan during the 1870s. He accused Eastern bankers of limiting the supply of money to the stock of gold. Since the money supply was finite and the Industrial Revolution increased production, the

United States was plagued by textbook deflation—too little money chasing too many goods and services. Jennings proposed to increase the money supply by introducing silver, a more plentiful metal, into the equation, which would have expanded the money supply and boosted prices paid to Western farmers for their produce.[1]

In addition to restricting the money supply, the gold standard subjects an economy to sharp increases in the money supply and inflation when new gold and silver discoveries occur.[2] It also places a significant amount of control of monetary policy in the hands of gold and silver miners, many of whom are foreign. The current system is flawed as well. As noted above, by setting short-term rates, the Federal Reserve often misses the mark and either spurs inflation (typically the case) or throws the economy into recession by raising rates too aggressively and restricting the money supply.

The New Federal Reserve: Setting Short-Term Rates

Allow Market to Set Short-Term Rates

During "normal" periods of time, the Federal Reserve should allow the market to establish the appropriate cost of capital, including the Fed Funds rate. Since the Fed Funds rate is approximately the interest rate that banks charge one another on overnight loans, the Federal Reserve should allow banks to establish the rates at which they are comfortable loaning and borrowing money to each other. In most instances, this rate of interest would represent some modest premium over the ninety-day T-bill (the shortest-duration government debt). The premium would acknowledge that banks would likely expect a modestly higher return on their interbank loans than the yield on federally issued debt, given the modestly higher default risk. However, it would not be significantly higher, since banks—often highly regulated—represent sound borrowers.

This rate would largely approximate today's current London Interbank Offered Rate, or LIBOR. LIBOR is the rate of interest that banks charge one another for short-term loans. Currently, LIBOR is influenced by the Fed Funds rate; it is generally slightly higher than the Fed Funds rate. However, if the Fed Funds rate were allowed to float, LIBOR would likely be less range bound as well and more subject to market forces.

Allowing Fed Funds to float would provide a self-moderating mechanism that should be superior to the present policy. During periods of strong economic growth, interest rates would likely rise based on market conditions. In this environment, banks would be eager to loan money. Accordingly, capital would become scarcer, and banks would charge higher rates on overnight loans. The same would hold true if inflation started to pick up. If that occurred, banks and other market participants would demand higher nominal rates to provide them with consistent "real" returns. In particular, if banks saw inflation increase from 2 to 3 percent, they would expect a 1 percent increase in short-term (and long-term) rates to compensate them for the loss of purchasing power on dollars. Otherwise, the banks' "real" returns (nominal interest rates, less inflation) would be reduced. Most market participants focus on their "real" returns, since this takes into account inflation over time.

During periods of economic weakness, the demand for capital would decline. And, just as long-term interest rates tend to decline during periods of current or anticipated economic weakness, so too would short-term rates. Sensing economic weakness, banks would not demand as high rate of returns on their loans to other banks (or to their customers). Thus, short-term (and longer-term) interest rates would normally decline during periods of economic weakness. The decline in interest rates would ultimately provide borrowers with lower debt service costs, which would boost the economy.

This system would also allow banks to take into account the credit quality of their counterparty to the loan. Interbank loans could have higher rates for lesser-quality borrowers and lower rates for better-quality borrowers, as determined by the lending institution. Since a bank is rated by the Office of the Comptroller of the Currency (OCC), the rating would be taken into consideration by a lender to determine the interest rate to charge on overnight loans.[3] This would encourage banks to manage their business more prudently and avoid having to pay higher borrowing costs in the interbank market. The self-moderating aspects of this system would create greater economic stability and provide the market with greater certainty than the current system. The market, rather than the Federal Reserve, possesses much greater insight and information to make decisions about the appropriate price for money, including short-term money.

Fighting Asset Inflation: Capital and Margin Requirements

The Federal Reserve should also use "capital requirements" (equity requirements for banks) and "margin requirements" (stock purchases) as the second great lever to cool or accelerate the economy.

Capital Requirements. Capital requirements are established by the Federal Reserve, subject to a global framework called Basel II. In general, capital requirements represent the equity capital a bank must maintain in relationship to its overall asset base, which includes loans. The higher the capital requirements, the less leverage a bank can use and the less credit available to the marketplace. That is, the Federal Reserve dictates how much equity a bank must carry on its balance sheet to support its loan portfolio. In general, the Federal Reserve requires that banks maintain about 10 percent in equity on their balance sheets. The remainder of their balance sheets can be in the form of loans, where banks take depositors' funds at the bank (CDs, checking accounts) and other assets and then make loans to businesses and consumers. So for every $100 loan a bank makes, it has to have $10 in equity (from its shareholders) to cover any potential loan losses. Obviously, the lower the equity requirement, the more loans a bank can make. This is demonstrated in chart 12-1.

By lowering the reserve requirements from 8 to 6 percent, the Federal Reserve gives banks the ability to increase their loan portfolios by more than 25 percent. While Basel II imposes a variety of risk-based

analyses of assets held on bank balance sheets, which would compli-
cate the foregoing example, the simple fact is that the Federal Reserve
has the ability to expand or decrease credit in the marketplace by lowering or increasing capital requirements.

Margin Requirements. Margin requirements work in much the
same way for those who purchase stocks as capital requirements do
for banks. Margin requirements dictate how much credit a stock investor can use to buy stocks. The Federal Reserve establishes margin requirements under Regulation T, which dictates that an investor can
only borrow a certain amount of the proceeds to buy stock. Today, the
margin requirement is about 50 percent. An investor can therefore buy
$100 in stocks using $50 in borrowed money. As with reserve requirements, by increasing (or decreasing) the margin requirement, the Federal Reserve can decrease (or increase) the amount of credit available
for stock market speculators, as illustrated by chart 12-2.

Again, the power of the Federal Reserve to increase or decrease
margin requirements in the stock market provides another lever to expand or contract credit and the size of the overall market.

CHART 12-1

Example of Bank with $100,000,000 in Equity Capital

	8% Reserve Requirement	6% Reserve Requirement
Equity Capital	$100,000,000	$100,000,000
Loan Portfolio	$1,150,000,000	$1,560,000,000
Total Assets	$1,250,000,000	$1,660,000,000
Increase in Loans	Not Applicable	25%+

CHART 12-2

Maximum Margin or Debt	50% Debt	60% Debt
Equity to Invest	$1,000,000	$1,000,000
Amount of Leverage/Debt	$1,000,000	$1,250,000
Total Assets	$2,000,000	$2,250,000
Increase in Equity Investment		12.5%

Recent History. The Federal Reserve has made very minor changes to the capital requirements of banks since the last recession in 1992.[4] It has not significantly modified margin lending requirements since 1974. Before that time, margin requirements were actively managed to deal with stock market speculation.[5] The Federal Reserve has largely left capital and margin requirements unchanged, despite an acceleration of asset inflation fueled partly by its own easy money policies.

In sharp contrast, the Chinese central bank has recently tightened reserve requirements in an effort to cool the red-hot Chinese stock and real estate markets fueled by speculative money, as well as overall consumer inflation. By requiring banks to maintain greater reserves, the Chinese authorities hope to reduce the overall level of credit in the marketplace, the first step in cooling asset values and inflation.

In the past, the Federal Reserve has also expressed concerns about asset inflation, indicating it would take into account asset values in establishing monetary policy. However, the Federal Reserve has re-lied almost exclusively on the lever of Fed Funds rate changes to combat inflation (deflation) and asset values. And, of late, monetary policy has been too accommodating on this front, causing asset inflation to soar.

Using Reserve and Capital Requirements to Regulate Credit. The Federal Reserve should use capital and margin requirements to reduce speculative excesses —particularly in the stock and real estate markets —or to boost such markets when they are deflating, as they are now. Toward this end, the Federal Reserve should establish a general range of capital and margin requirements and increase or decrease these requirements based on how expensive asset values are relative to their historical norms.

For example, the housing market has historically grown at approximately 3 percent per annum in "real" terms (i.e., after adjusting for inflation). However, housing prices escalated at an annual rate of approximately 20 percent from January 2002 through January 2006 (according to the S&P/Case-Shiller Home Price Indices of major metropolitan areas). During this time, short-term rates should have been allowed to "float," which would have averted some of the crisis. As important, the Federal Reserve should have slowly increased the capital requirements at banks in an effort to reduce the amount of credit available for the housing market. This would have cooled the overheated asset (housing) markets and debt creation, leaving the economy healthier and reducing the risk of a market collapse.

Obviously, the converse should be true as well. If the housing market is showing signs of deterioration and the banking sector is contracting, the Federal Reserve should gradually relax capital requirements to help increase the amount of capital available for lending. In particular, banks are writing off loans, meaning they are reducing shareholders' equity on a dollar for dollar basis for each dollar of bad loans written off. In doing so, banks have to either reduce their overall loan portfolios to get their debt-to-equity ratios back on line, or they have to raise additional equity. Either way, banks are now reticent to make new loans until they feel confident about their current loan portfolio and equity position. Credit, thus, is contracting significantly in the banking sector.

By relaxing capital requirements today, the Federal Reserve would provide banks with greater flexibility to work through the current credit crisis without having to worry as much about raising equity and/or deleveraging. Banks would be in a position to start extending credit to customers more quickly. Obviously, once the housing and credit markets started to recover, the Federal Reserve could gradually begin increasing capital requirements to more normal levels.

The same holds true for margin lending. If the stock markets start appreciating significantly, as they did in the late 1990s, the Federal Reserve could increase margin requirements, thereby cooling the speculative zeal in the markets. And when they are in free fall, as was the case from April 2000 though March 2003, the Federal Reserve should gradually relax margin requirements.

Modification to Capital Requirements. Modifications in capital requirements may require the US to change or opt out of portions of Basel II, the international framework governing the banking system. In addition, the proposed capital requirement regime should also be extended to cover derivatives transactions as well. As noted previously, the growth of derivatives has been significant over the past several years and the US regulatory framework has not been updated to address the growth of this sector.

What About Times of Crisis?

During times of economic crisis, the principal role of the Federal Reserve would be to ensure that the banking system remains functional. The Federal Reserve would have several policy tools at its disposal to achieve this end. In particular, during times of crisis, even creditworthy banks have trouble borrowing money. Since banks have a significant amount of debt on their balance sheets, their inability to borrow money from one another becomes problematic for the proper functioning of our credit markets. Thus, in times of crisis, the Federal Reserve should intervene and ensure that creditworthy banks have sufficient liquidity to conduct their business.

During most market panics, short-term interest rates on government securities would appropriately reflect the market's view of the panic. That is, interest rates on short-term government debt typically decline, as market participants flock to safety. However, the lending rate among banks might react in the opposite fashion and increase dramatically as banks horde cash and refuse to make loans to one another.

This is precisely what happened in August 2007 during the "subprime" credit debacle. Interest rates on short-term government debt declined markedly, as market participants flocked to government debt. Yet banks, fearing a squeeze on liquidity, shied away from making loans to other banks. This was evidenced by the marked increase in LIBOR. Typically, LIBOR tracks the Fed Funds and ninety-day US Treasury rates. LIBOR spiked because banks did not want to make loans to one another, due to fears about credit quality and liquidity concerns. This, of course, is not all bad. Under my plan, Fed Funds would float more freely and approximate LIBOR and would not be controlled by the Federal Reserve. Thus, if LIBOR or a market-based Fed Funds rate spiked, it would be because of general concerns about interest rates and market conditions. Banks that managed their liquidity well and kept adequate reserves would not be as impacted as those that did not. Accordingly, from a "moral hazard" standpoint, banks would have an incentive to run more conservative portfolios and maintain adequate liquidity to make it through the periodic storms characteristic to capitalism.

With that said, during times of crisis, the markets might dry up altogether and create situations where even creditworthy borrowers could not access capital. In these cases, the Federal Reserve would intervene on a selective basis. The best avenue for this type of intervention would be through the "discount window" or the Treasury Auction Facility (TAF).

The discount window is the Federal Reserve's means to provide loans directly to banks. At the discount window, a bank posts collateral and gets a loan from the Federal Reserve. The bank pays an interest rate to the Federal Reserve called the "discount rate." The TAF serves much the same purpose. Banks post collateral to the facility. They receive short-term funds in return, allowing them the liquidity to manage their affairs during times of market crisis.

In a new framework, the discount rate (charged at the discount window or by the TAF) would still be set by the Federal Reserve, but it would vary based on the creditworthiness of the borrowing bank. Since the Federal Reserve would have to step in and provide credit where the market would not, the rate of interest would be at a premium over the Fed Funds rate. Typically, the discount rate is at least 1 percent higher than the Fed Funds rate. But in the new framework, the discount rate would be priced at a premium over the Fed Funds rate based on the creditworthiness of the bank, as determined by the Office of the Comptroller of the Currency. The OCC rates each federally insured bank based on the bank's financial health. OCC ratings range from a 1 (soundest) to a 5 (riskiest). Most banks are either 2 or 3.

The Federal Reserve's discount rate might be structured in the following manner:

1. 0.50% over Fed Funds
2. 1.00% over Fed Funds
3. 1.50% over Fed Funds
4. 2.00% over Fed Funds
5. Negotiable

It is important to note that this framework provides general guidelines. During a time of market panic the Federal Reserve would be permitted to charge a higher or lower rate of interest. Given this system, banks would have a significant incentive to maintain relatively conservative ratings by the OCC in order to ensure that credit was available at a reasonable price during times of market crisis. A consistent theme of the new framework is that the market should largely control the price and flow of capital, rather than the Federal Reserve— critical to avoid the moral hazard problem that currently plagues the markets.

During his short tenure, Ben S. Bernanke has been more willing to use the discount window and other targeted ways (TAF) to provide liquidity than his predecessor, Alan Greenspan. As noted above, Greenspan preferred flooding the market with liquidity during times of market crisis, creating what some have derisively called the "Greenspan put." That is, market participants became conditioned that easy money would always be available to bail out foolish financial institutions during periods of market dislocations. The Greenspan put took the form of a cut in the Fed Funds rate. The cut was used to prop up the securities markets when Wall Street institutions got into trouble as a result of aggressive lending or investment activities.

Flooding the market with cheap money has had the impact of creating the next bubble, and at some point loses its desired effect of pulling the market out of an economic downturn. It should be noted that Japan suffered from fifteen years of recession. During the early part of the recession, the Bank of Japan cut rates from 6 percent (1989–1990) to 0.5 percent, where it remained from 1995 to 2000. Finally, it was cut to 0 percent, where it remained for six years (2000–2006).[6]

Rate cuts did not bail out the Japanese markets because the cuts allowed sick banks to survive, keeping bad loans on their books for well over a decade. Japanese consumers, fearing investment in a sick equity market, saved their money and put it in cash rather than risking it in a downwardly spiraling equity, fixed income, and real estate market. Since the sick banks stayed in business, the healthy banks had no pricing power, leaving these banks with lackluster profits and growth opportunities. The Japanese government should have focused on providing liquidity only to healthy banks that were just experiencing a temporary liquidity crisis, rather than the market as a whole. In that case, sick banks and companies would have gone out of business and allowed healthier companies to prosper and gain strength and market share.

In addition to the discount window and TAF, the Federal Reserve can also buy securities on the open market to provide banks with liquidity. This is a double-edged sword, however. While open market activities provide liquidity to market participants during times of market crises, such activities might also open an avenue for potential abuse by the Federal Reserve and market participants. Unlike the discount window, where the Federal Reserve is making short-term loans, open market transactions occur when the Federal Reserve makes outright purchases of securities, pumping liquidity into the market (albeit on a more targeted basis) through the purchase of securities.

This is often called the "monetization" of debt, since the Federal Reserve is trading a good asset (cash or treasuries) for an arguably bad one (debt or other securities held by the borrowing bank). Thus, the federal government is in effect issuing government debt to buy the assets in question, leading to the monetization of the bad debt. By pumping this liquidity into the market, the Federal Reserve risks a rapid growth of the money supply and the potential for inflation.

The Federal Reserve has the same issue with respect to making loans at the discount window. However, the stigma attached to borrowing money at the discount window is generally enough to keep banks away, except during times of market crisis. However, no stigma is associated with selling an asset to the Federal Reserve, given that there are no reporting requirements. This makes open market transactions a riper avenue for abuse and should be carefully monitored. For the current system (where the Federal Reserve sets short-term rates) or the proposed system (where the market in most instances sets short-term rates) to work appropriately, the economic data used by the Fed or the market has to be sound.

New Federal Reserve: Importance of Economic Data

Given the importance of sound and unbiased economic data, the Federal Reserve rather than the federal government should be responsible for posting basic economic data, which the market could then use to establish short-term (and longer-term) rates. Inflation, economic growth, and monetary growth are a few of the basic determinants of short-term interest rates. Policymakers and the market, use data supplied by the federal government and private sources to assess inflation and economic growth in order to establish interest rates. These numbers have to be trusted and respected by the market.

Unfortunately, the federal government has a vested interest in keeping inflationary numbers low. This incentive is due to the fact that most transfer payments (welfare, Social Security, etc.) have a cost-of-living escalator based on inflation. The federal government increases payments each year based on the increase in the consumer price index (CPI). CPI is calculated by the government and represents the inflation rate experienced by an average consumer. The inflation rate over the past several years has been relatively low (2 to 3 percent), particularly as compared to the 1970s and early 1980s (when inflation ran in some cases higher than 10 percent). At 2 to 3 percent, the annual in-crease on transfer payments is quite manageable for the federal gov-ernment, since the overall increase in benefits due to inflation is approximately $12 billion to $15 billion. However, if inflation was run-ning at 10 percent, as it did in parts of the 1970s and early 1980s, the increase in cost of social programs due to the cost-of-living increase would be much, much higher—about $60 billion to $80 billion per annum, if you also include reduced revenues.[6] The $60 billion to $80 billion difference represents a significant increase in the federal deficit.

In addition, the US government is the largest borrower in the world. It has over $9 trillion in debt (not including future obligations under Social Security and Medicare). Interest rates are comprised of two components: (a) a "real" rate of interest (usually 2 percent for gov-ernment debt) plus (b) inflation. Accordingly, higher inflation leads to higher nominal interest rates. Over the past twenty years, interest rates have been relatively low, and interest costs on the federal debt have consequently been relatively low (as a percentage of the overall fed-eral budget and of GDP). However, given that the level of federal debt has increased significantly over the past several years, (trending from about 50 percent of GDP to nearly 70 percent of GDP), any increase in inflation would have a profound impact on the level of interest costs paid by the federal government. If, for example, inflation increased from 2 to 3 percent to, say, 5 or even 6 percent, interest rates would in-crease by a like amount and borrowing costs by the federal govern-ment would increase by $100 billion to $150 billion per annum. This simple fact provides the federal government with a significant incen-tive to keep the *stated* inflation rate as low as possible and to manipu-late the inflation numbers to do so. This is precisely what many have been arguing for some time.

Government Has Changed How Inflation Is Calculated. Some have quite persuasively made the case that the US government has been understating inflation for years.[7] This is because the federal govern-ment has changed the manner in which it calculates inflation. Today, the government excludes food and energy costs from "core" inflation, the Federal Reserve's preferred measure of inflation. The stated rationale is that food and energy tend to be more volatile and ultimately find their way into the cost of most goods and services. So over time an increase in the price of food and energy will be priced into all goods and services, and "core" inflation will take these higher prices into account. By excluding them in the short term, inflation is smoothed out.

Also, the government now excludes housing prices from inflation. In place of housing prices, the government uses something called "owners equivalent rent" (OER), the cost of a person renting his house from himself. In effect, OER substitutes a rental costs across the nation for housing prices. Because until recently housing prices have greatly outpaced increases in rents, the substitution of OER for housing prices has had the effect of artificially reducing inflation.

The federal government also introduced a concept called "hedonics." This theory posits that with quality improvements, the cost of a particular good should be appropriately adjusted downward, as illustrated by the following example. Assume that a computer cost $1,000 in 2000 and a similar computer cost $1,200 in 2001 but provides two times the computing power. During the 1970s, the 20 percent price increase would be included in inflation calculations. However, today the government takes into account the quality improvements from 2000 and 2001 and reduces the price of the 2001 computer significantly, perhaps below the price of the 2000 computer. So the 20 percent price increase from 2000 to 2001 is magically transformed into a price *reduction* and inflation is lowered in the process.

Finally, the government introduced the concept of "substitution" to the calculation of inflation. Pursuant to this theory, the government assumes that as the price of one good increases, people will start using a lower-priced substitutable in its stead. For example, if the price of beef increases, people will switch to chicken if its price is more reasonable. This allows the government to substitute goods that are experiencing greater increases in prices with those whose prices are increasing at a less rapid pace, dampening inflation. Each of these changes has had the impact of reducing reported inflation. First, it is counterintuitive to eliminate food and energy prices in calculating inflation. Every American has to eat and most drive cars.

Second, reducing inflation due to hedonics is equally foolish. Technology improvements have occurred over time. My generation saw the transition from black and white TV to color TV and other technological advances. But inflation was not adjusted during the 1970s to take these into account.

Third, the cost of buying a house and rent factors should *both* be taken into account. This nation is filled with renters and home owners. If housing prices are declining but financing costs are increasing, as they are today, the cost of a home owner's mortgage payments for a house bought today may have actually gone up, given higher borrowing costs. The same holds true of rent. So the statistics need to take into account housing affordability and rental costs across the nation in proportion to the percentage of renters and home owners.

Fourth, the basket of goods and services should change from year to year, based on a survey of the American's consumptive patterns. Over time, our consumptive patterns might change. However, the theory of substitution should be more gradually implemented.

Finally, and most important, if changes are made to the manner in which inflation or any other significant economic index is calculated, prior years' inflation should be restated based on the change.

Today, politicians point to a low inflation rate and compare it with a much higher inflation rate in the 1970s. They declare all is well on the inflation front. However, if inflation was calculated today as it was in the 1970s, inflation would be much higher (as illustrated in chart 12-3 below.) For statistics to have any meaning, they need to be compiled in the same manner for comparative purposes. And if a new methodology is used, prior years' inflation should be restated and published for all to see so that the new standards cannot be measured against the old standards to mislead the public.

Powerful Incentive to Understate Inflation: Reduce Transfer Payments.
The following chart provides an outline of the impact of calculating inflation based on the older and more reliable methodology, vis-à-vis the current one.

If the older methodology was used reported inflation would be much higher today and the impact would be significant. Transfer payments would be increased by nearly $50 billion per annum. Further, US short-term and long-term interest rates would increase significantly, by as much as 7 percent. Interest costs paid by the federal government to finance its debt would increase dramatically, costing the federal government as much as $650 billion per annum or more in additional interest costs. The stated US budget deficit would soar from approximately $162 billion (2007) to approximately $850 billion.

Overstated Economic Growth. Higher stated inflation would also have had a profound impact on "real" economic growth over the past several years. "Real" economic or GDP growth is equal to the nominal growth rate, less inflation. If inflation has been understated, then

CHART 12-3

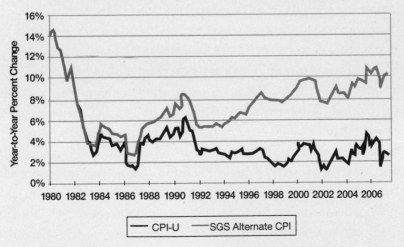

Annual Consumer Inflation - CPI vs. SGS Alternate

Source: Shadowstats, SGS, BLS

CHART 12-4

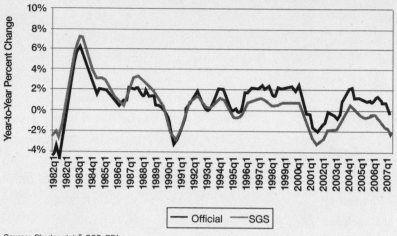

GDP Annual Growth – Official vs. SGS

Source: Shadowstats[B], SGS, BEA

"real" economic growth has been overstated by the amount of the understatement of inflation, as illustrated by chart 12-4.

It would mean that rather than 2 to 3 percent GDP growth over the past decade and a half, the total would have ranged from about 0 to 1 percent (or less), about the same as "old Europe" over the same time frame.

Federal Reserve Should Publish Economic Data. Some may argue that the US consumer should look the other way and allow the government to publish misleading government statistics for as long as possible. After all, if the US government were to publish more accurate inflation data, it would be more bankrupt than it already is. However, publishing trustworthy numbers is a prerequisite of a modern, advanced nation. At some point in the future, the market will figure out that the federal government is, at best, publishing faulty economic figures and demand a premium for holding US treasuries.

Given the importance of publishing accurate economic data, the task of compiling the data should be removed from the purview of the federal government, which has a vested interest in depressing inflationary numbers and overstating economic growth. Rather, the task should be entrusted to the Federal Reserve, which is more independent but already collects a significant amount of data to support its monetary policy activities.

Penalties for Manipulation of Financial Data. As with the proposed regime covering the financial statements published by the US government, Federal Reserve officials should also be subject to penalties if they provide US taxpayers and investors with false and misleading economic data.

Conclusion. Despite the problems in the late 1990s and early 2000s, investors realize that American corporations have among the best reporting standards in the world. The same cannot be said of the US government. By fundamentally changing the way it conducts its business, the US government can, like American corporations, be the envy of the world when it comes to transparency and providing reliable financial information.

CHAPTER 13

Addressing the Current Account Deficit

The United States ran a current account deficit of approximately $738 billion in 2007, or about 5.3% of GDP. The US current account deficit means that Americans consume more than they produce. Foreigners finance this excess consumption by making investments or loans to the US. So, America's current standard of living is dependent on foreign investment. Once foreign investment slows or dries up, Americans will see a dramatic decline in their standard of living and/or much higher borrowing or financing costs.

Policy Recommendations Will Improve Current Account Deficit

The United States runs significant risk that this foreign investment will slow or cease in the future, causing an extreme dislocation in the financial markets. The United States should take several steps to reduce the impact of this risk.

Improved Fiscal and Monetary Policy. The US government is the biggest borrower in the world; it borrows about $500 billion per annum to finance its operations. In addition, easy monetary policy has encouraged Americans to consume rather than save. By allowing the market to set short-term interest rates and reducing the US budget deficit, America can dramatically reduce the amount of capital being borrowed from abroad.

Energy. America imports approximately 11 million barrels of oil per day, or about $400 billion worth per year (at $100 per barrel). This represents over half of America's trade deficit. In the next chapter, I propose an energy tax equal to the cost of America's Middle Eastern military presence. This tax would be phased in over several years, but would be significant ($25 per barrel). By appropriately allocating the cost of America's Middle Eastern military presence, Americans would pay a market-based cost for oil. This higher price would reduce consumption and encourage a more rational debate about America's Middle Eastern military presence. It would also encourage America to find alternative energy solutions.

Restate the Current Account Deficit to Reflect Immigration. Throughout this book, I have made the point that the US government is publishing misleading economic statistics to make America's financial condition look better. With that said, I strongly believe that America's current account deficit is overstated because it does not take into account the impact of immigration.

Immigration represents the unilateral transfer of human capital from one country to another . The current account calculation includes a line item for net unilateral transfers from the United States to other countries. The US has a net outflow on this line item of approximately $100 billion. The outflow represents, among other things, US foreign aid and money being sent abroad by US residents to other private citizens (it is estimated that US residents of other nationalities send money back to their country of origin in the amount of $20 billion or more per annum). However, this line item does not take immigration into account—the single biggest unilateral transfer from other countries to the US. And this transfer is profound.

Taking our earlier example, the value of a worker immigrating to the United States is significant. Even an unskilled individual (aged eighteen) represents a significant value. In US dollars, it would cost approximately $150,000 to replicate this asset (the basic cost of educating, feeding, and clothing a person from birth to age 18).[1] This cost skyrockets if the person has a college education or an advanced degree and when the value of parenting is taken into account.

If one assumes that over 1.5 million people immigrate to the United States each year (legally and illegally)[2], this represents a unilateral transfer of at least $250 billion per annum (assuming about 300,000 immigrants are skilled).[3] When taking this into account, our trade deficit is reduced from a staggering 5.3 percent of GDP (2007) to as little as 1% of GDP, as illustrated by chart 13-1.[4]

Both legal and illegal immigration result in a direct transfer of wealth from developing nations to the United States. In addition, this human capital transfer comes at a time when this nation is aging, keeping our demographic problems in check.

The final advantage of including immigration in our current account balance is that it provides a strong sense of the value of a net inflow of immigrants to the US economy. Today, many Americans view immigration in a negative manner. If viewed appropriately, net immigration would be seen in a positive light, at least economically. The debate could then transition from being irrational and not supported

CHART 13-1

Current Account Deficit	2007 (formal)	2007 (adjusted)	2007 (adjusted for m1x benefit)
Current Account Deficit	$738 billion5	$738 billion	$738 billion
Less: Immigration[1]	N/A	$250 billion	
Less: Maximum Immigration[2]	N/A	-	$600 billion
Total	N/A	$538 billion	$138 billion
Percentage of GDP[3]	5.3%	3%	1%

(1) Average cost of raising a child to the age of eighteen in the United States, multiplied by the estimated number of legal and illegal immigrants per annum.

(2) Takes into account the value of parenting, as set forth in the chapter on immigration.

(3) GDP equals approximately $14 trillion[6]

by the facts (i.e., that immigration is bad for the United States from an economic standpoint) to where it should be. The immigration debate should be focused on issues of national identity, character, and assimilation.

Conclusion

America can dramatically reduce its current account deficit by taking measures that might be painful in the short term, but will benefit it over the long term.

By reducing its reliance on foreign capital to finance its excess consumption, America will regain control over its financial destiny and its currency—hallmarks of a superpower. If America does not, it risks economic deterioration and becoming the vassal of its creditors. It will lose its status as an economic superpower.

PART IV

ENERGY AND
ENVIRONMENTAL POLICY

- The Issues Driving Energy Policy Have Expanded

- Liberals vs. Conservatives

- Energy Plan: Near Term

- The "Manhattan Project" for Energy Independence:
  Longer Term

Introduction

Problems:

1. America and the rest of the world face severe shortages of oil, threatening economic growth.
2. America is not properly allocating the cost of disposing of wastes created by oil and other fossil fuels. This subsidy has created an incentive to burn fossil fuels over fuels that create less pollution.
3. The United States, through its Middle Eastern military presence, is subsidizing Middle Eastern energy producers. By not allocating the cost of its military presence to imported oil, the US government is effectively favoring Middle Eastern oil producers over domestic ones.
4. The environmental movement, while well-meaning, has focused on solutions (e.g., ethanol) that are largely energy inefficient or that are not viable economically vis-à-vis carbon-based fuels.
5. The energy and environmental situation will get worse as emerging Asia (China and India) dramatically increase their consumption of carbon-based fuels, particularly coal.

Imperatives:

- America must develop a comprehensive energy policy that addresses both global warming and its reliance on foreign oil.
- America must focus on fuels that do not reduce food supply (e.g., ethanol) or fan the flames of inflation.

CHAPTER 14

The Issues Driving Energy Policy Have Expanded

Three major trends will dictate American energy policy in the decades to come. The first is the environmental movement and the growing recognition about greenhouse gases and global warming. The second is that the Iraq war has highlighted the "true" cost of oil, in terms of American dollars and lives. The third is the rapid increase in the price of oil. Of these trends, the environmental movement is the newcomer on the scene, having moved from the fringe to the mainstream.

Environmental Threat Is Greater Than Terrorism

The global warming theory is a relatively simple one. Man is burning fossil fuels, emitting carbon dioxide (CO_2) into the atmosphere. Once in the atmosphere, CO_2 causes heat to be trapped between the earth and the atmosphere, permanently warming the planet.

Emissions of CO_2 have dramatically increased over the past century, as Western Europe and the United States have industrialized and burned increasing amounts of fossil fuels.[1] The carbon content in the atmosphere has more than doubled since the advent of the Industrial Revolution. As a result, the earth's temperature has steadily increased, as carbon emissions and the accumulation of CO_2 in the atmosphere have accelerated.

The Impact of Global Warming. Until recently, most studies warning about global warming were published by left-leaning think tanks. This trend is changing. A relatively recent and alarming study on global warming came from a surprising source: the US Department of Defense.

The report was completed in 2004 by a team led by Andrew Marshall, an octogenarian strategist who heads the Office of Net Assessment at the Pentagon. This group forecasts future risks and develops plans for the Department of Defense to combat those risks. Far from a left-leaning environmentalist, Marshall's conservative bona fides are strong. He has long been a proponent of a ballistic missile defense and a smaller and more mobile military to address twenty-first century threats—both popular among conservatives during Bush's first term. Due to his prescience in addressing future threats, Marshall is referred to as the "Yoda" of the Defense Department. Given this stature, then secretary of Defense Donald Rumsfeld tapped Marshall to study the long-term implications of global warming on national security. The findings challenged conservative orthodoxy about global warming.

Far from a whitewash, Marshall's report paints a bleak picture. The report, which remains classified, warns that global warming could cause major European cities to be submerged under water within the next twenty years and cause many farming regions to become unsuitable for agriculture due to increased temperatures. These changes would foment conflicts over increasingly scarce resources, such as food and water. *The report notes that this threat far outweighs that of terrorism.*

Marshall's report confirms a growing consensus among climatologists and other scientists. Unfortunately, it is far from the gloomiest assessment of global warming. In a worst-case scenario, the human race would face extinction before the end of this century. This view is advanced by Professor James Lovelock, a noted biochemist and author of the Gaia theory.[2,3]

Lovelock and Marshall both paint a dire picture of the future, but they are not alone. Many in the scientific community are deeply concerned about the threat of global warming.[4]

Simple Risk/Reward Applied to the Environment. Marshall's view that the risk of global warming outweighs that of terrorism is based on simple cost-benefit analysis. That is, even if the risk of global warming is relatively small, the magnitude of the risk is so great that it has to be addressed, as illustrated by chart 14-1.

On any risk-adjusted basis, the threat of global warming deserves attention. Even if US policymakers view the risk as minor, its sheer magnitude warrants a significant effort to reduce or avoid the risk altogether.

The cost (as a percentage of GDP) to avert the loss could be relatively moderate if the plan outlined below is adopted. And the costs associated with reducing greenhouse emissions would have the ancillary but very real benefits. These benefits include a reduction of America's dependence on foreign oil—a foreign policy and economic security necessity.

The True Cost of Oil

US foreign policy has been influenced by Middle Eastern oil for more than fifty years. During this period, the United States has extended its "military umbrella" to include the Middle East.

CHART 14-1

	Terrorist Attack	Environmental Catastrophe
Potential Loss of Life	3,000 to 500,000	Millions
Threat to Cities (US)	1 or 2 at a time	All coastal cities
Number of Displaced Citizens (worldwide)	5,000,000 to 10,000,000	Hundreds of millions
Other Threats	Global instability	Global instability, food supply, climate, weather patterns
Threat to Civilization	No	Yes
Cost If Not Avoided	Loss of a major city	Threat to civilization
Other Benefits of Policy (If Successful)	Stabilize the Middle East	Reduce energy dependence on the Middle East

Even before 9/11, the United States spent over $50 billion per annum on its Middle Eastern military presence. Today, it spends over $150 billion per annum.

The United States imports approximately 2.4 million barrels of oil per day from the Middle East. Thus, our current Middle Eastern defense costs equate to well over $150 per barrel of oil imported from the region. This cost does not include the considerable loss of life and casualties associated with America's military presence in the Middle East.

In sum, energy produced in the Middle East is highly subsidized by the US government, because the dependability of supply is largely predicated on the continued presence of the US military in the region. Simple cost accounting dictates that this cost should be allocated to the price of oil imported from the Middle East, a concept explored later in this chapter.

Demand Is Outstripping Supply.
Supply Increasingly Comes from Dangerous Regions

The third factor affecting future energy prices is the growing demand for oil by China, India, and other emerging economies. This demand growth is outstripping supply, causing prices to remain elevated. In this regard, today's energy crisis differs significantly from that of the 1970s. In the 1970s, oil prices spiked as a result of *supply* disruptions. As supply came back on line, energy prices receded. Today, supply and demand imbalances are being driven by higher demand. Oil producers can barely keep up with the increased demand from emerging Asia. Ominously, some prominent energy experts believe the world is nearing "peak" oil and that oil production will shortly go into permanent decline. If so, energy supplies will be declining at the same time that energy demand soars, ensuring an era of ever-increasing energy prices.

In today's world of tight energy markets, the risks associated with supply disruptions are acute. The price shock from the 1973–1974 Arab oil embargo and the Iranian revolution in 1979 resulted in a tripling of oil prices in each case. If a similar supply disruption occurred today, the United States would see price increases from $135 (May 2008) to over $400 per barrel, raising the cost of gasoline to as much as $10.00 per gallon.

Liberals and Conservatives Differ Significantly. Given these rather dark facts, the energy debate should focus on a reasonable, cost-effective manner to transition away from America's dependence on foreign oil for economic, national security, and environmental reasons.

However, the current debate is notable only for its shallowness and lack of any meaningful progress in formulating a comprehensive plan.

Thus far, the debate is being framed by two prominent camps. Liberals focus on "renewable" energy and conservation as the principal means to address the energy crisis. Conservatives support increased domestic oil supplies but until recently have largely ignored the value of conservation.[5] Both sides have sound points. However, given each camp's inflexibility, no meaningful progress has been made in formulating a comprehensive energy policy for the United States.

CHAPTER 15

Liberals vs. Conservatives

The purpose of this chapter is to formulate a better plan to address America's energy needs by fusing the best aspects of the liberal and conservative camps. The critical aspects of a comprehensive energy plan are (a) it must generate or save enough energy to make a difference, whether through energy production or conservation, (b) it must not be cost-prohibitive and must ultimately be supported by the fundamentals of the market, and (c) it must dramatically reduce carbon emissions over a reasonably short time frame (e.g., next twenty-five years).

Liberal Camp

Intent on curbing carbon emissions, environmentalists have yet to offer a comprehensive, viable program to do so. It is impractical to suggest that Americans are going to drive costly hybrids, ride bicycles, car pool, or take other measures—until it is too late. Further, the focus on "renewable" energy sources is equally quixotic.

A Drop in the Barrel: Alternative Energy

Despite the hoopla surrounding "alternative energy," the fact remains that less than 3 percent of all of US energy production comes from "alternatives" (e.g., biofuels, solar, and wind power). Even assuming the rosiest projections, this total is unlikely to be more than 5 to 10 percent of energy production by 2020. The reason is quite simple: alternative fuels are not economically viable without significant government subsidies. And nowhere has there been a bigger disconnect between economic viability and hype than ethanol.

The Ethanol Boondoggle

Ethanol has been the darling of the media, the greens and Midwestern farmers. But few "alternative" fuels make less sense than ethanol.

While clean burning, corn-based ethanol has many problems. First and foremost, it is energy inefficient. That is, it takes more energy to produce a gallon of ethanol than the gallon of ethanol itself produces.[1] Not only is ethanol energy inefficient, it cannot be transported through the nation's pipeline system because it erodes the rubber seals between each pipe joint. It must be transported via trucks or rail, a very inefficient manner to move the product.

Crowding Out Food Supply. Finally, by using corn for fuel, the US is taking corn out of the food supply, leading to significant increases in food prices.[2] In particular, in 2006, the US government outlawed MTBE (methyl tertiary butyl ether), a fuel additive blended into gasoline to provide additional octane, and mandated that corn ethanol take its place. Since that time, corn prices have surged by approximately 100 percent (from September 2006 to January 17, 2007). The problem is not likely to correct in the near term. The 2005 Energy Policy Act requires that 7.5 billion gallons of the nation's annual gasoline supply (about 5 percent) come from renewable fuels by 2012, a significant increase over current levels.

In effect, the transition to ethanol is pitting SUVs against corn, or food vs. fuel. Lester Brown, director of the Earth Policy Institute, notes that food will not be affordable to the poor if it continues to be used as a feedstock for fuel. Further, the costs associated with ethanol do not just relate to corn; the spillover effect has been significant. Since corn has increased in value, farmers have taken other crops out of production to plant it As a result, farmers have planted fewer acres of soy, wheat, and other agricultural commodities, and those commodities have seen their prices surge as a result.

Higher food and energy costs take a bigger bite out of the paychecks of the very poor. And these higher costs are not just relegated to the United States. Since agricultural commodities have worldwide markets, prices have surged around the world. These price increases have a profound impact on people in the poorest nations, which can ill afford higher food prices. A recent study by the World Bank estimated that an additional 100 million people slipped into deeper poverty and hunger due to the recent surge in food prices.

Wind and Solar Power. Wind and solar power have a powerful intrinsic appeal. The sun and wind represent the ultimate renewable energy sources. However, neither makes economic sense at the moment. Both require significant state and federal subsidies to make them affordable even for affluent individuals. Even with these subsidies, neither wind turbines nor solar panels are economically sound investments. They require large upfront costs ($25,000 or more[3] for a 3,000-square-foot house) and have a ten-to-fifteen-year "payback" period.[4] Since the average homeowner lives in a house less than ten years before selling it, the average homeowner will likely never recoup his or her investment.[5] Given these economics, it is unlikely that solar or wind power will have a high adoption rate in the near term.

Conclusion. Based on current technology, alternative energy sources are not economically viable and, thus, will not be broadly adopted by Americans without significant government subsidies. Worse yet, ethanol causes more environmental and societal damage than it alleviates. Without question, America should continue to explore and conduct research and development on alternative energy sources. But at the moment none of them offer a near-term means to dramatically reduce our reliance on carbon-based fuels. Thus, relying alternative energy sources in formulating a near-term energy policy is foolhardy.

The Conservative Position

Many conservatives believe that the best solution for the energy crisis is increased drilling in North America and tapping America's vast coal resources. Conservatives rightly point to the massive oil and gas reserves located along America's coastlines and in the Arctic National Wildlife Refuge (ANWR). Liberals have long opposed drilling in these areas due to the potential for oil spills and other environmental risks. While America should pursue both, neither offers a "silver bullet" in a comprehensive energy plan. Rather, drilling along America's coastline and in ANWR will represent just a piece, perhaps even a small one, in an overall energy plan.

By way of example, ANWR, located in northern Alaska, is considered one of the last great potential drilling sites in the United States. Yet even ANWR's massive reserves would not be enough to make much of a dent in America's oil consumption needs. If successful, it would generate about 600,000 to 800,000 barrels per day at peak production. But it would take about ten years to get this production on line.[6] The same also holds for increasing production elsewhere in the United States, even along its coastlines. Production from these areas is likely to just marginally offset the rapid decline in American oil and gas production elsewhere.

Coal has intriguing possibilities. America has vast reserves. However, when coal is burned, it discharges significant amounts of CO_2 and, in some cases, sulfur. Technology is being developed to eliminate much of these harmful emissions or to capture them and inject them back into the ground. Like alternative fuels, "clean coal" is not cost competitive at the moment, but continued research should be undertaken to develop these technologies and make "clean coal" cost effective. Despite their many problems, coal and increased domestic drilling represent two areas that America should pursue as a part of its near-term energy plan.

CHAPTER 16

Energy Plan: Near Term

The United States should adopt two energy plans: a near-term energy plan implemented over the next five years and a long-term energy plan implemented over the next twenty-five years. America's near-term energy plan should reduce America's reliance on imported energy through reduced consumption. It should also provide an incentive to increase domestic production and the development of alternative fuels by appropriately "costing" imported oil and applying a carbon-based tax.

Appropriately Cost Energy

As previously noted, oil prices do not reflect the true cost of the commodity. Middle Eastern oil producers benefit from the security umbrella provided by the United States, without having to pay for it. If the United States allocated this cost to Middle East oil imports, the cost would equate to over $150 per barrel.

A second cost relates to the environmental damage caused by burning carbon-based fuels. This relates not only to imported oil but also to domestically produced carbon-based energy. At a minimum, the United States should be willing to commit 1 percent of GDP ($140 billion) to reduce the effect of greenhouse gases due to carbon-based fuels. This cost should be borne by the users of carbon fuels in the form of a carbon tax. The tax should be based on the level of carbon dioxide emitted when burning a particular fuel and would apply to domestic and foreign fuel sources.

For example, if a power plant burns coal to generate power, the coal plant would bear a tax equal to the amount of carbon emissions generated from burning the coal. Since burning natural gas produces lower carbon emissions, a natural gas power plant would not bear as high a tax (or cost) as a coal plant. Thus, in effect, the tax would serve as a means to gauge the carbon cleanup costs associated with each fuel type. With a higher tax, coal would be more expensive to burn than natural gas, so people would burn less and/or pay less for it. However, if a coal-fired power plant used technologies to either reduce carbon emissions or "sequester" carbon emissions (by pumping CO_2 back into the ground), these "clean" coal plants would see their carbon tax either reduced or eliminated.

In sum, the near-term plan would appropriately cost carbon-based fuels for (a) the cost of our security umbrella (in the case of energy imported from the Middle East or outside the NAFTA region) and (b) the damage done to our environment by carbon-based fuels.

The Plan Implemented. A $150 per barrel tax for the Middle East security umbrella would not be politically or economically feasible. However, a $25 per barrel tax on all imports outside of the NAFTA region is certainly justifiable, particularly if phased in over five years.

In addition, carbon-based energy sources should also bear a carbon tax equal to $15 per barrel of oil equivalent. The carbon tax would equate to about 1 percent of GDP and represent the cleanup costs associated with fuels that emit carbon dioxide when burned. The tax would be adjusted when applied to other forms of carbon-based energy based on their carbon emissions when burned relative to those of oil. For most grades of coal, the tax would be higher on a heating equivalent basis; for natural gas, the tax would be lower, because natural gas emissions are lower. For the purpose of this discussion, the carbon tax will be discussed in the context of oil.

Under this plan, the cost of a barrel of oil would be increased by (a) $40 for oil produced outside the NAFTA region (security cost of $25 per barrel and environmental cost of $15 per barrel) or (b) $15 for oil produced in the NAFTA region (just environmental costs). The United States should also establish a floor on the cost of imported oil. The floor should be at least $80 per barrel, adjusted for inflation. The floor is important for the policy reasons discussed below.

Rationale. This cost reallocation—or tax, if you like—would have several benefits. First, it would provide a powerful incentive to Middle Eastern nations to find a solution to the turmoil in their region. At the moment, Middle Eastern despots have a powerful incentive to do just the opposite. They have an incentive to foment dissent to drive up oil prices. This is precisely what the president of Iran has done with great effectiveness over the past several years. For every $10-per-barrel price increase, his regime takes in about $10 billion in additional oil revenues per year.

Second, the tax and the "floor" would provide a planning tool for domestic producers *and* those who are investing in alternative fuels. Domestic producers would have a cost advantage over Middle Eastern oil producers, which would provide an incentive to develop and exploit reserves in the United States. This would include not only ANWR, but also America's coastlines—both of which should be open for oil exploration and drilling.

Those investing in alternative fuels would have a price target to beat in order to produce a commercially viable alternative to carbon-based fuels. In the case of oil, an energy alternative just 30 percent more expensive than oil would be commercially viable after the application of the carbon and security umbrella taxes. As important, oil would have a "floor" in its price, which would provide assurances that if there were a collapse in energy prices (which occurred during the late 1980s and for most of the 1990s) there would still an incentive to invest in alternatives.

The tax on foreign oil and floor also provides a stable and higher price environment. This provides incentive for investment in domestic (including Canadian and Mexican) production. The security umbrella tax of $25 per barrel would provide a significant cost advantage to domestic (as well as Canadian and Mexican) producers, who would be encouraged to increase their drilling activities and recovery programs in North America. At higher prices, more energy reserves become commercially viable to produce. These include oil trapped in the tar sands in Canada and oil reserves far off the US and Mexican shorelines—all of which are very expensive to find and produce. But the payoff in each of these areas could be huge. The Canadian tar sands are estimated to hold as many barrels of oil as Saudi Arabia.

The same theory holds true for alternative energy and developing technologies to burn traditional carbon-based fuels in a cleaner fashion. At higher prices, multiple forms of alternative energy, including "clean coal," become increasingly viable. Over the past few years, alternative energy companies have seen a flood of new investment. However, this investment will slow if the underlying fundamentals of alternative energy are not sound. And, just like oil exploration and development, these include (a) the cost of developing an alternative energy product, particularly solar and wind power and "clean coal," (b) the probability that the project will work, and (c) the price at which the energy can be sold. If prices remain relatively high, investment will flow into developing and commercializing new alternative energy forms. Further, since alternative energy and clean coal (and coal gasification) would be developed in the United States and ideally would not generate carbon dioxide (or as much of it), forms of alternative energy would have a profound price advantage over Middle Eastern producers ($40 per barrel equivalent) and, to a lesser extent, over domestic producers ($15 per barrel). This cost advantage is one supported by the market since alternative forms of energy do not require America's military umbrella and do not destroy the environment.

Both domestic energy producers and alternative energy would benefit from appropriately costing the commodity, enabling both to make the long-term investments necessary to develop domestic reserves and/or alternative energy technology.

Conservation

Conservation is the other aspect of the near-term plan. While some Americans will conserve because it is the right thing to do, the vast majority will not conserve until they are compelled to do so by the market. Yet conservation offers the most important means to reduce energy consumption over the very near term.

In the United States, energy usage is growing at approximately 2 percent per annum, about equal to population growth. This figure may seem trivial. But, the absolute amount is significant and represents about 400,000 barrels of additional oil usage per annum. This amount is nearly equal to what many believe ANWR would produce if it came on line.[1] The problem compounds over time. At this rate of increase, the United States would consume an additional 4.5 million barrels per annum in just ten years time. This is equivalent to the combined oil production of Iran and Iraq or about 50 percent of the total oil production of Saudi Arabia. China is anticipated to require the same or perhaps even a greater amount of additional oil over that time frame. So America will be competing in the global marketplace for energy with China and other developing nations. As noted in previous chapters, China is willing to do business with Iran, the Sudan, and other "bad" nations. Thus, it is in a much better position to secure the additional production necessary to meet its demand.

Given that, it is critical for America to promote domestic energy production (oil and alternatives) through higher prices, and change its foreign policy to promote trade with nations with whom it disagrees. But, this alone will not be sufficient. The United States must also promote conservation.

A recent study by one of the world's leading consulting firms, McKinsey and Company, indicates that America could save enough energy per year to nearly offset demand growth if America imposed more stringent energy conservation requirements in cars, appliances, power plants, lighting, etc. The McKinsey report noted that this goal could be accomplished through the use of existing technology. Thus, energy efficiency standards, such as the ones enacted by Congress in 2007, should be designed to offset, at least partially, anticipated increases in energy demand (i.e., reduce American energy consumption by 2 percent per annum). A prime example is a transition from incandescent lights (found in most homes) to fluorescent lights (found in most office buildings). This alone would reduce energy consumption by 1 percent per annum. These changes should be phased in over a five-to-ten year period so that there are no dramatic shocks to the US economy.

Cost to the Poor; Tax Rate

The near-term energy plan will come at a cost. Reallocating the cost of America's Middle Eastern military presence to imported oil (the security tax) and applying a carbon tax would impact the poor to a much greater extent than the wealthy. This makes it imperative that the energy plan be enacted in tandem with the new tax regime. The new tax regime would lower or eliminate taxes on the poor. Indeed, in most instances, lower-income workers would pay lower taxes than they do today, which would offset any higher taxes on energy.

Conclusion: A "Grand Bargain"

The near-term energy plan will require a "grand bargain" between liberals and conservatives. Liberals will have to concede the need for increased domestic drilling, including ANWR and along America's coastlines, to meet America's near-term energy needs. They will also have to abandon the foolish notion of taxing domestic energy companies through a windfall profits tax. This tax will either be passed to consumers or result in decreased investment by energy companies, neither of which make sense and both of which will result in higher energy prices over time. And conservatives will have to stomach higher taxes on energy imports and increased conservation efforts. By allocating costs appropriately through security and carbon taxes, liberals will see greater conservation once alternative energy companies are placed on the same footing as oil companies. Conservatives will see the possibility of production from ANWR and a resurgence of domestic energy producers, who will also be placed on sounder footing with Middle Eastern producers. And America will have an energy plan that meets its current needs, but also one that creates an environment to cut global emissions and wean America off imported oil in the future.

CHAPTER 17

The "Manhattan Project" for Energy Independence: Longer Term

Longer term, the United States should undertake a "Manhattan Project" for energy. Under this plan, America should establish a goal of eliminating its reliance on foreign oil by 2030.[1]

To address America's future energy needs, US policymakers must first define the major areas of energy usage and where oil usage is most prevalent. After doing so, US policymakers should assess what substitutes are likely to have the most dramatic impact on lowering oil consumption in the future.

Defining the Energy Markets

US energy demand falls into two categories. The first is energy needed for transportation. For the past hundred years, oil refined into gasoline has been the energy source of choice for automobiles. This is because any energy source used for transportation must have two characteristics. Namely, it must provide enough energy to propel the car. In addition, the fuel source must be small enough in weight and volume to fit within the automobile (i.e., the energy source must be transportable). Thus far, oil is the only commercially viable energy source that fits these two requirements.

The second category is the energy needed for power generation at power plants, which heat, cool, and provide electricity to homes, buildings, factories and other fixed assets. Since power plants are large and fixed, the transportability of the energy source is not as critical an issue as it is with a car.[2] Accordingly, the fuel sources available for use at power plants are much broader in scope. They include coal, natural gas, oil, nuclear power, wind power, hydroelectric power, etc.

Power Generation

Coal and Natural Gas. While America is largely reliant on imported oil to fuel its cars, it has significant and varied energy sources for its power generation infrastructure. America has vast coal and natural gas reserves to fire its power plants. In addition, it has significant uranium reserves, which can be used to generate nuclear power.

There are also a variety of alternative energy sources as well. Hydroelectric power generates about 6 percent of America's energy. In addition, America has vast expanses of land in the west and midwest that can be used for wind and solar power. At this point, neither wind nor power is commercially viable without government subsidies and neither will provide the United States with a significant percentage of its energy needs at any point in the near-to-medium term. Accordingly, at least for the near term, America will generate most of its incremental energy supply from one of the big three: coal, natural gas, or nuclear.

Coal is in abundant supply in the United States; current reserves could last this country for nearly two hundred years.[3] However, it is a carbon-based energy source with obvious environmental problems. Coal is perhaps the dirtiest of the fuel sources for power plants. Also, it must be mined, often from deep subsurface mines. Safety has improved dramatically over the years, but mining is still a dangerous job and deaths result.

Natural gas is a much cleaner-burning fossil fuel and is safer to produce. However, America's supply of natural gas is declining. At some point, the United States will be a net importer of natural gas. Importing natural gas poses significant logistical and safety problems.[4]

Health Costs. Coal and natural gas also impact health and safety at three levels: (1) deaths and injuries occur when coal is mined and natural gas is produced from wells (deaths are increasingly rare although they still occur), (2) deaths and injuries occur at power plants when these fuels are converted into energy (also relatively rare), (3) there are serious health issues (particularly with coal) relating to emissions from power plants burning these fuels.

When burned, coal emits carbon dioxide, sulfur, and other contaminants into the environment. The waste from burning coal is not being "stored" in a dump (like trash), but in the air we breath. Not surprisingly, the contaminants cause health problems, which typically involve the respiratory system.[5]

Coal Alternatives. New technologies have and are being developed to strip out the harmful sulfur from coal so that it is not released into the environment when burned. In addition, there have been attempts to "sequester" the carbon dioxide emitted from burning coal and pump it back into the ground to store it. Both solutions are extremely expensive.

As America becomes increasingly aware of the health and environmental issues posed by dumping carbon dioxide in the environment, it should impose a cost on this type of activities. This is not terribly dissimilar to the disposal of sewage. Not long ago, sewage was indiscriminately dumped into rivers and streams. Over time, Americans realized this posed health and safety issues. Typhoid and other ailments from drinking water contaminated with human waste claimed thousands of lives in the 1800s. As a result, Americans began to demand that sewage be treated. While more costly, the environment was made safer as a result. The damage being done to the environment through carbon emissions is analogous. The carbon tax outlined previously imposes a cost to carbon emissions. It will provide an incentive for carbon sequestration and the development of other technologies to find cleaner-burning fuels.

Nuclear Power

Despite its reputation, nuclear power offers the best medium-term alternative to produce economical energy without polluting the environment. Advanced with much promise during the 1950s through early 1970s, it suffered from a few high-profile accidents. While nuclear energy boasts a much stronger safety record than coal, these problems caused Americans to reassess it. Public opinion (led by environmentalists) swiftly turned against nuclear power and the United States has not built a new nuclear power plant in over twenty years.

Despite these problems, nuclear power has flourished elsewhere, particularly in Japan and Europe. France and parts of Europe and Japan derive as much as 70 percent of their electricity supplies from nuclear power, while it comprises just under 20 percent of US power generation.[6] Environmentalists rightly point to the lack of natural resources in Japan and Europe, making them a fertile market for nuclear energy. However, a closer look at the facts indicates that nuclear power is the safest, greenest, and most cost-effective power generation source available.

Nuclear Power's Safety Record. Environmentalists complain about the risks of operating nuclear power plants and disposing of nuclear waste. Both risks are overstated.

From an operational standpoint, nuclear power is among the safest forms of energy used for power generation. In general, nuclear, coal, and natural gas each have three main risks:

First, there are risks associated with finding and extracting the source fuel; these are relatively consistent among uranium, coal, and natural gas. Second, there are the risks involved in using the materials to produce electricity and power. The loss of life at nuclear plants has been lower than that at coal and/or natural gas plants. For Western countries, the risks of operating a nuclear plant are lower than those relating to the operation of a coal-fired power plant. In fact, despite the negative publicity this energy source received after the Three Mile Island incident, no deaths have resulted from operating a nuclear power plant in a Western country.

The final risks concern potential loss of life caused by an explosion or waste emitted into the atmosphere. Nuclear power is actually safer than coal and is arguably safer than natural gas. Actual nuclear plant explosions or "meltdowns" are extraordinarily rare. With 450 nuclear plants in existence, there has been only one plant explosion and meltdown causing loss of life—Chernobyl. And Chernobyl was an older plant that was built in the 1950s with antiquated technology. But, even including Chernobyl, the number of deaths associated with nuclear power is not anywhere close to the annual deaths caused by the emission of greenhouse gases and carbon into the environment. These emissions lower the air quality in cities throughout the United States, Europe, and Asia. The number premature deaths relating to air pollution is said to be over 300,000 per annum in Europe alone.[7]

Nuclear power does not generate carbon emissions, so loss of life from greenhouse gases is nonexistent. Further, there have been no deaths in over ten thousand nuclear reactor years of production in the West.[8] It seems clear that loss of life relating to carbon emissions will not slow appreciably, whereas loss of life relating to nuclear plant problems will likely be negligible, given that reactors today are much safer and more advanced than those built in the 1950s.

Nuclear Waste vs. Coal and Natural Gas Waste. Nuclear waste disposal is another area that receives criticism from environmentalists and others. Currently, nuclear waste is stored on site, though there is a proposal that it be stored in a geological repository under the Yucca Mountains in Nevada. Environmentalists believe this repository does not provide sufficient safeguards for future generations. Environmentalists have this concern despite the fact that studies indicate the waste could be efficiently and safely stored for as many as ten thousand years.

Even if this estimate is off by five thousand years, environmentalists should be more concerned about the imminent risk associated with carbon emissions and global warming. Many scientists believe that carbon emissions, if not addressed, will have a negative impact on the environment well before the end of *this century*. It would be wiser to store the nuclear waste and allow future generations to figure out a permanent storage solution for spent nuclear fuel, instead of continuing down the more certain, near-term road to disaster of storing carbon-based fuel waste in the environment.

We should be relatively confident that in 250 to 500 generations, mankind will be able to address the issues associated with nuclear waste buried beneath the Yucca Mountains, whether by sending it into space or some other means. We need to address a more pressing and near-term problem now—the potential for carbon-based fuel emissions to threaten our way of life.

Cost Effectiveness. The most troublesome issue is whether nuclear energy is cost effective. The cost of constructing nuclear power plants in the United States has increased dramatically. The permit process alone can take years and cost several hundred million dollars. The plants themselves cost billions more to construct and complete. However, a new generation of more cost-effective nuclear power plants is coming on line, starting in Japan.

These advanced reactors, developed by General Electric, provide a net output of about 1,340 megawatts of electricity per day—enough electricity for nearly one million households. (This figure is based on nuclear industry statistics that a 1,000-megawatt reactor provides sufficient electricity for 740,000 homes. [9]) As of year-end 2006, four new-generation nuclear power plants were in operation, all in Japan or Taiwan. Several have been proposed for the United States, although none have broken dirt on construction yet.

The reason, of course, starts with the hysteria that resulted from the Three Mile Island meltdown. After that, the US government imposed significant regulatory burdens on the construction of nuclear power plants. Each individual reactor must be licensed through a lengthy, costly, and laborious process. Japan and France, on the other hand, use a streamlined process for approval and construction. The United States is trending toward a more standardized approach.

The principal costs associated with power generation include (a) permit and construction costs, (b) fuel costs, (c) maintenance and operational costs, and (d) decommissioning costs. Based on an OECD study, nuclear energy provides a cost-competitive solution versus coal and natural gas. Measured against coal and natural gas, its cost is competitive across the world, even in the United States. The reason is that while nuclear plants are significantly more expensive to construct, the cost of nuclear fuel, uranium, is much lower than either coal or natural gas. Higher upfront expenses are recouped in lower fuel costs over the life of the plant.[10] The advantage of using nuclear power is accentuated if one assumes that the world is in a commodity "super cycle" in which commodity prices are trending ever higher. In that case, nuclear power then becomes more attractive given that its fuel costs are a lower portion of the overall cost. Gas- and coal-fired plants are more sensitive to rising gas and coal prices. Indeed, if fuels costs double, the overall cost associated with a nuclear power plant rise less than 10 percent, whereas coal- and gas-fired plants see increases of 31 and 66 percent, respectively.[11]

Further, no costs have been ascribed to the contribution to global warming by greenhouse gases emitted from coal and other fossil fuels. So nuclear power is fully loaded with costs, whereas coal, natural gas, and oil are not.

Indeed, once constructed, a nuclear plant's ongoing operating costs are modest and its environmental impact is negligible. But therein lies the rub. In the United States, constructing nuclear power plants is a costly and laborious process. The United States should look to Japan and France—both of which have thriving nuclear power industries—for guidance.

Using France and Japan as a Model. Japan and France have lower construction costs, shorter construction periods, and overall better safety records in nuclear power than the United States (although all countries with the exception of the old Soviet Union have a strong safety record in nuclear energy). Japan and France have lower construction costs and delays because of more streamlined governmental licensing and certification procedures.

In France, there is only one model of reactor that can be licensed. It has been extensively vetted and analyzed, assuring its safety. The same design is used throughout the country. Thus, the process of obtaining permits and construction is easier and less costly. Safety is also enhanced, given that the model has been thoroughly tested and the same construction procedures apply in each case. By perfecting the design and construction processes, mistakes are less likely to occur during the construction phase.

In the United States, each new plant has had a different design, making the process—from obtaining permits to construction to operation—different for each plant. Time delays and cost overruns have been the norm in the United States, not to mention the difficulties in constructing and operating the nuclear plants.

On a more positive note, the United States appears to be catching on. Recent legislation allows for "type-licensing" of reactors. This process is being used by General Electric and Westinghouse on two new nuclear reactor prototypes. In addition, the United States Department of Energy has introduced a program based on France's standard prototype licensing program. It provides applicants for nuclear power permits a subsidy of 25 to 50 percent of the cost overruns due to delays for the first six plants under the program. This will allow a standard prototype to be developed without one or two parties taking all the risks. Several applications have been submitted under this program and a couple of sites selected for new reactors.

If the United States can have a single design that can be replicated across the country, the costs associated with nuclear power will be reduced to the point where they are much more competitive than conventional fossil fuel sources of electricity. Better yet, nuclear energy is clean and does not emit carbon dioxide into the atmosphere.

Transmission of Nuclear Energy. The location of future nuclear plants might allay some concerns on the part of environmentalists. Current transmission infrastructure—alternating current power lines—loses considerable energy from the power generation source to the end user. The longer the transmission lines, the more power lost in transmission. This limits how far from population centers a nuclear power plant can be built.

However, direct-current power lines transmit power more efficiently, allowing power to be transmitted farther without as much loss. By using direct-current lines, new power plants can be built farther away from population centers, creating an even greater margin of safety.

The Time to Act Is Now

The alarm bells should be ringing on nuclear energy, but not in the way that you might think. Currently, nuclear energy provides approximately 19 percent of America's power supply, but many of the plants are old and will be decommissioned within the next twenty years. If we do not build new plants to replace existing ones, the percentage of electricity generated by nuclear power will start to decrease, with a resulting increase in carbon-fueled electricity.

Thus, even with greater conservation and more alternative energy, carbon emissions will continue to increase. However, America can choose another path. Over the next twenty years, the United States can build enough nuclear power plants to generate the same proportion of its electricity from nuclear power as France. If that occurred, America would reduce its greenhouse emissions by nearly 50 percent, even if energy consumption increased.

Ironically, if the United States had devoted the same resources to building nuclear power plants that it has to the war in Iraq, it would have over two hundred new nuclear power plants on line within the next ten years. These plants would have generated enough electricity to eliminate the need to burn any fossil fuels for power generation. This would have immediately reduced our need to import Persian Gulf oil and reduced greenhouse gases enough to have met all the requirements of the Kyoto Treaty.

In sum, the United States should proceed without hesitation to build enough nuclear power plants over the next twenty years to generate at least 70 percent of its power. Betting on unproven or uneconomical technologies is foolish, particularly given the risk of global warming and the national security threat posed by our reliance on Middle Eastern oil.

Integration of Nuclear Power Generation with Transportation Assets

The rapid expansion of nuclear power represents the first step: finding a reliable, home-grown and green energy source for power generation. However, America must also solve its dependence on imported oil to fuel its transportation assets.

General. To address the energy crisis in America's transportation fleet (cars and trucks), one must understand the issues associated with finding an appropriate energy source for these assets. Currently, cars and trucks generate power through an internal combustion engine. This engine serves as a mini power plant and transforms energy (gasoline) into power to propel the car.

Several issues are associated with the internal combustion engine. First, the fuel source needs to be transportable, and a car must carry enough fuel to power it for lengthy periods before being refueled. The average range of an automobile manufactured in the United States is between 250 and 400 miles. Second, the fuel source needs to be one that can be transported and stored at multiple locations throughout the county. Gas stations store gasoline and are scattered throughout the United States, making access to a fuel supply relatively easy for most motorists. Third, the internal combustion engine needs a fuel source that is relatively inexpensive and has a high octane level.

When added up, all these components mean that the best fuel source for cars is gasoline refined from oil. While coal is cheaper, it cannot be stored and does not have gasoline's octane levels.[12] Further, it is very costly to refine coal into liquid form. Natural gas offers promise. It has a relatively high octane level and can be stored within a car. However, America would have to make a lengthy and significant investment to retrofit its gas stations to accommodate natural gas.

To find a replacement for oil, the following factors should be considered. First, the cost of the fuel should be considered. Unless the fuel is cost competitive with gasoline, it is unlikely to be widely adopted. In this regard, the carbon and national security tax will open the door for several alternative fuel sources. Second, a substitute should have a favorable environmental impact relative to gasoline. Third, America should be able to roll out the substitute with a minimal amount of disruption and without having to modify existing infrastructure to any great extent. This will enhance the speed to market and address America's reliance on foreign oil and global warming in the near term. Finally, any substitute should eliminate or dramatically reduce America's reliance on Middle Eastern oil.

For the moment, there are few alternatives that meet all these requirements. In fact, there is only one option that meets all of these requirements—an electric car.

Benefit of Electric Cars over Internal Combustion Engine. An internal combustion engine is inefficient. It lacks the economies of scale of a full-scale power plant. If an internal combustion engine could generate power as efficiently as a large-scale power plant, a car would get over 130 miles or more per gallon on an energy equivalent basis. This degree of efficiency, even if generated from carbon-based fuels, would reduce America's oil consumption by 80 percent, eliminate the United States' reliance on foreign oil, and reduce carbon dioxide emissions from cars by the same amount.

The challenge is to translate the economies of scale of large-scale power plants to automobiles. But to do so you have to change the character of the car. In effect, a car would have to transition from a vehicle that *generates* its own power to one that *stores* its power. If a car can get its power from a power plant and store that power for use at a later time, you get the benefit of economies of scale in power generation and eliminate the need for an engine on board a car. This leads to a battery-powered car rather than an engine-powered car and an interesting plan.

The Business Case for the Electric Car

The next generation of car companies is being developed in Silicon Valley and elsewhere across the world. These companies are focused on developing a viable electric car. The following is an outline of the basic plan:

Battery Technology. A battery-powered electric car has been the Holy Grail of car companies for years. General Motors famously pursued one in the 1980s, only to drop it after some promise. The car fell victim to declining oil prices, cost overruns, a poor driving range, and internal politics.

Today, electric car entrepreneurs seem to be focusing on a different approach. Previously, car companies focused on inefficient alkaline battery technologies. The new companies, however, are focusing on lithium batteries. The logic is simple. Lithium batteries power everything from cell phones to computers. Given consumer demand and the proliferation of these devices, lithium battery technology has improved dramatically over the past five years and is likely to improve for many years to come. These companies believe they can build a commercially viable electric car using existing lithium battery technology. So, as battery technology continues to improve, these car companies believe they can deliver even better electric cars, with longer driving ranges and a lower price point. Indeed, the electric car revolution offers tremendous promise.

Prototypes. At least one of the electric car prototypes seems to manifest this promise. This car has a range of over two hundred miles. With the manufacturer's charge package, its battery charges within three and a half hours from a 220-volt electrical outlet. The prototype can go from 0 to 60 faster than a high-performance sports car and has a maximum speed of over 100 miles per hour. The cost of the car is high—over $100,000. However, once you factor in reduced fuel costs, the cost of the car is comparable to that of a $35,000 gasoline-powered automobile. Further, in the years to come, battery technology improvements should result in an electric car that is not only cost competitive, but actually cheaper than a standard automobile.

One electric car manufacturer is developing a roadster that has a high front-end cost but a low operating cost per mile. The car will sell for over $100,000 but cost about two cents per mile to operate. This means the car will get about 135 miles per gallon on an energy equivalent basis. The manufacturer is also coming out with a $30,000 sedan. The expense of the roadster and lower-cost sedan versus a $35,000 gasoline-powered car that gets twenty miles to the gallon are as set forth in chart 17-1.

Infrastructure. America has the infrastructure to accommodate electric cars. Of course, electric cars will need outlets to recharge their batteries. Fortunately, America has a greater density of electric outlets than gas stations. Every office building, restaurant, apartment complex, etc. has electric outlets and could have curbside electric ports established to recharge electric cars at very little cost. And electric companies could install these ports, complete with metering and credit card payment devices to provide energy for cars parked at these locations. Fortunately, the conversion costs would not be dramatic. Given the overall economics of the electric car the cost to have ports installed throughout the nation should be fairly reasonable.

Using Nuclear Power as the Power Source

Of course, the electric car must have an ultimate power source—a power plant. Many power plants in the United States are coal fired.

CHART 17-1

	Roadster	Sedan	Standard American Car
Cost	$109,000	$30,000 (est.)	$35,000
Miles Driven per Year	12,000	12,000	12,000
Years Owned	5	5	5
Resale (20% of Initial Price)	$22,450	$6,000	$7,000
Gas Prices	$4.00	$4.00	$4.00
Miles per Gallon Equivalent	135	135	20
Annual Maintenance Costs	$300	$300	$1,000
Cost Per Year	**$17,500**	**$5,000**	**$18,500**
Conclusion	The midrange-priced electric car is significantly cheaper to operate than a comparably priced US sedan.		

Even with coal, the electric car would be more efficient since the coal plant can generate power more cheaply and efficiently than an internal combustion engine. So, as noted above, a car with a battery that stores energy generated by a coal-fired plant will get the equivalent of over 130 miles per gallon and pollute much less than a standard gasoline-powered engine.

Nonetheless, a coal plant still generates carbon emissions, which pollutes the environment. However, if the United States transitions to a nation with nuclear power as its primary power-generation fuel, it would be able to dramatically reduce its greenhouse emissions. The reasoning is quite simple. A nuclear plant generates very little in the way of greenhouse gases. Thus, by powering electric cars through nuclear energy, the United States will have eliminated almost all greenhouse gases. The nuclear power plant, which recharges the electric cars' batteries, will not produce carbon emissions, and neither will the electric cars. Accordingly, the US can trend toward dramatically reducing carbon emissions and dramatically reduce the need for oil from the Middle East.

The Transition: The Energy "Manhattan Project"

This country's energy "Manhattan Project" should focus on building more cost-effective nuclear power plants and conducting research on more efficient battery-powered automobiles. In addition, the United States should develop a standard electricity port for a battery-powered car. This would avoid a series of competing ports that would make it difficult to have a fleet of quickly rechargeable electric cars.

If we build a sufficient number of nuclear power plants, greenhouse gases will decline. In fact, if the United States generated the same percentage of its energy from nuclear power that France does, the it would reduce carbon emissions by over 2,000 million metric tons of carbon dioxide—three times the carbon emissions generated by all cars and trucks on America's roadways.[13]

If we have a sufficient breakthrough in battery technology, nuclear power would provide the electricity necessary to recharge batteries and power electric cars. This would cut down on our use of foreign oil (and even domestic oil), and would also reduce greenhouse emissions by another 700 metric tons of carbon dioxide emissions per annum.

So the combination of using nuclear energy at the same rate as France in combination with the electric car would reduce America's greenhouse emissions by nearly 400 percent over the next thirty years. America would be energy self-sufficient and not have to import one drop of Middle Eastern oil.

The United States can and should devote significant resources to continuing to develop the electric car. The technology is available to make dramatic strides within a short period of time. There is already a prototype in place that is a viable alternative to the internal combustion engine. Once this electric car is improved upon and viable for mass production, the United States should start imposing more and more stringent gas mileage standards in a drive to transition the nation toward the electric car.

Through aggressive research and development (particularly as it relates to range, storage capacity, and charge time) and a standardized platform to recharge the batteries, the America can lay the foundation for the electric car to take over as the main mode of transportation within thirty years.

The risk to this plan is modest. First, nuclear power is proven. The technology works and it is safe and "green." There is therefore no technology risk associated with nuclear power.

Second, among the transportation alternatives, electric cars offer the best and most viable means to wean ourselves off foreign oil. The United States already has a battery-powered car on the verge of being commercially viable, and based on the advances in battery technology, these cars should be cost competitive within the next five years if not sooner. And since they run on electricity, the United States would not have to make a significant investment in infrastructure. It could rely more and more on nuclear energy to provide energy for both power generation and transportation.

Devoting resources to the electric car and investing heavily in its future does not carry a significant amount of risk, even if proven wrong or if a competing technology emerges. The primary focus will be on increasing the range of the car and reducing the amount of time necessary to charge the battery. This research will be undertaken in any event. There has been significant pressure by cell phone and laptop computer manufacturers on battery manufacturers to continue to make progress on battery life and charge time. These have dramatically improved over the past several years as a result, and it is highly likely that improvements will continue at a brisk pace well into the future.

Another "Grand Bargain"

To achieve this goal, liberals and conservatives will have to strike a yet another "grand bargain."[14] Environmentalists will have to accede to the fact that nuclear energy is the only fuel source that does not emit carbon dioxide, is commercially viable, and can produce enough electricity to meet America's energy consumption needs. Conservatives will have to accept that the US government should promote and perhaps subsidize research and development efforts for an electric car. If the United States spent as much developing the electric car as it did on the Manhattan Project, the entire $20 billion cost would still be less than the cost of three months in Iraq (inflation adjusted). It is hard to imagine a worthier or more strategic investment on the part of the US government.

PART V

AMERICAN FOREIGN POLICY

- Cold War Victory vs. Today
- Defining the Enemy and Why They Are Fighting
- New Foreign Policy
- Reconfiguring the US Military
- A New NATO and Regional Partnership to Address Human Crises
- Addressing the Palestinian Issue: A New Marshall Plan
- Addressing Iraq and Afghanistan

Introduction

*Goal: Global Stability to Reduce Security Threats
and Promote Commerce*

Imperatives:

- Identification of Principal Threats to National and Economic Security
- Clear Foreign Policy Tailored to:

    a. Reduce Tensions
    b. Enhance Trade and Promote National Interest

- National Defense: Narrow and Refine Focus to Better Address Principal National Security Threats

CHAPTER 18

Cold War Victory vs. Today

America's success during the Cold War can be traced to the foreign policy framework of George Washington. The United States won the Cold War by (a) defining early on America's chief national security threat, (b) developing a cost-effective military strategy to address this threat, (c) the superiority of its form of government and economic system, which provided a clear and superior alternative to the Soviet Union's for other nations to follow. This historical and rather recent precedent is a useful guide in assessing the current "war on terror."

Cold War vs. War on Terror

In this section, we will compare and contrast America's Cold War victory with its efforts thus far in the war on terror.

Clarity of Mission: Defining the Enemy

Cold War Era. During the Cold War, the United States had the benefit of a clear-cut enemy: the Soviet Union and its satellites.

Today. The world is more complex today, and certainly not bipolar. The United States is waging a war against Islamic extremists. In addition, it is fighting—whether through rhetoric, sanctions, or military action—a number of rogue states, including several carryovers from the Cold War era. Many of these states either support or have supported terrorism in the past. Finally, the United States is grappling with the emergence of China, and even India, as economic and military powers.

Challenge. America should define those nations or groups that truly pose a national security threat and develop a foreign policy to reduce the number of rogue states it has to worry about. Further, it should develop a foreign policy that better addresses economic threats and, to a lesser extent, military threats from China.

Cost-Effective Military Strategy

Cold War: America Bankrupted the Soviet Union. Early on, the architects of America's Cold War strategy realized that the greatest military advantage of the United States lay in its economic strength. Without question, it possessed a strong military during the Cold War conflict. But, based on conventional strength, the US military was never as big as the Soviet Union's. Many experts believe that if the Soviet Union desired, it could have taken control of Western Europe in a purely conventional war.

To offset the Soviet Union's conventional superiority, the United States developed and relied on a vast nuclear arsenal that served as a deterrent to the invasion of Western Europe. American policymakers understood that it was critical to develop a military strategy that used resources wisely and tailored the military in the most cost-effective manner. In the case of the Soviet Union, US policymakers rightly calculated that Soviet leadership would think twice about launching a conventional war if they knew that the United States would retaliate with its nuclear arsenal—assuring the mutual destruction of both nations.

Many experts also believe that the Soviet Union was spending over 30 percent of GDP on its military during the height of the Cold War. The United States rarely spent more than 5 percent of GDP. During this era, the Soviet Union faced two significant disadvantages. First, the US had a much larger and growing economy. Thus, the Soviet Union had to devote an increasing amount of its national wealth to maintain an edge against the United States.

Second, the Soviet Union invested more heavily in a more labor intensive and costlier conventional military, whereas the US relied extensively on its nuclear deterrence while also having a conventional military that was sufficient to provide some deterrent effect. Given the differential in military spending, the Soviet Union slowly bankrupted itself, while the US, given its economic strength, was able to maintain its level of military spending over a longer period of time. There are limits to how much of a nation's wealth can be devoted to national security without compromising its long-term economic health, a lesson that the Soviet Union and other historical powers have learned at the expense of their empires.

Today: America Is Bankrupting Itself. America is now following the opposite path. It is slowly bankrupting itself. The invasion of Iraq may go down in history as the most disastrous foreign policy decision ever by a US president, much akin to the disaster that befell Europe as a result of World War I.

World War I proved a watershed event for Europe, an unnecessary war that bled the continent literally and financially. Going into World War I, Western Europe was the world's economic and military power. After the war, Europe was heavily indebted to the United States and, worse yet, the war sowed the seeds for a broader, more disastrous war: World War II. The United States faces a set of similar circumstances today. The war in Iraq has been far less disastrous in terms of lives lost, but it has caused the US to become deeply indebted to China, its largest global competitor, to finance the war, just as Europe became indebted to the US to finance World War I. America is just now beginning to understand the full cost of this war.

The cost of the war has been staggering. The 9/11 Commission estimated that it cost Al Qaeda approximately $3 million to stage the 9/11 attacks. America, on the other hand, has spent well over $500 billion in response, a total expected to reach $1 trillion by 2010. This does take into account the higher energy costs that have resulted from the conflict. Energy prices have climbed steadily since the Iraq war started due to (a) decreased supply (Iraq's oil production virtually stopped when the United States invaded), (b) greater instability in the region, and (c) increased worldwide demand, particularly in emerging Asia.

Although the US invasion is not responsible for increased demand, one study estimates that the American consumer pays approximately $20 per barrel more as a result of America's invasion of Iraq. This, along with the hard costs of the war and other costs (e.g., lost productivity of soldiers), equate to about $1.5 trillion to date, and will result in a total tab for the war to over $3 trillion over time.

The United States has expanded a war started by Osama bin Laden to include Iraq and potentially Iran. It is expending hundreds of billions of dollars, with no end in sight. Indeed, President Bush has indicated that a long-term military presence should be undertaken, much like America's presence in Korea, which is now approaching sixty years.

One of Osama bin Laden's stated objectives is to bankrupt the United States by creating a situation where a terrorist attack that costs very little to plan and execute results in a costly and ineffective countermeasure. Indeed, Donald Rumsfeld, formerly secretary of Defense under President Bush, lamented that the economics of terrorism put the United States at an extreme cost disadvantage. Without a change in foreign policy and military strategy, the US will face a situation not terribly different than England, the USSR, and Rome before it. America's military commitments will slowly bleed the country, causing it to dramatically retrench its military based on economic crisis. Unlike England, however, the US may not have a friendly and aligned country that steps in and fills the void, as the US did when England's power waned.

As America fights a global war on terror, the Chinese are investing their resources into building a dominant economy. If the United States does not prioritize properly, it will find its status as the world's economic power eclipsed, compromising its economic standing and national security, just like the European powers a century ago.

Challenge. America should prioritize threats. It is no longer possible to defend against every conceivable threat, no matter how remote (e.g., invading Iraq). The United States must develop a national defense tailored to address true national threats in the most cost-effective manner possible.

Moral Clarity and Building Alliances

Cold War: America Accentuated Its Superior System and Provided a More Attractive Alternative. During the Cold War, the United States provided a clear and attractive alternative to the Soviet Union. It stood for freedom and economic prosperity, in stark contrast with the Soviet Union. The United States also invested heavily in Europe (the Marshall Plan) and Japan to rebuild their economies. This provided it with markets for its exports, but also—and as important—it provided the peoples of these regions with strong, stable economies and a reason to remain within the US sphere of influence.

Today: America's Haphazard Policy Provides Little Clarity. Europe Forges Its Own Path. China Provides an Alternative to America. The world is splitting into three spheres. America is forging its own path, hectoring the Europeans and other nations to follow its lead of nation-building, sanctions, and the spreading of democracy (at gunpoint, if need be). The Europeans seem to understand the threat of terrorism, given that they have dealt with this threat longer than the United States (whether from Islamic extremists or home-grown terrorists, such as Basque ETA (*Euskadi ta Askatasuna*) separatists in Spain or the Irish Republic Army in the United Kingdom).

But Europe and Japan are finding other differences with the United States, whether on human rights, the Palestinian issue, or the environment. These differences have driven a slight to modest wedge between Europe and America. Ironically, China has followed a foreign policy strategy that could have been taken straight from George Washington's farewell address: a policy based on establishing relationships with all nations and promoting economic trade. As China ascends economically, it has attracted a variety of nations to its sphere of influence, since nations respect a more balanced, even, and logical foreign policy. And nations flock to a winner.

Challenge. America needs to develop a more attractive foreign policy alternative to that of the Europeans and Chinese. America is ideally situated to provide a superior economic alternative to the Europeans and moral alternative to the Chinese. At the moment, it is losing on both fronts.

Overall Success of the Cold War. Tactical Failures

Regrettably, America seems to have largely eschewed the tactics that won the Cold War, while pursuing some of the more ineffective strategies employed during that era.

The Success: Collapse of the Soviet Union

In partnership with Soviet president Mikhail Gorbachev, who understood the dire economic straits of the USSR, President Ronald Reagan brought the Cold War to a close through active engagement backed by military strength. Through Reagan's efforts, the Soviet people came to realize two things. First, the United States meant the Soviet people no harm and, second, it had a superior economic system. Since profound fear was no longer an obstacle to rapprochement, the Soviet people began demanding economic liberalization to provide greater economic prosperity. The Soviet Union collapsed without a shot being fired.

Cold War Policy Failures

America's Cold War strategy ended in victory, without the predicted nuclear conflict with the USSR, yet the victory was not an unqualified one. The United States began the practice of punishing nations that did not conform to its interests or ideological views. Cuba is a prime example of this policy, which has carried forward and accelerated in the post–Cold War era.

The United States also started the dubious practice of establishing close relationships with nations or leaders that provided a check to Soviet expansion or that were considered strategic to US interests. In some cases, the leaders of these countries had little in common with the United States other than a desire to check Soviet expansion or provide the US with access to oil. Many of these countries (such as Iran under the Shah and Saudi Arabia) were ruled in a manner largely inconsistent with US moral and economic values.

In at least three of these instances, the United States helped sow the seeds of its current conflict with Islamic extremists, classic examples of "blowback." Blowback, is a term used by the CIA and is, in effect, the "law of unintended consequences." It occurs when the US takes an action supporting or opposing a nation or group to promote a particular strategic interest, only to have that action create new and much bigger problems down the road. The Middle East offers numerous examples of "blowback."

Iran. Both the United States and the Soviet Union realized the importance of the Middle East and—from the 1950s through the end of the Cold War—each worked hard to cement alliances with Middle Eastern nations to expand their influence in the region. Sitting in the center of the Middle East, Iran offered an enticing prize, particularly with its vast oil reserves and relatively sophisticated population. In the early 1950s, the Iranians overthrew the hereditary monarchy, and elected a prime minister named Mohammad Mossadegh who was focused on instituting democratic reform. However, Mossadegh also proposed to nationalize Western energy company holdings in Iran. Sensing a potentially unreliable ally, the CIA helped overthrow Mossadegh in 1953, and installed the Shah of Iran—the son of the previous monarch—in his place. For the next 25 years, the Shah was a reliable ally of the US. Unfortunately, he was also a brutal ruler, who was largely hated by his people, had a secret police (the Savak) known for torture, and was ultimately overthrown by Islamic fundamentalists in 1978.

The United States' and CIA's role in the overthrow of the more democratic Mossadegh and its support of the Shah was remembered by the fundamentalists who overthrew the Shah. These fundamentalists immediately took a staunchly anti-American position, a popular move with the vast majority of the Iranian people who identified America with the Shah's repressive regime. With the overthrow of the Shah, fundamentalists—largely college students—stormed the American embassy and took hostages. The United States broke off diplomatic relations with Iran and since that time has had little official contact with the government.

Afghanistan. The Soviet Union invaded Afghanistan in 1978, partly to quell Islamic extremism along its border with Afghanistan. After its stunning defeat in Vietnam (partially because of Soviet and Chinese support of North Vietnam), the United States was eager to repay the favor by providing assistance to the Muslim radicals fighting the Soviet Union, including a Saudi radical named Osama bin Laden. Armed with American sidewinder missiles and training, the Afghan freedom fighters proved tough adversaries, defeating the Red Army. This defeat certainly played a part in the fall of the Soviet Union by showing the vulnerability of the Red Army, straining the economic resources of the USSR, and turning public opinion against the Soviet leadership. The United States' support also created a group of well-trained, armed Islamic fundamentalists who would later turn their religious war on a new occupying power, the United States, in the aftermath of the First Gulf War.

Iraq. Shortly after the Soviet invasion of Afghanistan and the Iranian revolution, Iraq, sensing an opportunity, invaded Iran in 1980. It was a war that would last eight years. Stung by both the Iranian revolution and the Iranian hostage crisis, America began supporting Iraq and its secular leader, Saddam Hussein, in his war against the Islamic fundamentalists. The United States supplied military hardware and also the know-how and materials to make chemical weapons, which were ultimately used against Iran and the Kurds.

In 1988, with hundreds of thousands of lives lost on both sides, the war ended in a hollow Iraqi victory and a return to prewar borders. The United States might have felt some vindication. After all, Iraq was the much smaller country and had inflicted heavy losses on Iran. However, America's support of Saddam Hussein gave him the confidence to invade Kuwait in 1991. America and a broad coalition defeated Saddam in the First Gulf War, but left US troops in Saudi Arabia in 1992 as a check against further mischief. Sunni fundamentalists, including Osama bin Laden, viewed this as a desecration of their holy land (Saudi Arabia) by infidels, and shortly thereafter began a series of attacks on the United States, starting with the first World Trade Center bombing in 1993. The attacks have continued unabated.

Conclusion

America should develop a foreign policy and military strategy consistent with its principles and traditions. The Cold War represents a decisive US foreign policy and military victory. The United States should use the strategies that worked so well during the Cold War, refine them, and apply them today. The following chapters will focus on a strategy to (a) define who our enemies are, (b) develop a foreign policy designed to reduce tensions and military threats and promote economic trade, (c) build a more cost-effective military strategy, and (d) regain America's position of moral leadership through a series of related plans to address the Palestinian issue, Iraq, and Iran.

CHAPTER 19

Defining the Enemy and Why They Are Fighting

The first step in developing a post–Cold War foreign policy and military strategy is to define the threats facing the nation, whether current or prospective, and grade and prioritize those threats. In defining the threats, the United States should gain an understanding of the goals and objectives of each adversary or potential adversary. After doing so, it should develop a plan to address these threats, whether militarily and/or through a change in foreign policy, and then allocate resources to combat the threats based on the magnitude of the risk.

The Terrorism Threat

Without question, the biggest threat to America's national security is from Islamic extremists. President Bush has struck this note continually over the past several years. But he has used a broad and shifting definition that fails to precisely pinpoint our enemies.

America has historically faced threats from different sects of Islamic fundamentalists. Each sect has different leaders and objectives. Some sects engaged in attacks against the United States decades ago but have largely avoided confrontation for the last twenty years (e.g., Hezbollah, a Shiite sect aligned with Iran). Some were allied with America during the 1980s in the fight against Communism, only to turn against us in the early 1990s, partly because of the US military presence in Saudi Arabia after the First Gulf War (e.g., Al Qaeda).

There is no sense in waging a war against an entire religion when only a few factions are truly at war with the United States. Further, it makes sense to prevent a fight by avoiding policies or conduct that aggravate these sects, especially if the US does not compromise its national security in the process. American foreign and military policy should start with defining those sects of Islam that currently threaten the US.

Sunnis and Shiites. Islam has two main branches, Sunni and Shiite, which have been warring with each other almost since the inception of the religion. The schism occurred thirteen hundred years ago, shortly after the death of Islam's founder, the prophet Mohammad. The rift centered on who would succeed Mohammad, his cousin Ali or an unrelated follower. While religion has played a large role in the conflict, ethnic differences have also come into play. For example, Arabs are largely Sunni and have an antipathy toward the Persians (Iranians), who are largely Shiite. Indeed, the Saudis (Arab and Sunni) opposed America's second invasion of Iraq because they feared it would tip the balance of power in the region in favor of Iran (Persia and Shiites).

Based on population and dominion, Sunnis have reigned supreme. They comprise over 90 percent of the world's Muslims and dominate much of the Arabian Peninsula (Saudi Arabia and the other Gulf states), central Iraq, Afghanistan, Jordan, Syria, and large swaths of southeastern Asia (such as Indonesia). Shiites dominate Iran, Bahrain. and southern Iraq. Although they have fought one another for precedence in Islam for centuries, the two branches have united from time to time, typically to fight infidels periodically invading their sacred ground.

Who Is Fighting Us and Why Are They Fighting? President George W. Bush has cast the war with Al Qaeda as a war against "Islamic extremism," a war thrust on the United States by those who "hate our freedoms." This view has the allure of simplicity but is unfortunately well off the mark. As with most conflicts, the central focus is over territorial dominion, particularly Arab lands in the Middle East. These lands stretch from Iraq to Saudi Arabia to Syria (excluding Iran, dominated by Persians rather than Arabs).

As the majority in the region, Muslims want to control all land in the Middle East, particularly areas of religious significance. The United States, on the other hand, has for decades viewed the region as one of strategic importance, especially as it relates to energy. Many Arabs regard US interference in the region, particularly its occupation of Iraq and its military presence in Saudi Arabia, as unacceptable. In Osama bin Laden's 1998 fatwa, in effect his declaration of war against the United States, his principal grievance was America's continued military presence in Saudi Arabia.

Until the aftermath of the First Gulf War, the United States experienced little trouble with Sunni Muslims in general. In fact, from 1983 through 1993, after Reagan pulled the United States out of Lebanon in response to the Marine barracks bombing, America had few problems with Muslims.

In 1993, the period of dormancy came to an end when Sunni extremists bombed the World Trade Center. This began a period of fairly relentless terrorist activity against the United States that culminated with 9/11. What happened? Did, as President Bush suggests, the Sunni Arabs wake up one day in 1993 and decide to hate "our freedoms"? If so, isn't it coincidental that their hatred of our freedoms coincided almost perfectly with our decision to install military bases in Saudi Arabia, considered holy land by Sunni Muslims?

The Sunnis' grievances against the United States are much like those of the Shiites nearly three decades ago: our foreign policy and occupation of areas in the Middle East that they consider part of their dominion. Over the last thirty years, the United States has had a series of confrontations with Shiite and Sunni sects. The clear dividing line between the two sects should provide us with guidance in formulating new foreign and military policy.

Shiite Wars. From the late 1970s to mid 1980s, the United States was at war with Shiite Muslims, based largely on America's support of the former Shah of Iran and military intervention in the Lebanese civil war. It began with the overthrow of the Shah of Iran by Shiites led by Ayatollah Khomeini. This was followed by the storming of the US embassy and hostage taking by Iranian students for well over one year. Through the late 1970s to mid 1980s, the United States faced off with Iran and its proxies, particularly in Lebanon where the United States stationed troops as a part of a UN peacekeeping effort to pacify the Lebanese civil war.

Hezbollah, a Shiite sect, carried out attacks against the US. The worst attack occurred in 1983, when Hezbollah bombed the Marine barracks in Beirut, killing over 240 American soldiers. As a result of the bombing, President Reagan reassessed the need for a continued US presence in Beirut. After determining that the dangers outweighed the benefits, he withdrew all US troops from Beirut in 1983. Since that time, the US has suffered very little at the hands of Hezbollah or Shiite Muslims. The following chart illustrates the violence against Americans during the "warm" Shiite war and confirms the fact that after Reagan withdrew the troops from Lebanon, the US has had very little trouble with Shiite fundamentalists.

CHART 19-1

Attack	Date	Number Killed
US sends troops to Lebanon.	1982	N/A
US Embassy, Beirut	April 1983	63
US Marine Barracks, Beirut	October 1983	241
US Embassy, Kuwait City	December 1983	7
Reagan withdraws troops from Lebanon, March 1984.		
US Embassy, Beirut	September 1984	24
None	to present	0

It should be noted that Reagan also established relations with Iran in the 1980s, albeit through back channels. He supplied arms and other weapons to the Iranians during the war against Iraq (while later arming Iraq as well) in exchange for the release of hostages in Lebanon. By removing the source of Hezbollah's grievance and establishing a relationship with the Iranian government, Reagan avoided further violence at the hands of Shiite extremists. He correctly decided that the benefits of occupying Lebanon and squaring off with Iran were just not worth the cost to America. In explaining his decision, Reagan reasoned that "the price we had to pay in Beirut was so great, the tragedy at the barracks so enormous . . . We had to pull out . . . We couldn't stay there and run the risk of another suicide attack on the Marines."[1]

Sunni Wars. In this context, America should take a hard look at the sects and groups fighting us today and understand why they are fighting. Without question, the predominant sect fighting us today, and the one Osama bin Laden follows, is the Sunni branch. America's troubles with Sunni extremists began in the immediate aftermath of the First Gulf War. Despite some strong disagreements, particularly over Israel, the United States had previously experienced little difficulties with Sunni sects. Indeed, most Arab nations with whom the United States had strong relationships had a Sunni majority. Further, the United States had supported Sunni insurgents during the late 1970s and early 1980s, including Osama bin Laden, in their fight against the Soviets in Afghanistan. America's financial assistance and military aid turned out to be pivotal in this largely successful resistance movement. The guerrilla tactics taught to the extremists by the CIA proved critical. The US, from a distance, cheered these tactical successes. This alliance of convenience with Sunni extremists ended in 1993.

Shortly after the First Gulf War, the United States announced its intention to leave a military presence in Saudi Arabia to counter Saddam Hussein's Iraq. Iraq, while defeated, still represented a threat in the eyes of US and Saudi policymakers. Sunni fundamentalists such as Osama bin Laden did not care for the secular Saddam Hussein, but they also did not like the United States invading an Arab country. They were outraged over the continued US military presence in Saudi Arabia. (Saudi Arabia contains two of Islam's most sacred sites: Mecca and Medina.) It did not take long for this outrage to turn into action. Just eighteen months after the end of the First Gulf War, Sunni extremists bombed the World Trade Center. Fortunately, the bomb, set off in a truck in the basement, did not bring the building down. It did kill six people and injured over one thousand. The bombing started eight years of violence.

CHART 19-2

Attack	Date	Number Killed
US installs military bases in Saudi Arabia	1992	N/A
World Trade Center Bombing, New York, USA	Feb. 1993	6
Somalia	Oct. 1993	18
Khobar Towers, Khobar, Saudi Arabia	June 1996	19
Bombing of US Embassies in Kenya and Tanzania	Aug 1998	224
Attempted Bombing, Seattle, USA	Dec 1999	Failed
Bombing of USS Cole	Oct 2000	17
Attacks on World Trade Center, Pentagon—9/11, USA	Sept 2001	2,992
Attempted Bombing of Airliner (Shoe Bomber)	Dec 2001	Failed
Explosion of Synagogue,–Tunisia	April 2002	21
Car Bomb, Karachi, Pakistan	May 2002	14
US Embassy, Karachi, Pakistan	June 2002	12
Attempted Bombing of Tanker, Yemen	Oct 2002	1
Nightclub Bombings, Bali	Oct 2002	202
Suicide Bomber, Hotel Mombasa, Mombasa, Kenya	Nov 2002	16
Suicide Bomber, Riyadh, Saudia Arabia	May 2003	34
Bombings in Casablanca, Morocco	May 2003	33
Suicide Bomb, Hotel Jakarta, Jakarta, Indonesia	Aug 2003	12
Bombing of Housing Complex, Riyadh, Saudia Arabia	Nov 2003	17
Suicide Bombers, Synagogues in Istanbul, Turkey	Nov 2003	25
Truck Bombs, Istanbul, Turkey	Nov 2003	26
Train Bombings, Madrid, Spain	March 2004	191
Terrorist Attacks, Saudi Oil Offices, Khobar, Saudi Arabia	May 2004	22
Kidnapping of American, Riyadh, Saudia Arabia	June 2004	N/A
Car Bomb, Australian Embassy, Jakarta, Indonesia	Sept 2004	9
Terrorist Attack on US Consulate, Jeddah, Saudi Arabia	Dec 2004	9
Train Bombs, London, UK	July 2005	52
Suicide Bombers, Bali, Indonesia	Oct 2005	22
Hotel Bombings, Amman, Jordan	Nov 2005	57
Suicide Bombers, Police, Baghdad, Iraq	Jan 2006	20
Attempted Hijacking of Planes, London, UK	Aug 2006	Failed
Suicide Bombing, Algeria	April 2007	35
Suicide Bombing, Baghdad, Iraq	April 2007	8
Attempted Car Bombing, London, UK	June 2007	Failed

Note: Excludes attacks on US and Allied servicemen and women in Iraq and Afghanistan.

This period of violence culminated with the second attack on the World Trade Center on September 11, 2001. The sequence of events makes it clear that the United States is currently at war with Sunni extremists, a war declared, at least in part, because of the US military presence in Saudi Arabia.[2] This war has little to do with Islamic extremists "hating our freedoms."

Our Experience Is No Different Than That of Other Past Powers. The notion that Muslims are attacking us because they "hate our freedoms" is also undercut by research done on other targets of suicide bombings. This research shows that the United States is far from the only nation that has felt the pain of terrorism. Other powerful nations have dealt with terrorism, used as a tool by the "powerless" to fight the powerful for centuries.

In *Dying to Win: The Strategic Logic of Suicide Terrorism,* Robert A. Pape studied every suicide bombing that occurred from 1980 through 2003, in addition to suicide attacks waged against other past powers, dating back to ancient Rome. Pape found that the main reason for suicide missions was to effect a change in a more powerful nation's policy. Often those who carried them out intended to force a more powerful nation out of their homeland or protect their homeland from occupation. They believed these missions represented the most potent method to effect change.

The French experienced suicide bombing in Algeria, when they confronted native forces that wanted to end French colonialism. The United States faced kamikaze pilots at the end of World War II as the Japanese used ruthless methods in a futile effort to stave off imminent defeat. Following in this line, Muslim extremists started using suicide missions in the late 1970s, particularly in Palestine and Lebanon.

Mr. Pape's research indicates that in almost every instance, the suicide missions ceased when (a) the desired result was achieved and the occupying power left or the goal became impossible to achieve or (b) a better alternative was found. This (a) was our experience with Shiite extremists. As soon as Reagan pulled US troops out of Lebanon, the rash of violence against the United States declined, a lesson that should not be lost on policymakers in Washington.

Rogue States

The United States also faces threats from series of rogue states that align themselves with or support terrorist groups and/or contribute to the proliferation of nuclear, biological, or chemical weapons. Such nations include Syria, Iran, North Korea, Pakistan, and Sudan. Rogue states have one thing in common: their sole aim is self-preservation. Since dictators and their cronies often pay a high price—death—when there is a regime change, even rogue states have to show at least some degree of economic prosperity for their people or risk being overthrown.

Civilized states with functioning democracies have different concerns. The leaders of firmly established governments that are largely representative of the people do not have to worry about government stability or their lives. Rather, these leaders are more focused on global stability, which has a direct bearing on their nations' economic prosperity and safety. This is why terrorism is so deadly for civilized states in contrast with rogue states. Terrorism can grind the economies of civilized states to a standstill, threatening the safety and economic prosperity of their citizens. To rogue states, terrorism serves the purposes of (a) creating a more level playing field with industrialized countries and (b) currying favor with their population by demonizing the United States and other major powers.

The current manner of dealing with rogue states is irrational and counterproductive. The United States first brands the state as a "rogue" state, often severing diplomatic ties. Next we cut economic ties. Then we impose sanctions and/or seek "regime change," whether through military action (Iraq), covert actions, or other means (current policy with regard to Iran). This foreign policy not only emboldens the leaders of these states, it also provides them with a means to garner popular support. When the United States severs diplomatic ties, a leader portrays

the United States as an enemy of the state. When we impose trade restrictions, a leader uses this as evidence to support earlier claims that the
US is out to hurt the people. And if the United States uses military
force against the rogue state or another rogue state in the same camp,
a leader claims that the US is intent on killing civilians in states that oppose US policy. Dictators are almost never popular. Yet the train of logic
set forth above provides dictators of rogue states with the means to garner popular support by demonizing the United States. Regrettably,
America's economic sanctions typically do not harm the leaders of these
states, only the people, underscoring the dictator's logic.

Conventional Foes: The Emergence of China

The Bush administration has been troubled by the increasing milita-
rization of China. China's growing military might should be cause for
concern, but it is hardly surprising or unexpected. Indeed, it is inevitable. As nations become wealthier, they tend to spend more on
their military. As China continues its transition to a developed, industrialized nation, its military spending will increase, just as the
America's did as it became a superpower.

Further, US policy, particularly over the past five years, has caused
many nations, including China, to grow more concerned about US
power. America's invasion of Iraq and willingness to saber-rattle has
created an atmosphere in which other nations are moving away from
the US. They are seeking other security arrangements, outside of
America's sphere of influence, partly to check America's power and
unilateralism.

China is among those nations. Not only has it substantially increased its military budget over the past five years, it has also been in-
strumental in forging new alliances in the Far East to counterbalance
US power. China has taken the lead in developing stronger economic
and security relationships with India and Russia.[3] These three countries
comprise over 35 percent of the world's population and will be among
the top five economic powers within thirty years, if not sooner. This

group has also made overtures to other nations to join a semiformal military alliance of Pan-Asian countries. Membership is highly coveted, with Iran actively lobbying to be included in the alliance at this year's meeting. The purpose of this alliance is to address regional security matters in a collective manner, without consulting or including the West.

The critical question is whether the United States will enlist China in a concerted effort to maintain global stability or whether it will see China as an adversary and promote an arms race and otherwise increase tensions. Thus far, the US reaction has been mixed. It is critical that the US works with China to maintain global stability. The alternative is another arms race and tensions on three levels: terrorism, rogue states, and between the US and China.

CHAPTER 20

New Foreign Policy

The United States should have a foreign policy to address the threats outlined above, incorporating the elements of the Cold War strategy that worked. The mistakes of the Cold War and of the past several years should be avoided. The threats of terrorism, rogue states, and the rise of China must be addressed in different ways but with a largely consistent foreign policy and military strategy.

Terrorism

Terrorism must be battled on three levels. First, America must win the ideological battle with terrorists, just as it won the ideological battle against the Communists. Reducing popular support for terrorists on the Arab streets will be a critical step in the strategy. Second, America must eliminate the support provided to terrorists by rogue states. Third, we must develop a cost-effective military strategy to battle the terrorists. If the United States is successful in the first two challenges, the military strategy becomes easier, particularly if it can enlist other nations in the fight.

Winning an Ideological War against Terrorism and Rogue States

Like the war on Communism before it, the war on terror is as much an ideological war as a military one. Without questions, the US military will play an important role, but the war will be won or lost on the basis of the superiority of America's values, ideals, and economic system. By this administration's own admission, America is losing the public relations battle in the current war on terror. The loss is across the board, from the developed world to the developing world. Given this sad fact, America's approach must be rethought. A new, more coherent, and logical approach must be developed. The strategy used to fight the last great ideological battle—capitalism vs. Communism—should be the starting point.

War on Communism as a Guide. After World War II, America provided assistance to rebuild the shattered economies of Germany and Japan. This policy had three benefits. First, America was viewed by these nations and much of the rest of the civilized world in a positive light. Second, America created strong, market-based economies that provided opportunity, hope, and prosperity after World War II. This stood in sharp contrast to the aftermath of World War I, where Germany collapsed under punitive reparations. Third, by providing economic prosperity, these nations became stable and clearly aligned with the United States. A similar vision has been lacking in the post–Cold War era. While the US has undertaken to rebuild Iraq, the result has been disastrous, underscoring a widespread belief that America—or more precisely, the Bush administration—is incompetent or the unfair perception that the war was about oil.

To regain its standing, the United States must focus on three things: (a) a peace plan for Israel and Palestine, (b) a plan to stabilize Iraq, and (c) a plan for economic redevelopment of the region. By addressing Palestine and Iraq, the United States would eliminate considerable criticism and slowly begin to build a reputation in the region for a more even-handed handling of diplomatic affairs. As the region stabilized, the US military could dramatically reduce its presence, further easing tensions. In offering a plan of economic reconstruction along the lines of the Marshall Plan, America would provide greater economic hope to a region in need of it. Each of these components to the overall plan will be addressed in subsequent chapters.

Rogue States and Other States

Dealing wisely with rogue states is a vital component of American foreign policy and national security. These states (including Iran, Syria, Sudan, Cuba, Venezuela, North Korea, Pakistan and, until recently, Libya, Iraq, and Afghanistan) have historically created mischief. Through attacks against their neighbors, providing sanctuary to terrorists, and/or through arms proliferation, these states disrupt and destabilize the world's geopolitical framework. America's goal should be to bring these nations into the economic and political mainstream, yet its foreign policy over the past several decades has promoted just the opposite.

An Ineffective Foreign Policy Regarding Rogue States

America has meddled in the internal affairs of many of these nations. It has chosen sides in civil wars and backed some factions over others, often with disastrous results. America has used sanctions, harsh rhetoric, or even military action to promote regime change, tactics not lost on the dictators and autocrats who rule these nations.

This habit will be hard to break. The United States has long abandoned George Washington's admonition about the evils of favoring some nations over others. Meddling has become the norm for liberal and conservative administrations alike. For the past sixty years, liberals and conservatives have sought to use America's foreign policy strength to support and reward "good" governments and punish "bad" governments. This has been the one foreign policy constant throughout Democratic and Republican administrations over this era.

Unfortunately, the United States often makes mistakes about

which government is good and which is bad. Good governments may not be good in a general sense, but good only within the context of the alternatives. America supported Saddam Hussein in the 1980s, since he was a secularist and believed to be better than the fundamentalists who ran Iran. Thus, Saddam was only "good" when compared to the Iranians and only while he was opposing Iran. He became "bad" when he invaded Kuwait and threatened the world's oil supplies. Today, America supports President Pervez Musharraf of Pakistan, despite his aiding and abetting the Taliban before 9/11 and his spotty record on combating terrorism since then.

The same holds true of Saudi Arabia, which is ruled by the Saudi royal family with a repressive secret police very much like that of the Shah of Iran. President Musharraf appears on his way out, and, absent significant reform, the House of Saud will most assuredly fall as the shah of Iran did. If this occurs, what will the replacement regimes look like and how friendly will they be to the United States? We might not like the answer to this question, just as we did not like the regime that replaced the Shah.

Even more devastating is our policy of punishing "bad" governments. Bad governments include Castro's Cuba, Kim Jung-il's South Korea, and the fundamentalist Islamic state of Iran. *In each of these cases we have opposed the leaders of these nations. And in each of these cases the government has remained in existence for decades.* We have yet to learn that these governments remain in existence partly because of America's policies, not despite them. While America sharply criticizes these nations and imposes sanctions, other nations are more than happy to fill the void. So while America alienates the peoples of these nations through sanctions, it simultaneously gives global competitors an unfair trade advantage.

While America follows a policy of imposing sanctions, China is securing vast quantities of natural resources from these nations. The leaders of rogue states prosper while their people and America's economy suffer. With these economic ties firmly established, China is also in a better position to pressure the regimes in these states to make changes.

Given this reality, the United States has increasingly relied on China to broker change in North Korea and more recently Iran. Without a dramatic change in America's foreign policy, it will continue to see erosion in its foreign policy and economic clout relative to China.

Shift in Foreign Policy: Following George Washington

US policymakers would do well to consult the teachings of George Washington in developing critical aspects of foreign policy. In his famous farewell address, Washington stressed the importance of not punishing nations and seeking commerce with all nations. He understood the animus resulting from meddling and the benefits derived from trade, particularly for a country with an industrious people, natural barriers to invasion, and a superior economic system. Taking Washington's advice, the United States should develop a broad plan to establish trade and diplomatic relations with these nations over time. In particular, over the near-to-medium term, the United States should move to recognize Cuba, Syria, Iran, and North Korea, installing ambassadors and establishing full diplomatic and economic relations with each. In the case of Iran and North Korea, the United States could move to establish diplomatic relations as a part of a plan, outlined in the next chapter, to reduce nuclear or military tensions.

Increasing Pressure on Rogue States

The movement to recognize these nations, ultimately including North Korea and Iran, would serve the self-interest of the United States by placing pressure on the rogue states. A move by the United States to establish diplomatic and economic ties would put pressure on these regimes on two fronts. First, it would eliminate a significant plank, the demonization of America, used by these regimes to gain public support. Second, through trade these nations would start to develop market economies and experience greater economic prosperity, the fundamental underpinnings of democracy. Further, with greater commerce with America, the people of these nations will be exposed to Americans in an entirely different and positive fashion.

As for the leaders of rogue states, the United States should make it clear that it is committed to democracy at home and believes the destiny of all nations should be determined by their people. But America should also stress that it will no longer interfere in the internal affairs of sovereign states unless its national security is threatened. Nor will the United States impose sanctions or trade restrictions, which tend to only hurt the people. Thus, the leaders of rogue states would not be *directly* threatened by the United States. Through its leadership the United States would offer an example to the people that would apply great *indirect* pressure on these leaders. By ratcheting down the rhetoric and interference, America would reduce tensions with these states and open the door for economic prosperity and ultimately democracy. Indeed, the transition from an autocracy to democracy tends to follow economic development.

In particular, states do not transition from autocratic rule to democracy in one swift stroke. Rather, the transition is gradual and coincides with economic development. The trend toward democracy tends to follow economic development, especially when shared on a broader basis. In some cases, the wealthy elite provide the catalyst for change and power sharing, typically with an autocratic regime (e.g., a monarchy). The middle class provides a base that has a shared interest in the continued prosperity of the state. They support the wealthy elite to create a system where power is diffused more broadly. Over time, a more democratic state emerges (e.g., through the establishment of a parliament to govern alongside the monarch). This was the pattern that emerged in Western Europe as many of its nations transitioned from monarchies to parliamentary democracies.

In other cases, an autocratic regime goes along with the tide of economic development and opportunity to create jobs for its people and greater stability for itself. This appears to be what is occurring in China, Vietnam, and other Communist or autocratic states in Asia. These Communist governments understand that to survive they must promote opportunity and economic growth for their people, lest the people revolt against the state.

Build on America's Successes: The Lesson of the Soviet Union, Vietnam, and China

The United States has had a multitude of foreign policy successes over the past fifteen years that illustrate the benefits of a foreign policy based on active engagement and promoting economic development.

USSR. The Soviet Union collapsed in no small part because its people got a taste of our way of life and the superiority of our system. This was due to engagement by the Reagan and first Bush administrations, which sought to promote stronger diplomatic relations and trade. As a result, the old regime collapsed without a shot being fired.

China. China offers another example. Besieged by Watergate, President Richard Nixon reached out in 1973 and engaged China, at that time ardently Communist. The Mao-led regime was hostile to the United States, having assisted Communist regimes in both North Korea and North Vietnam in their fight against America. Internally, Red China represented perhaps an even more repressive regime than the Soviet Union. Despite criticism at home, President Nixon visited China and relations between the two powers started to thaw. China began its path toward a market-based economy.

Another pivotal moment in Sino-American relations occurred less than twenty years ago in 1989, when the Chinese government butchered hundreds of pro-democracy protesters in Beijing's Tiananmen Square. With approximately 1.5 billion people in China, the government feared unrest would unleash democratic torrents that would threaten the regime. The world watched as students bravely tried to stand down the tanks in the square before being scattered and massacred by the army.

President George H. W. Bush, a former ambassador to China, understood the government and the people running it. Although he roundly condemned the government's actions, he decided to maintain trade and diplomatic relations with China. He was criticized in many circles for not cracking down more on the Chinese government. In retrospect, he handled the situation as well as it could have been handled and his actions proved wise.

China's development has exploded over the past eighteen years, and it has emerged as one of the great world powers. With economic development, its people have seen their living standards improve. And dissent, while not welcome, no longer invites an *automatic* death sentence. China has also proven a valuable ally in addressing regional concerns, such as North Korea and potentially even Iran.

If the United States had taken a harder line under former President Bush, this progress would likely have been shunted aside, and America would have an entrenched enemy in Beijing. The lives of hundreds of millions of Chinese would be the worse for it. Further, the US would be facing a less stable China, a large country hostile to the United States and its interests. So while the policy of continued engagement outraged liberals and conservatives at the time, it was the right decision.

Vietnam. Vietnam offers another positive example of the benefits of engagement over punishment, illustrating the sharp contrast between the two policies. After a nearly decade-long war, in 1975 the United States withdrew from Vietnam once and for all. For over twenty years, the US did not have diplomatic relations with Vietnam. It instituted a trade embargo that lasted from 1980 through 1995. Human and economic tragedy beset Vietnam and its neighbors during this era. The Khmer Rouge regime dominated its neighbor, Cambodia, and slaughtered millions from 1975 through the early 1980s. The Vietnamese people suffered from starvation and economic deprivation.

In 1995, the Clinton administration normalized relations with Vietnam after the Vietnamese government agreed to help the United States locate the remains of American war dead. After recognizing Vietnam, American businesses began to stream into the country, along with other foreign investment, and Vietnam has become one of the great success stories among emerging nations over the past ten years.[1]

The lesson seems quite clear. When the United States uses its economic power and the superiority of its systems and institutions for contructive engagement, it creates a more stable world. Germany, Japan, Russia, China, and Vietnam are all products of this philosophy. When America imposes sanctions and rattles its saber, it creates resistance and solidifies rogue regimes. Iran, Cuba, Syria, and North Korea spring to mind.[2] And, finally, when the United States actively supports groups and governments that are inconsistent with its ideals, it tempts fate and inevitable blowback. This is precisely what happened when we supported the Shah of Iran, Saddam Hussein against Iran, and Osama bin Laden in Afghanistan.

New Marshall Plan. Middle East Stabilization

The catalyst for dramatic reform in the Middle East should be a US-sponsored plan similar to the Marshall Plan, aimed at stabilizing the Middle East and offering its citizens economic hope. With one bold and proven plan, the United States would create further goodwill and provide a growing number of people with hope for a better tomorrow. This hope, combined with a less intrusive foreign policy, would differentiate the United States from terrorists in an entirely positive manner. And it would provide an important bulwark against the terrorists on Arab streets. Such a stabilization plan will be discussed in a later chapter.

Conclusion

The irrefutable conclusions are to (a) stay out of the internal affairs of other nations (i.e., do not promote regime change), (b) recognize diplomatically all nations that have a functioning government (e.g., control the land that they govern), (c) promote trade among all nations, including rogue nations, as a means to promote economic development and regime change, and (d) spur economic growth in the Middle East through a new Marshall Plan (to turn the Arab street against the terrorists).

Some might consider this naïve, but the track record of this approach (China, USSR, Vietnam, etc.) trounces the alternative of saber-rattling and sanctions (North Korea, Iran, Syria, Cuba, etc.). A critical component of this effort would be a plan to address Iraq, North Korea, Iran, and Palestine. A clearer, less confrontational foreign policy should result in less incentive for these nations to harbor terrorists, further isolating of terrorist groups.

This strategy alone, however, will not cure the current ills in the Middle East and elsewhere. US foreign policy is only part, albeit a significant one, of the equation. In addition, America must address a series of problems that plague the world geopolitical scene, particularly in the Middle East and Sudan. It must transform its military from one tailored to fight conventional wars with the Soviet Union to one that is quick-hitting and focused on fighting asymmetrical foes such as Al Qaeda, which is the subject of the next chapter.

CHAPTER 21

Reconfiguring the US Military

This chapter discusses US military policy and examines (a) the circumstances in which the United States should commit its military to action, (b) the threats facing it faces today, (c) how the US military is currently configured, and (d) the need to tailor and appropriately size the US military based on these threats and America's economic base.

Introduction: Historical View

The United States maintained a small standing army throughout much of the nineteenth century, since it faced few if any external threats. Other than during the Civil War, America's standing army was smaller and less costly than those of the major European powers during this era. By devoting more resources to expanding its economy, the United States entered the twentieth century as an emerging economic power, while its European counterparts, straining under the burden of expansive militaries, were on the verge of decline. So goes the ebb of flow of superpowers. Nations that reach this plateau achieve it through either economic or military means, but no superpower has been able to sustain its preeminence indefinitely, a point made in Paul Kennedy's book *The Rise and Fall of the Great Powers*.

The failing of all superpowers centers on their inability to balance their economic might with their military might. They tend to commit themselves militarily beyond their economies' ability to ultimately pay for it. Less long-lived superpowers, which tend to reach that status through their military rather than economic policies, often do not have the economic base to support the military for even a century. The Soviet Union, a superpower for a mere thirty-five years following World War II, reached that status through its military policy. The USSR's economic base, a fraction of the United States', was unable to sustain the military. The USSR collapsed because it could not indefinitely devote 30 percent or more of its GDP to supporting its military. The strain was too great.

The most successful superpowers in history have done a much better job of managing the tenuous balancing act of having a strong enough military to protect their interests while not overstretching their economic base. Professor Kennedy called it "imperial overstretch." Rome and Great Britain, two of the longest-lived superpowers in history, underscore this point.

Rome. Rome was able to maintain its empire through a brilliant system of administration. It taxed the locals to pay for its military occupation and let them administer their own affairs, under a Roman governor for the province. So long as the locals paid the punitive taxes and maintained some semblance of order, the Romans allowed them to administer their affairs as they chose. Kings retained their thrones and the people worshiped their own gods.

This was an effective system of government for maintaining an empire, and the Romans used it for nearly a thousand years. Ultimately, Rome's economic and moral underpinnings could not support a far-flung empire. It was not able to maintain control over increasingly hostile and independent-minded vassal states and Rome fell.

Great Britain. The English model was a variation of the Roman model: exploitation of the local population to maintain military and economic power. India, Australia, and parts of the Middle East, China, and Africa (and prerevolutionary America) were all under British dominion at one time or another. Through taxation and economic exploitation, England maintained an empire for several hundred years. The empire started to crumble when the weight of England's military commitment started outstripping its imperial revenues. World War I and then World War II sapped England economically. After those wars it just did not have the resources to keep local populations at bay. Sensing this, many countries moved toward independence after World War II, and the British Empire began its rapid but largely peaceful dissolution.

The United States, if it maintains its current course, will have a different and less sustainable model. The US maintains a worldwide military presence but does not tax or exploit the local populations to pay for (as the Romans and British did). Rather, America's military presence throughout the world is a relic of the Cold War and today's war on terror, as noted in chart 21-1.

America's far-flung military raises several questions: (a) is the scope of this military presence necessary to face today's threats? (b) is the US military presence, through heightened tensions, actually creating more risk than it is preventing? and (c) can resources be better allocated to address America's threats, allowing greater resources to be devoted to maintaining its economic base?

After all, economic might is the fundamental underpinning of military might. If the United States devotes too much capital to its military, it compromises its economic might, which in turn undermines its ability to maintain a strong military over time. Balance and prioritization are the watchwords for designing a military. The first step in achieving this balance and prioritizing is to define the mission of the US military.

CHART 21-1

Nation/Area	Troops	Threat/Comment
Asia (South Korea / Japan)	100,000	North Korea, China, Russia
Europe	90,000	Russia, Middle East
Middle East	200,000	Terrorism, Iraq, Afghanistan, and Iran
Rest of the World	10,000	
Total	300,000	

Defining the Mission

The mission of America's military includes (a) national security (i.e., direct threats to the United States), (b) preemptive strikes against nations believed to threaten the US, (c) spreading democracy and nation-building, and (d) humanitarian missions. The expansion of the US military' mission is a relatively recent phenomenon. It started after World War II when the United States undertook military action to contain the spread of Communism, when arguably no direct threat to the United States existed. President Bush took this a step further, arguing that America's military should make preemptive defensive strikes against nations believed to threaten the US and to spread democracy.

There are two sound reasons for limiting the role of the US military to combating direct national security threats to the United States, rather than using it to "spread democracy" and for nation building. One is the Constitution; the other is practical.

US Constitution. The US Constitution does not provide for nation-building or humanitarian missions by the US military. The reason is quite simple. Our founders did not believe in it. They were quite clear during the post-Revolutionary period that US foreign policy should avoid entanglements abroad unless national security was directly threatened. James Madison was clear on this point in the debates that raged over the adoption of the Constitution. Even those who supported a strong, vigorous federal government, such as Alexander Hamilton, did not have an expansive a view of the US military. This view was confirmed in George Washington's 1796 farewell address to the nation, in which he framed US foreign policy for his and subsequent generations. In this address, Washington made it clear that the United States should avoid foreign entanglements and alliances and should promote trade with all nations.[1]

Practical Reasons: Public and Military Support. The second critical reason for limiting the use of the military to repel invasions or attacks is to ensure public and military support. Few people would argue that the most critical role of the US military is to combat those who attack

us. Once the mission is expanded beyond that point political considerations come into play, and it is difficult to unite the nation during
wartime. Some will oppose the use of the military for humanitarian
reasons. Others will oppose the use of the military for nation-building.
Yet almost all will support the use of the military to address direct
threats to the United States.

The invasions of Iraq and Afghanistan are instructive on this front.
The Bush administration pushed for military action against
Afghanistan immediately after 9/11. The entire country and much of
the rest of the civilized world supported the US. The Taliban regime
had harbored Al Qaeda and thus bore at least some responsibility for
in the attacks of 9/11. The US public and its allies still remain solidly
behind the Afghanistan war.[2]

Iraq presents the other side of the coin. The Iraqi invasion was
based on a potential threat—weapons of mass destruction (WMD)—
and was aggressively sold to the American public and the world on
this count. When no WMD were found, the war was then sold on the
basis of humanitarian and nation-building. The war was initially supported by a majority, but not overwhelming majority, of the public. As
the rationale for the war has changed and shifted, the war's popularity has declined. Worldwide support for the war, never high to begin
with, has collapsed as well.

How Should the United States Go to War?

When the United States commits to war, the commitment should be
unconditional and fall broadly on the American people, not just the
military. The first step in the process should be a declaration of war by
Congress, as required by the Constitution.

Declaration of War. There is no more solemn or grave decision made
by a leader than the decision to go to war. The founders believed that
the powers to declare war and wage war should be separate. For the
sake of efficiency, they believed the president and executive branch
should manage wars. By placing this power in one person's hands, a

war could be prosecuted under the direction of one person, thus avoiding the pitfalls of management by committee. For example, interference by Congress could lead to inefficiencies and difficulties in prosecuting a war. However, the founders also believed in checks and balances, reserving for Congress, the people's representative, the sole and exclusive right to determine if and when the United States should go to war. By vesting this power in Congress, the founders placed an important check on the power of the president.

Despite this rather clear-cut constitutional delegation of authority, Congress has not declared war since December 1941, although this nation has fought four major conflicts since that time (a "major conflict" being defined as a confrontation in which more than 100,000 troops were mobilized). These conflicts include Korea, Vietnam, and the First and Second Gulf Wars. In these undeclared wars, America has lost over 100,000 men and women, representing more deaths than in all *foreign* wars during the nineteenth century combined. Worse yet, the United States record in undeclared wars since World War II is a dreadful 1-1-1, with Iraq II still outstanding.

By shirking its constitutional responsibility to declare war, Congress has abdicated its responsibility to frame wartime goals and objectives, a key failure of American policymakers in almost all of the undeclared wars. Congress has also enhanced the power of the executive, arguably allowing the president to use America's military might to fight wars in a manner consonant with his objectives, rather than the people's.

Iraq II may have finally taught Congress a lesson it should have learned from Vietnam. In Iraq II, Congress did not declare war. It gave the president a relatively broad and open-ended mandate to fight the war. The authorization of force empowered the president to use "all necessary force" to disarm Saddam Hussein after the president had exhausted diplomatic efforts.

This authorization created a series of problems. First, it was open ended. Congress has been hamstrung since that time by an administration that has shifted the rationale for the war and shifted definitions of victory. Every effort to check this power has been rebuffed, leaving Congress with only the draconian lever of cutting off war funding to effect change. Any attempt to narrow the scope of the war would be met with not only hostility but also a presidential veto.

Second, Congress should provide that it, and it alone, shall define victory or the need for an exit. Perhaps this was not necessary fifty years ago when wars were fought among established states and victory or defeat were relatively easy to determine. Going forward, America's wars may be more asymmetrical. It may be fighting loosely confederated groups not bound by a state; they may reside in and conduct their operations from many states. Given this context, Congress needs to be more cautious in declaring war by (a) defining the objectives of a war and (b) providing some basis to conclude a war. Otherwise, the president can use a declaration of war as an open-ended invitation to wage war until he, rather than the legislature, is satisfied it is complete.

Third, there should not be any conditions precedent to the declaration of war. In the last authorization of the use of force, Congress indicated that the president could use force if he had exhausted all diplomatic efforts. This allowed the president to determine whether the process had been exhausted. It would have been better had Congress waited until after the president had "exhausted" the diplomatic process before considering a declaration of war.

Taking the Nation, Not Just the Military, to War. Not surprisingly, as Congress has increasingly avoided its duty to declare war, America has asked for less and less sacrifice on the part of Americans in waging war. The burden of fighting wars has fallen onto a narrower and narrower segment of the population, just as wars were increasingly fought by a narrower and narrower segment of the citizens of the Roman Empire during its decline. In general, if a war is worth fighting, the nation as a whole should be asked to sacrifice. And the nation should be asked to mobilize for war, just as our parents, grandparents, and great-grandparents did during World War II. Many have cast the war on terror as equivalent to the World War II. President Bush has compared the tyranny of Saddam Hussein, among others, to that of Hitler. Yet he has asked for little sacrifice from Americans outside of the US military, particularly when compared with past wars.

Iraq II more closely parallels Vietnam, where there was no clear mission or objective and an uneven sharing of burdens. In both cases, national support collapsed as America's leaders have been unable to articulate a clear rationale for the war or a plan for winning it. They have incongruously hyped the war as necessary for this nation's survival while asking Americans for little or no sacrifice. By contrast, during World War II there was a clear mission and a broad sharing of the sacrifices of war. To be sure, there were ebbs and flows in support during World War II, but it is clear that the nation was more united in that war than, for example, the war in Iraq.

The contrasts between Iraq II/Vietnam and World War II illustrate the need for policy changes in the next war. If America's next war is too long, and one sold as necessary for this nation's survival, America's leaders should clearly define the mission, define who our enemy is, tell us how the war will be won, and ask for shared sacrifice to achieve the desired result. If America's leaders are not capable of doing this, Americans will likely conclude that the war is probably not one worth fighting. That will be the right conclusion.

Shared Sacrifice. In taking a nation to war, Congress should not only declare war but also mobilize the nation for war, asking for broad and shared sacrifice, including:

- *National Conscription.* If a war is to be a long one, the nation as a whole should contribute the necessary manpower to win the war. This means national conscription. In Iraq II, most Americans faced little risk, and their representatives asked few difficult questions. If a broader segment of America faced the risk of war, I believe Congress would have asked more difficult questions, exposing the flimsy case for war offered by the Bush administration. As it was, reportedly just six US senators bothered to read the National Intelligence Estimate (NIE) report, which outlined the Bush administration's detailed case for the war.[7] It is striking that at least one senator who did read the NIE indicated that he voted against the war based on the flimsy case presented in the NIE study.[8]

- *Rationing Resources.* The burden of fighting a war should not only fall on the young or those waging it. If a natural resource is needed to wage the war or is at the heart of the war, Americans should be required to conserve that resource. That would mean either rationing or a significant tax on oil in the current Iraqi war. This would have the effect of reducing our consumption of oil and our dependence on foreign sources, which is at the fulcrum of our problems in the Middle East.

- *Raising Taxes.* If this generation believes that a war is worth fighting, it should pay for at least some of it. Unlike President Roosevelt during World War II, President Bush *cut* taxes, and now the United States is borrowing money from the Chinese and other foreign nations to wage the war on terror. This is not to say that the government should not borrow during times of war; we should and always have. But the United States should not give the current generation of Americans a tax cut during wartime, thereby passing most of the bill for the war to future generations.

While more minor conflicts might be waged without resorting to these measures (e.g., Afghanistan), broader conflicts, particularly ones portrayed as this generation's World War II, should undergo extensive scrutiny and be borne by the nation as a whole. If not, the United States will be doomed to repeat the mistakes of Iraq II and Vietnam, wars without a real purpose or, unfortunately, an end.

Tailoring the Military to Meet Threats and What We Can Afford

Defining when and under what circumstances the United States will commit its military is critical. It provides the basis for defining the size and scope of the US military. If the United States determines that its military should police the world, engage in nation-building, and undertake humanitarian missions, the US military will have to be expanded and taxes should and will be increased to pay for it. However, I believe the US military should only be used for national defense based on the Constitution, the practical grounds outlined above, and the simple cost-benefit analysis discussed in this section.

In fashioning a military focused solely on national security, US policymakers should consider the threats faced by the United States and then tailor the US military to address these threats in the most cost-effective manner possible. The threats to US national security can now be divided into two broad categories: (a) those posed by organized states and (b) those posed by asymmetrical foes.

Threats from Organized States. Conventional Wars. The United States faces threats from organized states. The first threat is a conventional attack against the US by a major military power. With the collapse of the Soviet Union, the prospect of another large-scale conventional war is remote. The United States might have smaller wars, such as Afghanistan and Iraq II. But, it is unlikely that it will have to fight Russia, China, India, or another great or emerging power in a large-scale conventional war.

In particular, the threat posed to the United Sates by its principal two Cold War foes has declined significantly over the past twenty years, as the world has become increasingly integrated economically. China and Russia are now significant players in the world economy, and a large part of their global strategies depend on maintaining and enhancing their economic might. China is now the United States' largest trading partner and one of the largest economies in the world. Russia's largest trading partner is Europe, which it supplies with energy from its vast reserves. Both China and Russia have governments that are not democratic by Western standards, but are committed to competing in the global marketplace. They know they have much to lose from engaging in a global or even regional conflict.

Also, unlike most countries, the United States has natural barriers that make invasion not only impractical but virtually impossible, even today. The Atlantic and Pacific Oceans provide us with this luxury.[9] Despite the natural barriers and reduced threats posed by organized states, the United States spends more on national defense than any other nation. Chart 21-3 provides an estimate of US versus worldwide defense spending.

Due to a military strategy ill defined by America's civilian leaders and deployments abroad that are largely a residue of its Cold War strategy containment, the United States spends more on its military than all other nations combined.

By contrast, China does not have natural barriers to invasion. And like many nations, it has historical enemies situated along its borders or in proximity. Despite this, China spends less than 2 percent of its GDP on defense, about 60 to 70 percent less than the United States in relative terms and about 90 percent less in nominal terms. The critical question for the US is whether it can continue devoting in excess of 5 percent of its GDP to defense, when its economic competitors, particularly China, are spending less than 2 percent, or whether it would be better served tailoring its military to meet real rather than remote threats.

The United States has made little effort to assess risks and make judgments about the necessary size and scope of its military to address those risks, just as it has been loath to make difficult decisions in sizing its entitlement programs. The United States wants to protect against all risks, no matter how remote, just as it wants to have an entitlement system that covers every American regardless of need. Unfortunately, it

CHART 21-3		
Country	Amount (% of GDP)	Bordering Countries
United States	$700 billion (>5%)[10]	Mexico and Canada
China	$50 billion (<2%)	Russia, Iran, Mongolia, North Korea, India, etc.
Europe (as whole)	$200 billion (<2%)	Russia (east of Poland)
World ex-US	$450 billion (<2%)	

can no longer afford to spend 5 percent of GDP on its military, when its global economic competitors are spending less than half that.

If the United States chooses to focus its military on the real threats facing it and adopt a more sensible, nonconfrontational, and unintrusive foreign policy, it should be able to downsize its military considerably without compromising its national security. *Indeed, by downsizing its military dramatically and improving its focus, the United States would have a more effective military that would better address its current national security threats.* The United States could devote the savings in military spending to more productive economic uses and delay the onset of imperial overstretch, the disease that besets all superpowers sooner or later.

Protection against Asymmetrical Foes. While the United States faces a relatively modest threat from organized states, it does face threats from terrorist groups and rogue states. These threats should decline with the advent of a more sensible foreign policy, a new Marshall Plan, and a withdrawal of troops from sensitive regions (proposed in the following chapter). But, even with a more rational foreign policy and reduced military presence abroad, these threats will still exist and should be the focus of the US military going forward.

Reducing the US Military's Global Footprint

The US military could greatly reduce its military presence in the world without materially compromising America's national security. The current US military footprint was developed to combat the spread of Communism through the policy of containment. It required the Unites States to maintain troops (forward deployment) throughout the world as a check against Soviet expansion. With the collapse of the Soviet Union, the US military has scaled back its troop levels, but still has over 200,000 troops stationed throughout the world (excluding Iraq and Afghanistan) to combat an increasingly unlikely event: a large-scale conventional war with either Russia or China.

In some respects, the US military presence is not reducing the risk of war, but increasing it. Russia and China as well as other nations are wary of US military might, particularly given the rather bellicose rhetoric of this administration and the largely unilateral invasion of Iraq. The United States should not withdraw *all* of its troops from abroad, but it should withdraw a substantial portion of them. The plan should focus on a gradual withdrawal from certain regions of the world. It should be undertaken through a series of agreements that actually enhance the United States' national security and, ideally, address regional conflicts. The following is a broad outline of the proposed plan.

Korea. The United States maintains approximately 30,000 troops in South Korea. They have been stationed along the border between North and South Korea for over sixty years. The rationale for this military presence is to protect against a North Korean invasion, potentially supported by the Chinese and/or the Soviets. However, the 30,000 Americans troops have only a modest deterrent effect. They would quickly be overrun by a North Korean assault, given that the North Korean army has well over 2 million troops (about a 60-1 differential with the US force) and is supported by heavy artillery. The real deterrents to an attack during the Cold War era were the United States' nuclear arsenal and the threat of World War III. This kept the North Koreans as well as their patrons, the Chinese and Soviets, honest.

The situation is little changed in one respect and greatly changed in another. The situation is little changed in that the United States could do little to stop a North Korean assault. But the risk that a North Korean assault would be accompanied by Chinese and/or Russian support is growingly increasingly remote. China, more likely, would be violently opposed to any incursion by North Korea into South Korea, given that it would create chaos in the region and most likely have a negative impact on China's booming economy. In addition, any attack would likely cause North Korean refugees to flood into China, which it fears.

The US presence creates friction with the Kim Jung Il regime of North Korea and is increasingly causing tensions with the government of South Korea. The only thing keeping the US force in place is a Cold War mentality that pervades not only the Pentagon, but the American public. Even Donald S. Rumsfeld questioned the wisdom of having US troops stationed in South Korea.

Given that the US force provides little deterrence beyond our nuclear capabilities, the United States should broker a deal that would formally end the Korean War, which was concluded in a cease-fire over sixty years ago. There was never a formal treaty to end the war, so technically the war is still ongoing. The parties to the treaty would consist of all the parties to the cease-fire: Russia, China, South Korea, North Korea, and the United States.

The treaty would end the war on the following conditions: (a) a gradual reduction of North Korean conventional forces, (b) mutual economic cooperation among all parties to develop North Korea's economy (particularly between North and South Korea, which is already occurring), (c) US recognition of the North Korean regime, (d) an agreement by the US to change its tone from one of regime change to a more general tone that the North Korean people should determine their own form of government, (e) a withdrawal of US troops from South Korea over a five-year period (or whatever time frame provides an expeditious but not disruptive withdrawal; the time frame should be tied to the reduction of North Korean conventional forces), (f) an agreement on the part of North Korea to shut down its nuclear program and submit to inspections by the International Atomic Energy Agency and international inspectors, and (g) the North Korean government's agreement not to aid any other country with military or nuclear technology.

From the United States' standpoint, this bargain would have the dual benefit of reducing risks associated with the rogue regime while also greatly reducing our costs in the region. It would have the additional benefit of thrusting the burden of containing the rogue regime where it belongs: on China and South Korea. Both of these countries have the most to lose if North Korea continues making mischief. The

North Korean regime would gain some breathing room to develop economically and potentially transition into a reasonably respectable member of the world community over the next decade. And, the United States would not lose any significant degree of deterrence. Its fleet and bases in the Pacific could serve as a launching pad for air strikes, which is the only realistic means of striking North Korea to begin with. In addition, the US retains its biggest deterrent—its nuclear arsenal.

Withdrawal from Europe. The United States should undertake a similar withdrawal from Europe. The Cold War is over. Russia's GDP is about 10 percent that of the US. Russia's conventional might is no longer a threat to Europe. Indeed, Europe is Russia's biggest customer for its goods and services, principally energy. Given that, it is highly unlikely that Russia is going to invade Western Europe anytime soon.

If it did, Europe should be in a position to defend itself. The European Union has about the same GDP as the United States and should have the resources to build a military to defend itself against a power that is economically 10 percent its size. The US would also maintain a strong nuclear arsenal as a backstop.

A broad agreement should accompany the US military withdrawal. First, Russia should agree to leave the Eastern European states, including the former Soviet republics, alone. This would include the Baltic states and the Ukraine as well as the former East Bloc (Poland, Czech Republic, etc.). Second, the United States should be permitted to contribute troops to an expanded NATO force (which might include Russia over time) as it has historically done, although at much more modest levels. Third, the US would drop its plans to provide Eastern Europe with a missile defense shield. To begin with, the missile defense shield is far-fetched at this point in time, and is needlessly inflaming policymakers in Moscow. (The US should, however, continue research and development on the defense shield at full pace). Finally, the United States would withdraw its troops over a reasonable time frame (meeting various benchmarks) and redeploy a portion of the withdrawn troops to Turkey and perhaps Afghanistan— two "hot" areas that should have troop deployments—with the remainder coming home. This arrangement should result in reduced tensions without a corresponding increase in risks.

Middle Eastern Military Presence. The US military presence should be dramatically decreased in the Middle East, as outlined in the next two chapters. The reduction would ease tensions without compromising US economic or national security interests. In fact, the reduction would probably make the United States both more secure and economically sound, given that it would save $150 billion per annum and withdraw troops from Arab soil, a hot button with Islamic radicals.

Other Bases. The United States should focus on an effort to close down bases throughout the world, just as it has at home. America undertook an effort to consolidate its domestic bases over a decade ago. The trend accelerated in 2005 with a new plan to close another thirty or more large military bases. Even with these closures, the United States will still have over three hundred domestic military bases. Efforts to close US bases are often accompanied by fierce lobbying on the part of local communities and their congressmen. The reaction to the closure of foreign bases would not be as pronounced. Indeed, in many cases, these closures would be welcomed.

The United States should close bases throughout the world. Those that remain should be consolidated into a handful of bases to support the army in a few hot spots and the navy in its main theaters of operation. This would mean having a handful of Pacific bases and Indian Ocean bases, particularly in the Persian Gulf region. The result would be fewer bases supporting a smaller, more mobile military tailored to meet the major threats facing the United States.

Reducing Costs Without Significant Decline in Security

The United States can no longer afford to maintain its global military empire, particularly given that conventional threats have declined markedly. Rather, it needs to tailor its military to the one threat significant to its national security and economic might—terrorism. The US can then divert the resources used to maintain a global military empire to sustaining its economic base. In short, America is fighting two wars. One is with global Islamic extremists. The second is an economic war with China, India, and other emerging economic powers.

If the United States did a rational job of reducing costs associated with its military empire, the impact on overall military spending would be profound. The savings from the reduction of its military presence could be as much as $300 billion per annum, or about 2 percent of GDP. Even with these savings, the US military would still be by far the largest in the world, spending about $400 billion per annum (about 3 percent of GDP). And during peacetime the US should always target a 2-to-3-percent-of-GDP military budget. This amount seems reasonable to meet the national security needs of a country that has a lack of internal strife and natural barriers to invasion.

What Should the US Military Look Like?

The principal threat facing the United States is an attack by a asymmetrical enemy, whether by Islamic fundamentalists or other terrorist groups. Given that, the question is, what type of military is best suited not only to address such an attack, but to prevent it? The answer is multifaceted. First, the military should be redefined along the lines suggested by the Bush administration (led by then secretary of Defense Donald Rumsfeld)—before its disastrous invasion of Iraq. That is, the US military should be a quick-strike, lighter force that is mobile and uses technology to knock out terrorist cells throughout the world. Second, the US military should also be used to secure the United States' borders and to guard its sensitive infrastructure, whether ports, refineries, or nuclear power plants. Third, the US should continue its lead in nuclear weapons and missile defense. Making America secure within its borders should be the ultimate objective of US's national defense.

Newly Configured US Military. A military armed to fight against terrorists and other asymmetrical foes would not look like the army of yesteryear, which was configured to fight two conventional wars simultaneously. It would not need to take, occupy, and hold large bodies of land as it did during World War II. This is not to say that the Untied States does not need sufficient troop levels to launch a major offensive; the US should have this capability. But America should not design its military consistent with the national security threats of yesteryear. It is unnecessary and America cannot afford it.

Rather, if America has the foresight to change its foreign policy, its military will become quick hitting and stealthy. In addition, America should continue to consolidate its intelligence apparatus by integrating its intelligence gathering into military operations. America's military intelligence should be the best in the world, and America should use this intelligence to knock out terrorist cells regardless of where they are. A quick-hitting military, smaller in numbers but armed with greater intelligence and firepower, would be ideally suited to fight asymmetrical forces.

Granted, going after terrorist groups may mean attacking cells in a country with which the United States has diplomatic relations. But despite a mandate to have an "agnostic" foreign policy, the US should always be proactive about eliminating real threats. It should not be afraid to launch attacks within the borders of other countries if need be. But America should be wary of occupying nations, as this new type of military will not be well suited for such an endeavor.

In short, the US military should be sized to confront the United States' most likely threats, not theoretical ones. These threats are most likely to be from terrorist groups and rogue nations. This would require a smaller, more mobile military. To the extent that the United States faces a conventional threat, it should have enough troops between its standing army and the National Guard to address a regional conflict, like Afghanistan or Iran.

If the conflict is larger in scale (unlikely but possible), the standing army and National Guard should provide enough manpower to fight the initial stages of the war. This would allow time to raise and train more troops, whether by increasing enlistment or a draft. This is precisely what happened in World War II. The United States instituted a draft at just about the time the Japanese bombed Pearl Harbor. It relied on its standing army to fight until drafted reinforcements could be trained and sent into the war zones. The task during World War II was even more daunting than today, given that the US had a much smaller standing military and the war spanned the world. Although it took about a year to get on full war footing, the regular army and navy was able to hold its own until drafted soldiers starting flooding into the war zones.

US Army Focused on Securing the United States. The US army should take up its traditional role of securing the US mainland, first and foremost. The US military has historically had a role in protecting the mainland; for example, manning forts within the United States and patrolling the borders for incursions. Currently, much of this is being handled by other government agencies (e.g., US Border Patrol) and/or private contractors.

The strategic plan would call for troop reductions abroad (closing down bases and reallocating some of these troops; redeploying of some of those troops to theaters that are of more pressing importance to US interests). The remaining troops from abroad could be stationed back in the United States at lesser cost; there would be some attrition as troops left the military and reentered civilian life. Given their superlative training, these men and women would be highly sought and have excellent career paths.

As for those stationed domestically, their duties would change, with a significant focus on protecting the mainland:

a. *Securing Our Borders*. Immigration policy was addressed in a previous chapter, but one of the key elements of the immigration plan is to promote a free flow of immigration into the United States, so long as it is monitored and controlled. The quid quo pro is that America would focus a great deal of effort to secure its southern border with Mexico.

The plan would require building a double fence along the US-Mexico border with sensors that would detect illegal immigration into the United States. With a sophisticated border fence, the US military could man the monitoring stations along the border and also actively patrol the border along the fence, responding where sensors indicated potential illegal crossings. The Army Corp of Engineers should undertake its historical job of building infrastructure aimed at securing the US mainland. It should oversee the construction and maintenance of a double fence along the US-Mexico border. A small portion of the savings from the reduction in our troop levels abroad could be used to build the fence. A portion of the troops withdrawn from overseas could be redeployed to patrol the border.

b. *Secure Sensitive Infrastructure Assets.* The US military could also protect and secure assets sensitive to attack by terrorists, such as nuclear power plants, airports, etc. It would identify those assets most at risk for attack, the most likely types of attacks, and the best manner to protect the assets. Notable examples of assets at risk for attack are (a) nuclear power plants, (b) refining assets (major hubs), (c) power plants, (d) major airports (the perimeter), (e) water treatment plants, and (f) other infrastructure assets.

If there are a hundred nuclear power plants and five hundred to a thousand other sensitive projects, the US military could deploy 20 to 50 troops per asset, comprising about 25,000 to 50,000 troops at most. The troops (drawn from existing troops) could be deployed from bases located near the assets. Troops stationed in the US could handle this assignment. The troops could balance training with stints protecting these assets.

In all, this balance would be consistent with what the US military has historically done: protect American interests on native soil. This was done during the 1800s, when the US military built small forts throughout America to protect either settlements or strategic assets in the west and southwest. Our modern-day forts are our bases, and our strategic assets are the power plants, etc. that need to be protected against foreign threats.

c. *Ports.* The most significant area of focus aside from the border would be to secure, monitor, and patrol our ports. The US port system seems a likely target for terrorist attack. Containers and goods come to the United States from all parts of the world. The US inspects very little cargo coming into it from other parts of the world, not having a sound plan to screen or monitor these goods.

America needs a plan to ensure that we do not suffer an attack on a major American city through the shipment of a dirty bomb or some other deadly agent or device into the United States. This would require the development of a plan to ensure the cargo is inspected before it is shipped from a foreign port and certified by a third party when loaded at that port. The certification could be electronic and approved by the foreign government or third-party contractor operating the foreign port.

If the products or cargo come from a sound, stable nation (e.g., England), the cargo should pass through a detection device and be randomly checked in the United States. If it comes from a suspect government, the cargo should go through a detection device and be inspected more closely. The US military could develop a plan to secure our ports and the inspection of imported goods, along the lines set forth above.

The military would also man the stations at the major ports that interfaced with foreign ports and/or governments or contractors that would transmit information to us regarding the cargo being shipped to the United States. In addition, the US military could oversee the inspection process of imported cargo and also periodically tour and inspect ports from which products are sent into the US, to test them for compliance with our policies and procedures. Technology could be developed to assist the military in this endeavor. The military, in conjunction with the private sector, has been at the forefront of developing technology for its own use. This should be no different.

The duties outlined above might seem a bit strange for the US military, but they would be in keeping with its historical role before the US transitioned into a hyperpower and military empire after World War II. Before that, the US military was largely stationed domestically. Its duties in protecting US interests ranged from patrolling the border (even as late as the early 1900s) to protecting US assets and civilians (the fort system scattered throughout the US).

By devoting what was necessary to provide security within its borders but not overextending the military, the United States transitioned from an economic backwater to an economic powerhouse. It should revert to this more focused national security effort and devote the savings in manpower and money to maintaining its economic superpower status. After all, without that, America will not only see a decline in its standard of living, it will not be able to defend itself if and when a serious conflict arises.

Missile Defense. One of the great victories of the Cold War was the United States' decision to rely on the deterrent effect of its nuclear arsenal rather than a larger, more costly conventional force. To be sure, America's standing army was large and far-flung, but it was modest compared to that of the Soviet Union. By keeping its costs lower, America had a more cost-effective defense. Eventually, the US bankrupted the Soviet Union.

The United States should maintain its nuclear arsenal. Any calls to eliminate it are foolish. America's nuclear arsenal and its natural barriers are the biggest deterrents against attack by an organized state. A sealed border and more secure ports will make it more difficult for a terrorist to smuggle in a nuclear or dirty bomb. This is why it makes tremendous sense for the US military to patrol our borders and ports and to develop a more rational immigration policy that tracks all immigrants in the United States.

However, America will be vulnerable as nations become nuclear powers and develop the capacity to deliver nuclear warheads to the US mainland. Given this, the United States should not only maintain but increase the effectiveness of its missile defense shield. In doing so, the US, as it did during the Cold War, can use technology to cost effectively defend this nation.

Conclusion

The German war theoretician Carl von Clausewitz indicated that war is foreign policy by other means. Conversely, foreign policy also offers a state a means to assert its national interests by means other than war. In that regard, the United States should address its foreign policy short-comings and develop one that (a) is consonant with its ideals and values and (b) is efficacious in achieving peace, economic stability, and national security for itself and the rest of the world.

US foreign policy should be focused on a general recognition that the United States should not intervene in the affairs of other states, since it only breeds animosity. Rather, the United States should recognize all governments and promote trade with all nations, since economic prosperity among nations promotes greater stability and provides the underpinnings necessary to transition from autocracy to democracy. To avert human crises, the United States should work with its allies to expand the membership of NATO to all nations that share its and Western Europe's commitment to some minimal level of human rights and free trade. NATO should be used to promote these ideals (but not in a unilateral fashion) and on occasion to intervene in major crises, such as mass genocide.

Finally, the United States should continue to work with partners in each region of the world to address conflicts and rogue states, rather than undertaking action by itself. The six-party talks with North Korea offer a useful road map. In these talks, the United States partnered with China, South Korea, Russia, and Japan to address North Korea's nuclear ambitions. This shares the burden of global stability with partners in the affected regions, shifting the cost and responsibility away from the United States while still maintaining US involvement.

Before undertaking this significant change in foreign policy, the United States would have to confront two significant issues: Iraq and Palestine. The former is a mess very much of our own making. The second is less so, but our actions in the region have certainly not helped matters. Addressing the Palestinian issue would provide a boost to any efforts to resolve the Iraqi mess.

CHAPTER 22

A New NATO and Regional Partnership to Address Human Crises

Global stability should be the focal point of US foreign policy as well as that of other civilized nations. Stability can be bred through a more sensible approach by the United States in how it deals with other nations. By establishing relationships, engaging in trade, and keeping out of their internal affairs the US could avoid needless conflict with other nations. It could actually promote economic development and the more orderly progress of nations, including rogue nations, toward democracy.

There will be instances where human crises and/or the pursuit of nuclear or other weapons becomes too pronounced for the United States and the civilized world to ignore. To address human crises and weapons proliferation at their early-to-intermediate stages, the United States should strive to work in an organized fashion with other civilized states. In the case of national security threats (such as weapons proliferation or direct threats), the US military should be used as a last resort, but it should be tailored to meet those threats, as noted in the previous chapter. Establishing a new framework for the twenty-first century, in which the United States plays a central role among and *in partnership* with other nations, will be a critical counter to the growing influence of both China and Europe.

North Atlantic Treaty Organization

Since World War II, the United States has promoted multilateral relationships to preserve peace and create order among nations. This started with the creation of the United Nations (UN) and North Atlantic Treaty Organization (NATO) shortly after World War II. The UN has had its moments and certainly has provided a forum for nations to speak to one another, even when they are enemies. But the UN is viewed with deep skepticism by many Americans, for good reason. Almost any country can gain admission to the UN, even some of the worst human-rights offenders. And these nations often block productive measures that would ultimately hold them accountable for the treatment of their citizens or the actions of their governments. It is clear that the UN is incapable of halting human crises or even handle world security matters to any great degree.

NATO, on the other hand, has been an unqualified success. Unlike the UN, NATO does have membership criteria and has provided a framework that has promoted peace and prosperity in Europe for sixty years. Going forward, NATO should continue to be expanded and serve as the model for handling regional and global human and security crises, not the UN. This will require the United States and its partners in NATO to expand NATO's mandate from a regional one to an increasingly global one. In particular, NATO should become a more proactive force to ensure global stability and security as well as to address humanitarian issues.

The New NATO

NATO represents much of what has been good about US foreign policy during the last sixty years. While not explicit, the common values of NATO's members have provided the alliance with a foundation. These shared values include a respect for Western values as they relate to democracy and human rights. Given this, NATO should be become more global in its membership and mandate. This should follow the trends put in place by a series of US presidential administrations, but pushed the hardest by the current Bush administration, which has or-chestrated a dramatic increase in NATO membership. New partners should include Japan, South Korea, and possibly the newly emergent powers China, India, Russia, and Brazil.

Admission to NATO should be based on a few fundamentals. A nation should be committed to global stability and the protection of basic human rights—the foundation of the United States' and other civilized nations' foreign policy. The membership bar should be set high enough so that members provide their citizens with fundamental rights and the vast majority of their citizens are treated with dignity and respect, but not so high that NATO excludes emergent powers such as India, China, and Russia. These nations are making their way to a more democratic form of government, but it will take some time. In the meantime, the United States should not exclude them from the table of civilized nations but rather use them to assist it and the rest of the civilized world in maintaining global stability. After all, India and China have as much, if not more, to lose from global instability as other nations.

Over time, membership standards should be tightened. NATO could be used as the appropriate forum to address global threats or is-sues, such as global warming, as well as the protection of basic human rights. Initially, these topics would be the subject of conversation, since making any firm commitment on these issues would likely take time and divert NATO from its first and foremost role of promoting global stability. However, NATO should have a mandate to address future problems that can only be addressed by a multilateral body of civilized nations.

The other key difference between the new NATO and the current one is that it would not be a defensive alliance. An attack on a mem-ber state would not necessitate a response by the alliance as a whole. This would be disastrous, committing nations to participate in wars they might have little interest in. This would also create the kind of entanglements against which George Washington warned. Rather, the new NATO would be an alliance focused on global stability and addressing humanitarian and regional issues, as discussed and agreed upon by its members.

In this regard, NATO would become much more akin to the UN, with some degree of consensus among the member states needed in order to take action. But unlike the UN, the member states would at least have to meet some minimal threshold in providing their people basic human rights. Given this, membership would have meaning and would likely be coveted, thereby encouraging nations to meet basic levels of respect for human rights. In this regard, the new NATO would promote the very conduct that was the purpose of its existence: global stability and orderly conduct. Another key difference with the UN would be its ability to expel members. Upon a vote of the member states, a nation could be expelled for human rights abuses or other activities inconsistent with the NATO charter.

Of course, the United States and other member nations would be free to pursue their own national interests outside of NATO. If the US or any member was attacked or believed that preemptive military action was in its interests, it would be entitled to act. The US should not cede its sovereignty to any nation or institution and should always have the latitude to act alone if need be. Ideally, this would be the exception rather than the norm.

Use of Regional Partnerships to Address Local Concerns

Another achievement of the present Bush administration is the use of a regional partnership to address North Korea. The United States partnered with China, Japan, South Korea, and Russia to discuss nuclear disarmament with North Korea. This was rightly done on an ad hoc basis. Regional partnerships also offer a way to address regional problems, such as a rogue state, in partnership with countries that have the most to lose if the rogue state creates problems.

North Korea is instructive on this point. While North Korea has made threats against the United States, the impact of a war between North Korea, the United States, and South Korea would be felt heavily by China (which borders North Korea) and even Japan. If war broke out, trade in the region would grind to a halt, damaging China and Japan. Refugees, particularly from North Korea, would flood into China and China would have a disaster on its hands. Logically, China, which has the most influence with North Korea, has a great deal to lose and should take the lead in figuring out a balanced solution to the problem. The Bush administration has wisely determined this and put responsibility for fixing the problem squarely in the hands of the Chinese.

A similar strain of regional partnerships figures prominently in the chapter on the Middle East, and addressing the Iraqi and Palestinian crises. There are players in the Middle East—particularly Saudi Arabia, Iran, and other wealthy Gulf states—that have gotten a free pass so far. In fact, US foreign policy has been so destabilizing that these nations have actually profited from instability through higher oil prices. By putting the situation in the appropriate context, the United States can show these nations that they have a great deal to lose in the event of a "hot" war and enlist them to at least attempt a comprehensive plan to stabilize the region. The following chapters will address this plan.

CHAPTER 23

Addressing the Palestinian Issue: The New Marshall Plan

The United States has made a mess of the Middle East. It must develop a better-reasoned plan to address the chaos that pervades the region. The first step in stabilizing the Middle East is a resolution of the Palestinian and Israeli crisis. Although Iraq occupies US headlines, the Palestinian issue has become a cause célèbre among Arab and Islamic moderates and extremists alike. Before addressing the Israeli-Palestinian situation, it is critical to have an understanding of the history of the region from biblical times to the very recent past and outline the claims of both the Arabs and the Israelis.

The Arab View

Arabs view Palestine, which includes modern Israel, as theirs. They controlled it for well over a thousand years until the nineteenth century. During that period, they endured the Crusades, an attempt by western European Christians to recapture the Holy Land. The Crusades ended in a truce between Christendom, represented by King Richard, and Islam, represented by Saladin. The Peace of Ramla held that the Arabs would occupy Palestine, including Jerusalem, but that

Jerusalem would be an open city that would accommodate pilgrims. This truce was struck in 1192 and held for centuries.

By the nineteenth century, the Arabs had lost control over much of their lands to the British and French. World War I represented a mixed victory for Arabs. It resulted in the creation of Saudi Arabia but also started the Zionist movement in earnest as well as the continued sub- jugation of Turkey, Syria, Iraq, and Northern Africa to French and British rule. Following World War I and World War II secular lead- ers in Islamic states saw remarkable victories. These included Ataturk in Turkey after World War I and Nasser in Egypt after World War II. With the French and English retrenching, whether by choice or by force, Arab self-determination was on a very successful run with one exception: Israel.

Israel was created in 1948 after a successful war waged by Jewish Zionists and as a result of pressure by the United States and the United Nations. Although Arabs could point to numerous successes, the cre- ation of Israel represented a stinging blow, particularly after Israel won war after war with the Arabs, from 1948 through the early 1970s.

Putting this anger into context is difficult for the United States. Quite simply, the Arabs view much of Israel's territory as their own, believing displaced Palestinians should have a right to return to their historical homes. And history certainly does indicate that Arabs con- trolled Palestine for well over a thousand years, which lends credence to the Arab position, just as Israel's ancient claims to Judea lend cre- dence to its position. The Arabs, of course, are not without fault. In their efforts to eliminate Israel, they have lost three wars and more and more territory. Further, the Arab world is filled with authoritarian and repressive regimes, with which most Americans have difficulty iden- tifying. By virtue of religious, cultural, and historical reasons, the US logically and rightly identifies closely with Israel and has steadfastly supported it almost without reservation. However, to win the war on terror and broker a peace agreement in the Middle East, the United States will have to *understand* long-standing Arab grievances and claims, as well as those of Israel.

The Israeli View

The Israeli position is also grounded in history, some ancient and some more modern. As most people know, the Jews were the chosen ones in the Old Testament. They occupied Palestine and Judea for over two thousand years (from the twenty-fifth century BC to AD 70). However, the last five centuries of this era were not happy for the Jews, as they faced domination by a series of powers, the last being the Roman Empire.

The Jews bravely revolted against Roman rule twice, the last time in AD 70. The second revolt proved disastrous. Although Judaism was a small religion, and a relatively insignificant one within the context of the Roman Empire, the Romans did not brook dissent.[1] The Romans took punitive action and obliterated the Jewish resistance. They slaughtered the rebels at Masada, razed the Second Temple, and sent the Jews into exile to Babylon (today's Baghdad). The Jews proved resilient, the most resilient religion and culture in the history of man. Despite the crushing blow from the Romans and exile to Baghdad, Jews spread across world, most notably into Europe and ultimately the United States. Some even found their way back to Jerusalem.

The dream of reestablishing a Jewish state with Jerusalem as its capital was never extinguished. The modern Zionist movement started in earnest in the 1800s and accelerated in the aftermath of World War I. Zionists found a sympathetic ear in the West, although this sympathy was hardly enough to force the creation of an Israeli state, until World War II.

The Zionist movement gained special stature after World War II, as the world recoiled from the atrocities committed by the Nazis. After the genocide of the Jews, those who were historically in favor of a Jewish state (perhaps for religious reasons) were joined by those who wanted to do so for humanitarian reasons. In Western countries, particularly the United States, the desire to create a Jewish state was borne from a complex mixture of sympathy, religious identification, and national interest (to check potential Soviet influence in the region). The notion of a Jewish state was boosted in 1948, with UN resolutions calling for the creation of Israel. It was solidified when the Israelis defeated Arab armies late that year. It was cemented with the United States' recognition of Israel in 1948.

Since recognizing Israel, the United States has been Israel's most ardent Western supporter, and Israel has proved a valuable ally over the years. During the Cold War era the United States relied on Israel as a check to Soviet expansionism. Israel was also useful as to thwart a consolidation of power in the region by any one Arab state, a constant threat to worldwide oil supplies and the United States' economic well-being. Israel's bombing of the Iraqi nuclear reactors in 1981 represented one of the crowning achievements on this front.

In addition to the hard realities of realpolitik, the United States' relationship with Israel also has a religious element to it. To many Americans, particularly Christian conservatives, US support of Israel is unquestioned because it is grounded in biblical prophecy. This is despite the fact that in some cases Israel's interests have *quite logically* diverged from those of the United States. One of the worst espionage scandals in US history involved a spy for the Israeli government, Jonathan Pollard. As an American, I do not view the Pollard case sympathetically but believe Israel has the absolute right and obligation to further its national interests, which may entail spying on the United States.

Despite an occasional divergence of interests (which affects all alliances), it is in both America's and Israel's best interests to maintain a strong relationship, given the volatility in the Middle East. Finding a permanent solution to the tensions in the region is in both countries' best interests.

Addressing the Palestinian Situation

Addressing the Palestinian issue is the linchpin for Middle Eastern peace. The United States should embark on a new Marshall Plan. This plan would be balanced and promotes economic development in Palestine and the broader Middle East. US economic aid and recognition of a Palestinian state would be predicated on a like commitment by the Arab states. That is, the Arab states would have to contribute aid to Palestine *and* recognize Israel. The broad outline of the plan is as follows:

Economic, Not Military, Aid. Currently, the United States provides Israel with about $2.5 to $3 billion worth of aid per year. This makes Israel the largest beneficiary of US foreign aid.

Several issues are at play. First, Israel is hardly an impoverished country. Its GDP per capita is the highest in the region and one of the highest in the world. In fact, Israel's GDP per capita is only modestly less than that of France and Italy, which, not surprisingly, receive no US aid. Second, the United States provides aid to Israel largely in the form of military hardware and munitions. Israel has the unquestioned right to exist and defend itself. However, further militarizing the Middle East is poor policy, particularly when those arms are used against groups and countries already wary of the US.

The sale of US arms is not relegated to Israel alone. The US is also selling arms to Saudi Arabia ($20 billion worth of arms over the next ten years) and providing arms to Sunni groups in Iraq.[2] The rationale for the United States' militarization of the Middle East is fairly clear: the US government is promoting exports by US military hardware manufacturers (or the "military-industrial complex," as President Dwight D. Eisenhower dubbed it). Between the recent commitment of arm sales to Israel and Saudi Arabia and other states, the US is slated to sell over $50 billion worth of arms to Middle Eastern states over the next ten years, excluding arms being funneled into Iraq. If America's aim is to stabilize the Middle East, these arms sales and grants may not be the best means to achieve that goal. If the United States wants to give aid to Israel, it should be in cash and the string attached could be that the money be used to purchase goods from US manufacturers. That might effectively mean US arms. But at least it would be one step removed.

Finally, the US should use foreign aid to promote a Middle East peace plan. It should also include a like promise of aid to the Palestinians, funded by the US and Arab states. As noted, the US currently gives Israel nearly $3 billion in aid per annum. The US should enlist other nations to provide a like commitment to Palestine.

In particular, the US should commit $1.5 billion to Palestine, which would have to be matched dollar-for-dollar by other regional powers, including the Arab Gulf States, Iran, China, and Europe. This would result in $3 billion in aid to Israel and $3 billion in aid to Palestine. This would both leverage US support and also make other countries invest in the success of the Middle East.

The US government has subsidized the region for far too long. It should be assisted by other interested parties who should have the opportunity to express their support in both word and deed. A more stable Middle East benefits the entire world, not just the United States. The aid should be in cash, but there should be stipulations that the dollars contributed should be used to trade with the countries that contributed the dollars in the first place. So if the United States gave 75 percent of the dollars and the rest were given by Arab states, Iran, Europe, China, etc., the aid should be spent with those partners in roughly the same percentages. This would promote trade among the various parties, which would foster (a) economic development in Palestine and Israel and (b) cement economic relationships among the parties (Israel with the Arab states; Palestine with Europe and the US; etc.).

The economic aid should focus on infrastructure and economic development. For example, a pipeline could be constructed from Saudi Arabia to transport natural gas and/or oil to Palestine and/or Israel. Palestine and/or Israelis could build a liquid natural gas (LNG) plant and refineries along the coast, creating construction jobs and future jobs. The plants could then supply the United States and other nations with petroleum products. The series of relationships created would not only promote economic development but also trading relationships in the region.

Second, Israel would make an open city of Jerusalem—creating an international city open to all faiths. This would continue the ancient truce of Saladin and Richard. Israel could still have its capital city in Jerusalem, but so too could the Palestinians, in East Jerusalem. Significantly, Jerusalem would be administered by the state of Israel.

Third, the Palestinian-Israel borders agreed upon at Camp David by the United States, Israel, and Palestine under President Clinton would become the recognized borders. These borders are largely the pre-1967 war borders and conform to the original UN resolutions that outlined the creation of Israel.

Fourth, at Israel's option, it could maintain its settlements in Palestinian areas, provided that it compensated displaced Palestinians for their loss of property. The Palestinians would have no further right to this property, accepting payment for their damages and resettling in other areas of Palestine.

Finally, and most significantly, the Arab states, Iran, and Syria would recognize Israel and its right to exist and sign a treaty to that effect. The European Union, China, and Russia would also be signatories, given their influence in the region, particularly with Iran. The end result would be a more stable Middle East. It is critical for the United States to regain it reputation and credibility in the region.

Further, since each of the Middle Eastern states would have a vested interest in the success of this endeavor, the chances of the plan succeeding would increase significantly. And by enlisting the Middle Eastern states to put their money alongside their rhetoric, America would leverage the amount of total aid given to the region. Palestine would have the assistance necessary to gain a foothold and become a more prosperous area, where enough opportunity existed to forgo temptations to further violence and bloodshed. This has been sorely needed for some time. Providing the citizenry of Palestine and other countries in the area with more opportunity is the surest way to reduce violence in the region. This plan would provide Israel with the security it needs to ensure its continued existence. For Israel, this is a must.

Israel may be militarily superior today, but it faces two ominous trends First, the wealth creation in the Middle East is resulting in ever-increasing arms purchases, including from the United States. This is certainly not good news for Israel—or the US if it thinks beyond today's profits. Most of these states are not on the steadiest ground and, while today they may be controlled by moderate governments, there are no assurances that will be the case tomorrow. In fact, it is unlikely that all the current regimes will survive the trend toward more aggressive Islamic fundamentalism in the region. So absent a firmly established, economically driven (through trade), lasting peace, the US and Israel may well find themselves on the other end of the very same weapons the US is selling to the Middle East today.

The second issue relates to demographics. Israel is a state of 7.1 million (approximately 5.4 million are Jews).[3] Palestine and Israel have 2.9 million Palestinians.[4] Saudi Arabia has a population of 27 million,[5] Iraq 27.5 million,[6] and Iran 65 million.[7] Including the other states in the region, the Islamic states have a combined population of 323 million,[8] most under the age of twenty-five. This younger population in Arab states is growing at a much faster rate than Israel's. Forecasts estimate that the number of Muslims in the region will increase substantially, while Israel's Jewish population will remain relatively stagnant. Unless a plan is initiated that provides a framework to stabilize the region and, more important, to promote a *broader-based* economic prosperity in the region, Israel will face a soaring population of Arabs with limited opportunities but with an incentive to make things difficult for the more prosperous West.

George Marshall understood that the millions of unemployed Germans in the aftermath of World War I made Hitler's rise more likely and perhaps even inevitable, so he developed a plan to promote economic prosperity in Germany after World War II. Marshall believed that an investment by the United States in Germany would result in greater stability. The US and Israel should look at the results of post-war Europe to see the light, and the wisdom, of a similar plan in the Middle East.

CHAPTER 24

Addressing Iraq and Afghanistan

As with Palestine, the United States should create a plan for the stabilization of Iraq. US policymakers have grown frustrated by the lack of progress on the part of Iraqis to resolve internal differences. This frustration is shared by Democrats and Republicans alike. Both have developed plans based on the notion that the responsibility for the failed state of Iraq rests on the Iraqi people, rather than the United States. In general, the American position seems to be that "we made this mess, now *you* need to clean it up." The plans offered, one by the Bush administration and one by the Democrats, presuppose that the Iraqis can build a central government capable of governing Iraq. Both plans are flawed for the same reason: the Iraqis will not be able to reconcile, given their long-standing differences and grievances.

The Democrats' Plan

The Democrats have called for a phased withdrawal from Iraq, given the Iraqi government's failure to govern effectively and its consequent deterioration. (To be fair, some Democrats have offered a variant of the plan set forth below, but the two major Democratic presidential candidates have promoted a phased withdrawal).[1] The principal problem with the Democrats plan is that it would leave Iraq in chaos. The plan places the blame for the current situation on the Iraqi people, rather than on the US government, where it belongs. Given this, the Democrats plan would destroy what little credibility the United States still has in the region, create a situation conducive to mass genocide, and ultimately result in an Iraqi state controlled by the Shiites, the majority ethnic group. Further, given the tensions between the Kurds and Turks along the northern Iraqi border, the US would invite Turkish intervention into northern Iraq. The plan would also encourage Iranian interference in southern Iraq since Iraq's Shiite majority might naturally align with Iran's Shiite majority.

Bush's Plan for Iraq

President Bush's plan is not much better. He plans is to infuse additional troops into Iraq, particularly into Baghdad, to create a more stable environment. The hope is that greater security will create an environment that will allow a stronger central government to emerge. Bush has warned that if the "surge" fails, then Iraq will be lost and chaos will result, a logical conclusion. This plan presupposes two things: (a) the surge can last long enough to create an environment conducive to reconciliation among the various ethic groups and (b) that in fact, a strong central government can actually emerge and bind the nation together.

Time Frame. Based on troop rotations and the demands placed on the US military, the surge could only last through 2008 or perhaps 2009 without unduly placing strain on the US military. Without question, the military portion of the plan providing a safer, more stable environment is working. It should work for so long as America can maintain its current troop levels, basically through 2008. The National Intelligence Estimate published in August 2007[2] confirms that. Thereafter, absent a stronger government, the security gains achieved by the US military may well melt away as the troop reductions occur. So the general time frame to achieve a stronger government by 2009 is short.

Odds of Stronger Government. The surge is supposed to create a security blanket, which will provide time for the Iraqis to create a stronger Iraqi federal government, one capable of providing basic fundamental services (i.e., security, electricity, gas, etc.). The current government, led by Prime Minister Maliki is the horse the United States is betting on. Unfortunately, this is wagering on a fiction. The Maliki government, a government in name only, cannot provide its people with security or basic services. Security is being provided by America and basic services are spotty, at best.

Some suggest that Iraq is in the midst of a civil war. However, the situation in Iraq does not meet the traditional definition of a civil war: a government struggling for survival against an organized opposition. Rather, Iraq does not have a fully functioning central government. Further, the opposition to the government is multifaceted. Anarchy would be a better definition of the situation in Iraq. No government exists, and several warring groups vie for control over all or part of Iraq. So the US is attempting to transform a government that does not exist into one that does, in a very short time frame. Even if the cost in terms of lives and money were not so high, this bet would still be a foolish one. The prospects that the Maliki government will succeed are low. The reason the Maliki government will fail has little to do with the man himself. It is because of the history and composition of Iraq.

Recent History of Iraq

Iraq is an artifice of British colonialism, created after World War I pursuant to the Treaty of Versailles. Winston Churchill drew the boundaries of modern Iraq, fusing together territories inhabited by three different and warring ethnic groups: the Kurds (north), the Sunnis (central) and the Shiites (south). Since the creation of Iraq in 1919, the country has been ruled by either a puppet of the United Kingdom (King Faisal II) or a strongman (e.g., Saddam Hussein). In many respects, Iraq is the Middle East's version of Yugoslavia: a patched together country of hostile ethnic groups. And, as in Yugoslavia, the hatreds of the various groups were kept in check by repressive regimes.

Once those strongmen either died (Tito of Yugoslavia) or were deposed (Saddam of Iraq), the age-old hatreds surfaced and ripped the country apart. Just as Europe was powerless to keep Yugoslavia together, the United States is powerless to keep Iraq together. We should ask ourselves why it is in our interests to keep Iraq together and whether the its ultimate dissolution of Iraq would provide a better alternative.

The Example of Yugoslavia

Like Iraq, Yugoslavia was created in the aftermath of World War I. Historically, the principalities that comprised Yugoslavia (except Serbia) were a part of the Austro-Hungarian Empire (previously the Hapsburg Empire). As such, these principalities—Bosnia-Herzegovina, Macedonia, Slovenia, Croatia, and Montenegro—had some degree of autonomy in this sprawling empire. After its defeat in World War I, the Austro-Hungarian Empire was dismantled and the principalities were fused to form a pan-Slavic nation that would become known as Yugoslavia.

The decision to create Yugoslavia ignored the historical animosities among several of these principalities and their peoples, most notably the Serbs and the Albanians who shared the Kosovo region. This animosity was largely kept in check for the next sixty years, as a series of strong rulers kept the lid on the ethnic tensions. Marshal Tito ruled Yugoslavia for thirty-five years. After his death in 1980, problems began to arise, even before the rise of Slobodan Milosevic in Serbia in 1987. The principal problem stemmed from the historical claims that both the Serbs and Albanians had to Kosovo, a quasi-independent Serbian province. In an effort to stir Serbian nationalism, Milosevic persecuted the Albanians and began a movement to drive them from Kosovo in a notorious "ethnic cleansing." The population of mixed ethnic and religious groups in Kosovo, Bosnia, and other Yugoslavian provinces proved to be a toxic brew.

Faced with the massacre of Muslim Kosovars by the Serbs, NATO ultimately intervened in 1999, but did not invade. With air cover, the Muslims were able to avert further massacres and fend for themselves. This ultimately led to a treaty that provided a cessation of the ethnic cleansing and led to some degree of stability in the region. Thus Yugoslavia was ripped apart once a strong man was no longer around to hold the country together. The lesson here is that it is better to allow an artificially created country to splinter into a series of ethnically and religiously coherent states. This is painful in the near term, in terms of both violence and the dislocation of ethnic minorities. But over the long term, giving individual peoples and ethnic groups a higher degree of self-determination should result in greater regional stability. It is instructive that since the conclusion of the violence in Bosnia and Kosovo, the Balkan region has been relatively peaceful and prosperous, although the fate of Kosovo remains in play. The same could well hold true in Iraq if we allow it to naturally split apart along religious and ethnic lines.

Self-Determination

Using Yugoslavia as an analogue, America has to define the best alternative, both for Iraq and itself, and then develop a plan to come as close as possible to achieving that end. Stability in the region comprising Iraq is the best possible outcome for both the US and the Iraqi people. At this juncture, America should not focus on Iraq's form of government, as it has over the past few years. The US should instead focus on a political plan that provides stability and security to the people within Iraqi borders.

In particular, the United States should not impose its views on which form of government is appropriate. It may well be that democracy is not feasible or desired at this point. The US only has to look at Palestine to see the law of unintended consequences in full force. After having touted Lebanon as a case in point for the democratization of the Middle East, the Bush administration was then forced into sharp retreat on the issue when, in democratic elections, the Palestinians handed over control of parliament to Hamas, a terrorist organization.

The United States faces a similar challenge in Iraq and, indeed, the entire Middle East. America's quest for democratic rule could hand control of the Middle East to religious extremists, who tend to be well organized and who have significant support on the Arab street.

Solution for Iraq

To achieve stability and avoid a situation where all of Iraq is controlled by a Shiite theocracy, the United States should promote a solution that allows the various ethnic and religious groups within Iraq a high degree of self-determination. This would lead to a more satisfied populace and greater stability. Ultimately, this means that Iraq should be split into several states. Each would be drawn largely along religious, ethnic, and/or sectarian lines, much like what occurred in Yugoslavia. In the case of Iraq, three separate and independent states would result: a Kurdish state in the north, a Sunni state in the central part of the country, and a Shiite state in the south. Not only is this the "right" solution, it is already happening. Ironically, America is trying to stop the best alternative for both the US and Iraq. America should not fight the natural dissolution of Iraq. Rather, it should do whatever it can to accelerate this trend, since it represents the natural order of things. The end result of this division would not necessarily be bad for the United States. Actually, the outcome could be quite beneficial because it would result in greater stability in the region and in at least one thriving democracy, the Kurdish state in the north.

Transitioning to Three States

The United States should convene an international conference on Iraq, with NATO in the lead (see discussion on NATO above). The purpose of the conference would be to bring together the various constituents in Iraq, work out a plan for a more stable situation in the region.[3] Although the US should come to the conference with a blueprint for the country, it should be prepared to accept the desires of each of the constituent groups in Iraq.

The blueprint for a new Iraq should call for the transition to three independent states. They would operate as sovereign states with complete control and dominion over their territories and natural resources.

The most problematic state would be the central state, encompassing Baghdad and the western province of Anbar. It is in an area with no proven oil reserves to speak of, although some believe massive reserves are hidden under the desert. It would therefore, become a relatively large and poor country dominated by Sunni Muslims. But it would include the largest city in Iraq: Baghdad.

It would be impractical at this point to provide for a sharing of oil revenues from the more prosperous northern and southern states. That would only promote instability in each of the three nations, as the southern and northern states would fight to keep their oil reserves. Accordingly, the United States and Arab states should develop a plan to provide the Sunni state with foreign aid to rebuild its shattered infrastructure, largely a result of our invasion and Saddam's decades of neglect. The aid package, while large, would be much less than the US is currently spending militarily. If this central country had 10 million residents, the United States could spend $5 billion per year for the next ten years on reconstruction and that would still be fraction our current *annual* expenditures in Iraq: $100 to $150 billion per annum. If the money were spent on rebuilding the country's infrastructure, it would create Iraqi jobs and result in a country with the necessary infrastructure to prosper. The United States could also use part of the money to foster exploration for oil and gas in the region. With the proper investment, this commodity could provide the new central state with oil riches comparable to other countries in the region.

The second state would be a Shiite state in the south. This state would have significant oil reserves and include the port of Basra, an important gateway to the Indian Ocean. Without question, America should prepare for a fundamentalist Shiite state, perhaps one aligned with Iran. But this is going to occur regardless of what America wants.

And there is a chance, perhaps a decent one, that this state would retain some degree of independence from Iran, even though both would be dominated by Shiites. This is because Iraq is dominated by Arabs, whereas Iran is dominated by Persians, and distrust exists between the two ethnic groups. Further, bitterness lingers from the Iran-Iraq war. In any event, American should recognize the resultant state, establish full diplomatic relations with it, and trade with it.

The Kurdish state to the north will likely be democratic and prosperous, given the oil and gas reserves that it would possess. It is currently being dragged down by the unrest in other areas of Iraq. Once relieved of the uncertainties relating to the central state of Iraq, the Kurds would be free to create an independent state and oversee the development of their oil reserves. The principal issue with the Kurdish state would be the presence of Turkey on its northern border. The Turks have a large Kurdish population and fear an independent Kurdish state. A Kurdish separatist group, the Kurdish Workers Party (PKK), has initiated attacks within Turkey, causing tensions to flare. The Iranians also have a large Kurdish population in the northern part of their country. Both the Iranians and Turkey would have concerns about a rebellion in their Kurd-dominated regions. This will be addressed in the following section.

Conditions

Several conditions should be attached to this blueprint for the Middle East:

1. *NATO Force.* Ideally, the US military should be augmented by NATO forces in Iraq. This would give the plan greater credibility. For America's NATO allies, America could ensure that they would not have any more troops in Afghanistan and Iraq than they do now. America could do this by shifting a portion of US troops in Iraq to Afghanistan, replacing allied troops that would be redeployed in Iraq. While the overall troop lev-

els of America's allies would remain relatively constant, the force would become internationalized in Iraq and led by NATO, rather than the United States. This would take the US out of the equation and lead to a more credible force and plan. Overall, the goal would be to internationalize the force if possible. If our NATO allies balked, the US would be no worse off than today. That is, it would station troops in Iraq long enough to transition it into three autonomous countries.

2. *Security Umbrella.* The US military (or NATO) would provide a general security umbrella for the implementation of the plan, ensuring that ethnic minorities in each state were relocated to a state better suited to them. For example, Shiites living in Baghdad might relocate to the Shiite state in the south. After a grace period, ethnic minorities who remained in lands dominated by another majority would be doing so at their own risk. (Although the plan would call for respect of ethnic minorities by each state, the US would have little power to enforce that edict.)

3. *Reducing the US Footprint in Iraq. Relocating Troops to Non-Arab Lands.* Ultimately, the United States needs to reduce its troop presence dramatically. US military bases in the region should be relocated to the new Kurdish state or to Turkey. By moving troops from central Iraq, the United States would not be occupying Arab lands, one of the stated reasons for the 9/11 attacks.

4. *Kurdish State.* In consideration for formal recognition by Iran and Turkey, the Kurdish state would agree not to foment unrest in the Kurdish regions of Turkey and Iran. The Kurdish state would have to denounce the PKK and provide Turkey with assistance in ensuring that attacks by the PKK were not launched from its territory. Iran should be warned that any mischief on its part would nullify this promise.

5. *Turkey.* If Turkey were agreeable to the previous point, it should gain some stature with respect to being admitted to the European Union.

6. *Inclusion of Other Nations.* China, India, and Russia should be part of this plan.

7. *Noninterference.* The US and Gulf states, including Iran, would agree not to interfere in the internal affairs of the sovereign states resulting from the partition of Iraq. With China, Russia, and the EU behind this plan, the threat would carry additional weight. In addition, we would tie Iran's support of the plan to the stipulation that the new Kurdish state would not stir up unrest in northern Iran. If Iran did not agree, all bets would be off on this point.

8. *Noninterference in Each Other's Affairs.* The states resulting from the partition of Iraq would have to agree not to interfere in each other's affairs.

9. *Economic Aid.* As noted above, the US and the Sunni Arab states should promise economic aid to the central Sunni state, given that it has been hardest hit by war and does not have any significant oil revenues. This economic aid should be equal to what the Sunni state would have otherwise received in oil revenues. The other two states would have sufficient oil revenues to move forward without any significant foreign aid. The aid to the Sunni state should be directed toward rebuilding the nation's infrastructure and be put under NATO purview and administration. The Arab states might be amenable to this because most of them are also Sunni states and probably want a reasonably strong Sunni state to counterbalance the southern Shiite state and Iran.

The United States should pay for a large portion, because the American invasion caused a great deal of the destruction of the nation's infrastructure in the first place. A total aid package of $10 billion per annum, funded 75 percent by the United States and 25 percent by the Arab states, would equate to a fraction of the current cost of the war. The package would last for a specified time period, say ten years. The lone stipulation by the US and the other participants in the plan would be that the aid should be used to procure services from the countries providing the aid. However, the allocation of those funds should be at the discretion of the Sunni Iraqi government, and not the United States. This would, again, cut down on the concerns that many might have about the US misallocating aid and resources, a claim made by many during US reconstruction efforts in post-invasion Iraq.

10. *Protection of Ethnic Minorities.* Each state resulting from the partition of Iraq should agree not to persecute ethnic minorities that remain in their countries, and provide freedom of passage at any time should any of these people want to leave.

11. *Consummated by a Treaty.* The plan should be embodied in a treaty signed by the three newly created states, Iran, the Gulf states, the US, the EU, Russia, China, and possibly NATO. By including China, Russia, the EU, and Iran, the treaty should carry a great deal of weight. That is, if any of the resultant Iraqi states or Iraq breached the treaty, they would not only have to deal with the US, but also the newly emergent powers of Russia and China.

12. *US Acquiescence.* The United States should accept whatever forms of government emerged in the three states. It should recognize each state diplomatically and try to conduct trade with each, consistent with the new US foreign policy. The Shiite state almost certainly would be Islamic, and the United States would need to accept that.

Clearly, this plan would be modified over the course of the conference. But its essence, autonomy for each major ethnic and religious group, should withstand scrutiny. Further, there is something in this plan for all major outside powers. The Arab Gulf states would have a Sunni state to check the growing Shiite influence in the region. Turkey would get a firm guarantee with respect to its border with the new Kurdish state, something it very much wants. And it would get more consideration in its bid for EU membership. The United States would have at least one democratic state in the region and the prospect of another stable one.

The alternative is to continue losing American and Iraqi lives, spending hundreds of billions of dollars, and supporting a state that will become increasingly unstable once the US military begins its drawdown. The result will either be a lawless state or one dominated by Shiites aligned with Iran. The latter is the worst-case scenario for the United States.

Using the surge and the temporary buildup of our troops to create a stable framework for Iraq would be far better than trying to hold the currently unstable country together. With a strategic plan, the United States could use its troops wisely to transition all or part of Iraq to a more stable future, rather than sowing the seeds of a future civil war. If the country were partitioned along the lines set forth above, some fighting might still occur, but at least we would have moved to the endgame and cut down on the level of violence. Further, this plan would likely gain worldwide support.

Afghanistan Is a Bigger Risk. Need for American Troop Redeployment

One of the most critical reasons for resolving the Iraqi situation is to reduce overall US troop levels in Iraq and redeploy a portion of these troops to Afghanistan. The rest would go to the new Kurdish state or back to the US. Afghanistan represents a bigger risk than Iraq. A political solution exists for Iraq and stability should follow at some point in the future. Afghanistan is much more homogeneous and has the potential to be a more unified country behind a theological regime, such as the Taliban, if America is not successful. Moreover, the prospects for a healthy economy are poor unless the country is stabilized. Currently, Afghanistan's largest industry is the cultivation of opium poppies, used to create heroin.

A theological regime in charge of an economically depressed country whose principal source of revenue is heroin would create a significant risk for the United States. The Taliban regime consolidated power in Afghanistan and established a radical theological regime that trafficked heroin and supported global terrorism. That regime ultimately harbored Osama bin Laden while he planned and executed 9/11.

Worse yet, a theocratic regime in Afghanistan could spill over into Pakistan. Unrest on the northwest frontier and the reemergence of the Taliban would provide an ominous threat to Pakistan and the West. Given that Pakistan is a nuclear power, the idea of a theocratic regime in Pakistan should strike fear in US policymakers. It should provide the US government with the impetus to make every effort to ensure Afghanistan's success, keeping it from falling into chaos and threatening more instability in the region.

Without the distraction of Iraq, the United States could focus on Afghanistan. The US only has 25,500 troops in Afghanistan (NATO has about 50,000 in total), far too few to help stabilize it.[5] And reports indicate that the country is falling back into disarray. With more troops, the chances of success should increase, but time is running out. The strategic plan described here would call for reducing troop levels in Iraq by half, to 80,000. Sixty thousand would be sent home and the other 20,000 redeployed to Afghanistan. This would nearly double the US troop level in Afghanistan and provide a better opportunity for success. And by reducing overall forces in the region by 60,000 troops, the US military could take some of the strain off of an already strapped army. In the end, this would be the best allocation of a finite pool of resources.

PART VI

CONSTITUTIONAL AND ELECTORAL POLICY ISSUES

- Rome as a Guide
- The US Constitution and the Forgotten Amendments
- The Constitution and the New Deal
- Constitutional Fidelity: Changing the Tone
- Congressional Appointment

Introduction

The United States of America. Americans say the name reflexively, as a proper noun rather than a descriptive one. But the name has profound importance in explaining the very nature of this country. This nation was created through the union of several sovereign states, each of which ceded some sovereignty to gain the benefits of a stronger overall nation. This created a union of sovereign states. However, as noted in the Constitution, these states did not cede all their sovereignty, but just a portion. The same is also true of the people. This is consistent with the social contract theory of the Enlightenment.[1] Our constitution makes it clear that the creators of the United States nation are "we the people" who "in order to form a more perfect Union" ceded certain powers to the states and the federal government.

Most Americans learn about the Constitution in school. Yet, it remains an increasingly unknown document, although it represents the foundation of the America's government. Federal officials, from the president to each congressman, take an oath to uphold the US Constitution. Despite this oath, few of them seem to have a clear understanding of this document or our system of government. Quarrels over the constitutionality of bills today, if they occur, generally revolve around whether the president is trampling on Congress's turf or vice versa. The debates are rarely about whether either Congress or the president is trampling on the rights of the states or the people. This is certainly a departure from the government outlined in the Constitution. Our founders,[2] looking to ancient precedents, believed the United States had to have a central government to function effectively. However, recalling the lessons of ancient Rome, they realized that if the federal government became too strong, the prospects of tyrannical rule increased.

Accordingly, the founders set up a system of divided government. Power in the federal government would be shared by the executive branch (president), legislative branch (Congress), and the judiciary branch (the courts, led by the Supreme Court). The powers would be shared among these branches to provide a series of checks and balances to ensure that no branch became too powerful. Most Americans know about these checks and balances, since this is the one area that is still subject to an occasional constitutional debate.

What is less clear to most Americans is that the Constitution sharply limits the powers of the federal government. In particular, the federal government received its power through a grant from the states. Each of the initial states comprising the Union was an independent, sovereign state after the Revolutionary War. In forming the Union, each state gave up a portion of its sovereignty to the federal government but retained all powers that were not specifically granted. This grant recognized that there were certain powers the federal government was better equipped to exercise on behalf of the states. These activities included: defending the nation, negotiating treaties, protecting intellectual property, and waging war. Beyond these and other limited powers, the states and the people retained all other powers. These retained powers included: laws focusing on morality, criminality, and other matters that might be influenced by regional differences.

Until relatively recently, federal lawmakers debated the constitutionality of bills with fervor. They argued the merits of a bill in the context of whether Congress had the authority to pass it. A president carefully reviewed the constitutional merits of a particular bill to determine whether signing it into law would breach his duty to uphold the Constitution. In this era (largely before FDR), lawmakers understood that the powers of the federal government were limited. If a power was not expressly provided for in the Constitution, most lawmakers rightly concluded that the power was outside the constitutional mandate of Congress. Moral issues were largely left to the states. The federal system allowed for regional differences on moral issues. This enabled each state to fashion laws on moral issues that fit the values of the citizens of that state. During this earlier era, debates over moral issues were largely left to the states and decided at a level of government closer to the people. More important, the federal government was not debating a single moral standard would apply to the country as a whole and inflame regional differences.

Over the years, the federal government has encroached on the powers of the states and the people, and today few powers are off limits to it. Since this has been a gradual process, very few people are aware of it or even care. However, the ramifications are profound: individuals' loss of power and a breakdown in civility. To understand why many of the founders would take a dim view of a federal government with virtually unlimited powers and an extremely strong executive, one has to understand the development of the Constitution and its antecedents, which takes us back to ancient Rome.

CHAPTER 25

Rome as a Guide

General

"All roads lead to Rome." This saying was a testament to Rome's status as the ancient world's superpower and its position as the center of the known world for nearly ten centuries. Rome's influence did not die with its destruction by barbarians in AD 476. It lived on. To understand the United States and its birth, we must take a road back to ancient Rome.

Our Founders

Our founders were products of the Enlightenment era that followed the Renaissance, a period that saw the spiritual restoration of ancient Rome and Greek traditions that had lain dormant for nearly a thousand years. Everything, from the architecture of our capitol to our constitution, finds its roots in ancient times. Ancient Athens is often viewed as the model for the United States. However, it was ancient Greece's younger and more successful brother, Rome, that set the most influential precedent for America. Our founders viewed ancient Athens' noisy democracy as much too anarchistic to be a reliable form of government. Our founders, who were mostly affluent, were more

comfortable with a republican form of government, which was tanta-
mount to an oligarchy. The Roman republic, with its grandeur and august oligarchy, offered a more palatable and successful precedent for
our founders.

The Roman Republic

Ancient Rome conjures up a variety of images for Americans. To de-
vout Christians, it represents the repressive regime that ruled ancient
Judea and oversaw the death of Jesus. To historians, ancient Rome was
the superpower of its era, ruling most of the known world with administrative efficiency and rapacity. To students of military conquest,
Rome maintained its military might for centuries through innovation,
mobility (good road systems), and discipline. To engineers, the Roman
Empire is worthy of awe. Indeed, its technological progress would not
be equaled in some instances until the eighteenth century.

For our founders, the Roman Republic offered not only a road map
for success, it also provided insight on the problems and pitfalls of self-
government. Rome provided a strong case study for developing our
own constitution.

The Parallels of Roman and American History

As with the United States, the Roman republic grew out of a spat with
a tyrannical king: King Tarquin. Tarquin took liberties with the daughter of a Roman nobleman. Taking offense, the nobleman and others
ousted the king, vowing to abolish one-man rule forever. With that, the
Roman republic was born in the fifth century BC. For the next four
hundred years, the Roman republic was governed by an unwritten constitution that was formulated, developed, and refined over the years.
Within this constitutional framework, Rome was ruled informally by
a strong legislature, its senate. The senate (derived from the word *senex*,
or "old man" in Latin) was comprised of three to four hundred of
Rome's leading citizens, each of whom vied aggressively for a seat.

A Limited Executive

Mindful of the perils of one-man rule, Rome had a weak executive branch. Rome was generally led by two executives, called consuls, who each served a single one-year term. They alternated days at the helm of state, another limitation on the executives. Consuls were elected by the senate, typically from its own ranks. A consul could serve longer, or alone, only during times of crisis, such as war or revolt. In these cases, the senate could declare a dictatorship of limited duration and one man could take control of the state and lead it through the crisis. After the end of the crisis, the executive responsibilities of the state would revert back to two consuls.

A Strong Legislative Branch; Officials of State

The people were represented through the senate, and also by tribunes. The senate was elected by Roman citizens. While Rome had a representative democracy, the scope of the democracy was fairly narrow. For much of the first four centuries, Roman citizenship was confined to inhabitants of Rome who owned land.[1] Over time, citizenship was expanded to include many outside of Rome, starting modestly with inhabitants in the Italian countryside. Eventually, even those from Rome's most far-flung provinces could become citizens. The genius of Rome was its ability to attract talent individuals and integrate them into the social fabric of the state, thus turning enemies into supporters of Rome.[2] While the senate represented Rome's elite, tribunes represented all inhabitants of Rome. They had the power to veto any law proposed by the senate that was not in the people's interest.

Transformation from Republic to Empire

This unwritten and sometimes chaotic system of representative democracy lasted for four centuries, until Julius Caesar rebelled in 44 BC. He began Rome's transformation from a representative democracy to an empire over which one man would rule. The transformation was not an overnight affair, as is often imagined, but a gradual process. For the fifty years prior to Caesar's famous reentry into Rome, the Roman republic endured a series of internal squabbles and was tested by men seeking to consolidate power and rule the city-state themselves.[3] It was in this highly charged environment that Caesar came of age. Coming from a family with a glorious, albeit distant, past, he established himself quite early as a man on the move. Holding numerous offices at a relatively young age, Caesar attained the position of consul, the pinnacle of Roman success, in his early forties. His tenure was filled with intrigue and accusations of misconduct.

After his term as consul ended, Caesar was accused of accepting bribes. But rather than confront the popular Julius Caesar, the senate had a better idea. Why not give the young, ambitious Caesar an impossible task and let him fail? The impossible task was to serve as military governor of Gaul. By exposing Caesar to the rigors of one of Rome's toughest military theaters, the senate believed it could break him and his popularity with the people. But Caesar did not fail. Instead, he subdued Gaul over his five-year term as military governor, becoming more popular than ever. As the time for Caesar's return to Rome neared, the senate voted to impose charges against him for accepting bribes. Caesar's chief lieutenant, Marc Antony, tried to veto the charge in his role as tribune. However, the senate bypassed the veto. With nothing to lose and Rome to gain, Caesar crossed the Rubicon River and led his army into Rome.[4] Civil war followed. Caesar easily crushed his adversaries and established himself as the lord of Rome He turned the senate into his puppets until a group of senators assassinated him in 44 BC on March 15, the ides of March. With his assassination, the republic, however, was not restored. Caesar's adopted son, his great nephew later known as Augustus, proved himself a worthy heir and a much better administrator. Effectively consolidating power, he led Rome, more or less as dictator, for over forty years. He outlived the living memory of the Roman republic and began a long line of emperors who led the Roman Empire for the next four hundred years. While Rome reached its zenith during the empire era, many historians since that time have reserved their praise for the republic.

The Patina of the Roman Republic

With this model in mind, our founders began developing a system of government for the United States. Like their Roman forbearers, our founders threw off the yoke of an oppressive king, King George III. Having done so at great personal risk, the founders were not keen on substituting a homegrown autocrat for a foreign one. Nor were they enamored with the idea of installing a noisy, chaotic democracy like that of ancient Athens. Rather, our founders believed that a representative democracy—a republic—was the best alternative. A republic would provide stability and protect the state from mob rule. With this in mind, our founders began to develop a system of government with three branches and a series of checks and balances, much like the intricate Roman constitution two millennia earlier.

CHAPTER 26

The US Constitution
and the Forgotten Amendments

In developing the US Constitution and our system of government our founders had several considerations:

Limited Federal Government. The founders did not want a strong central government for several reasons. First, a strong federal government posed the greatest risk to individual liberties and freedoms, as evidenced by the European monarchies and the more tyrannical states in the ancient East. Second, the United States had to have the support of the states, each of which considered itself a sovereign country. Each state jealously guarded its sovereignty; initially, the citizens of each state regarded themselves first and foremost as citizens of their state, not of the United States.

For those who wanted to build a single country, this posed a problem: how to convince each state to give up some degree of sovereignty to a new nation in consideration for the benefits of being part of a union. The founders understood that the states would not agree to cede too much sovereignty to the new union. They had to walk a fine line between getting enough powers from the states to make the new union viable, without overreaching. That meant a relatively weak central government. Finally, the founders rightly believed that the government that governs best is closest to the people. This meant that state and local governments should make as many decisions as possible, leaving just a few big-ticket items (e.g., defense, coining money, roads, foreign relations, etc.) to the federal government.

Scope of Federal Government. Once the appropriate scope of federal powers was determined, the founders then took the additional step of creating a three-branch federal government to further mitigate the risk of tyranny. The three branches were the legislative branch, the executive branch, and the judiciary. The roles of each are simple:

Legislature. Makes laws (including taxing, spending powers, and declaring war);

Checks: The Constitution, people, judiciary, and the chief executive. The Constitution limits the powers of the legislature. The people elect legislators and have the ultimate authority to kick them out of office. The judiciary considers whether a law is constitutional, a check on any attempt by the legislature to overreach constitutionally. The chief executive can veto laws he believes are either unconstitutional or not in the national interest.

Executive. Enforces laws and conducts foreign relations (including waging war, after it is declared).

Checks: The Constitution, the legislature, and judiciary. The Constitution limits the powers of the executive. The legislature defines the scope of his powers; that is, the executive cannot enforce laws that are not made or that are repealed. So the executive generally has to work within the boundaries prescribed by the legislature. Also, the legislature has the power of the purse, which further limits the power of the executive. The judiciary rules on actions taken by the executive and whether the actions are constitutional.

Judiciary. Considers the constitutionality of laws. Judges and justices receive lifetime appointments.

Checks: The Constitution provides both the legislature and the executive with important controls, or checks, on the judiciary. Congress controls the establishment of the federal courts and their composition. Congress can expand the Supreme Court, or as justices retire, reduce the size of it. Further, Congress can impeach and remove judges and justices for high crimes and misdemeanors. The president has the right to appoint judges and justices, subject to confirmation by the Senate.

The First Experiment: The Articles of Confederation

Despite the road map provided by the Roman constitution, the US Constitution did not come into existence immediately. Political realities dictated that an intermediate step be taken, in the form of the Articles of Confederation. The Articles of Confederation was the first official governing document of the United States. It was a failure in the sense that it survived less than ten years. However, the founders were working with a blank slate. Nothing like this had been attempted for nearly two millennia. Further, the founders were not conducting an experiment on government in a laboratory or classroom, where a system of government could be forged without political considerations. They were working in a highly charged political climate, where each constituent state jealously guarded its sovereignty. As an attempt to balance these competing considerations, the Articles of Confederation proved too weak to succeed. But in another sense it provided an intermediate step necessary for the sovereign states to transition to a unified country.

Articles of Confederation: Led by a Three-Person Executive

The Articles of Confederation looked very much like the unwritten Roman constitution. The executive branch was lodged into the hands of three coequal executives, each nominated and elected by the states legislatures. These coexecutives served one-year terms and had limited powers to oversee the affairs of state, much like the consuls of ancient Rome. The legislature held much of the power of the federal government, but even that was limited. The US legislature did not have the ability to levy taxes without each state's consent and did not even have the ability to raise a standing army. Each state retained a high degree of sovereignty and could levy tariffs on goods imported from other states as it saw fit. This proved a significant advantage to the more rural states in the South when importing manufactured goods from the North, but a disaster when trying to build a unified nation. In addition, states coined their own money and had their own court systems. Criminals who fled from one state to another could not be extradited without a treaty between the two states in question. Not surprisingly, the Articles of Confederation led to confusion and squabbling among the constituent states.

Transitioning to the Constitution: Constitutional Convention

In 1788, after seven years of the largely ineffectual Articles of Confederation, the founders realized that American system of government needed to be changed. They proposed a constitutional convention with the fairly narrow scope of modifying the existing Articles of Confederation. The chief concern was the belief that the United States had to have a stronger, more effective executive and a more powerful federal government in order to provide for a common defense and to administer the affairs of state. Yet the founders remained wary of a strong executive, given their experience with King George III.

It was within this context—the need to modify the Articles of Confederation to provide for a stronger federal government—that the Constitutional Convention was called. Heeding the call, the states each sent delegates to Philadelphia. However, the organizers, including the brilliant Alexander Hamilton, had other designs in mind. They wanted to reorganize the country's government and provide for the far stronger and more effective central government that many had originally contemplated. After much deliberation, the Constitutional Convention developed a system of government that would address the shortcomings of the Articles of Confederation by creating a stronger central government and a more effective executive.

The founders drafted a constitution that delineated powers between the federal government, the states, and the people but also provided for a more powerful federal government. The federal government itself was divided into three equal branches, each branch providing checks and balances to the others. Most important, the US Constitution was written and clear, unlike its Roman predecessor. The executive branch was to be headed by one person. He would have the power to execute the laws enacted by Congress, wage war, and conduct foreign policy in consultation with the Senate. The consolidation of war and foreign policy in the hands of one person made sense, particularly since it would take congressional action to declare war (House and Senate approval) or ratify treaties (Senate approval).

Comprised of two houses, Congress was to control the nation's purse strings. It would have limited rights to pass legislation. All legislation had to fit within fit into one of Congress's enumerated powers. There were just sixteen enumerated powers or areas of responsibility, which sharply limited Congress's ability to pass laws. In addition, the Bill of Rights further proscribed the power of Congress and the president, making it clear that the people and states had significant rights and would retain all rights not specifically granted in the Constitution. The judiciary was to assess the constitutionality of laws passed by the federal and state legislatures, as well as serve as a check on executive or legislative overreach on constitutional authority.[1]

For the first 150 years of this nation's existence, the executive, legislature, and judiciary took a limited view of the federal government's power. There were continual debates about whether a proposed or existing law was constitutional. It was understood all too well that the powers and authority outlined in the Constitution were limited in scope. Unless a specific power was granted to the president, Congress or the courts, that power was expressly reserved for the people and the states.

The Limited Power of the Purse

Congress, then as now, wielded the power of the purse. However, the purse strings were, by design, tight indeed. Congress could not pass a tax that did not fit neatly and specifically within its sixteen enumerated powers, as set forth in Article I, Section 8 of the Constitution. These included the powers to tax, borrow money, regulate commerce among states and foreign nations, declare wars, establish the court system, and coin money. The Constitution also provided Congress with a catch-all power. It could make all laws "necessary and proper" for carrying out the foregoing powers. This final power provided a loophole exploited during the New Deal era to greatly expand the scope of congressional authority.

It is significant that Congress's power to tax was limited. Until 1913, it did not have the constitutional power to levy an income tax on individuals. Rather, most tax revenues were generated through tariffs, duties, and other taxes levied on the importation of goods and occasionally through an estate tax. With a restricted ability to tax and spend, the federal government remained rather limited for its first 130 years. *In fact, revenue for the US Treasury reached its highest point in 1866 at $310 million, just after the Civil War ended. It would not reach this amount again for nearly fifty years (1911).*[2] Federal revenues accelerated in the early part of the twentieth century, after passage of the Sixteenth Amendment, which gave Congress the express authority to levy taxes on personal income. Such authority had been struck down as unconstitutional by the Supreme Court in 1895.[3]

Congress Gets Its First Credit Card

Even with its newfound authority, Congress still had to contend with a fairly narrow set of enumerated powers that constrained its ability to spend. So, even though Congress got a credit card, it had a fairly low limit. That, of course, would change with the New Deal.

CHAPTER 27

The Constitution and the New Deal

From the Civil War to the late 1920s, the United States muddled along on its path to superpower status. The federal government largely kept out of the way. Progress was relatively strong, with a periodic panic, recession, or even depression thrown in. In other words, the United States followed the path of an emerging market transitioning to a developed state. Absent a few conflicts here and there, the United States largely heeded the founder's caution against entangling itself in European conflicts, the Spanish-American War being a notable exception.

This is not to say that the United States was not expanding. It was. But it was expanding relatively efficiently, without a significant loss of life or treasure. The United States bought Louisiana from Napoleon so that he could finance his disastrous war against England. Overnight, the Louisiana Purchase doubled America's size. Texas was annexed in 1848. And the rest of the West was settled through a series of wars, battles, and skirmishes against the American Indians. By the 1870s, the continental United States was largely the nation it is today in terms of land mass. And by this time, the United States had begun focusing on industrialization. For the next fifty years it transitioned from a largely rural nation to an increasingly industrial one.

Within this time frame, the United States had a series of mediocre, caretaker presidents, Theodore Roosevelt excepted. As any school child will tell you, recalling the seventeenth through twenty-seventh presidents is a difficult exercise, given the limited achievements of the group. But, in a sense, this is precisely what the United States needed. The US did not need an activist government led by strong, visionary men. It was the vision of the founders that had created the system that would lead the US to greatness. The job of these presidents was to maintain enough order to avoid anarchy and to promote growth. Nothing more, nothing less.

In many ways, the United States of this period was much like many emerging markets today: a wide-open land of opportunity without many rules. During this period, the United States started challenging traditional Western European powers. It is significant that the US government was not soaking up the nation's resources as it is today. During America's transition from a rural backwater to an industrial power, the US government consumed less than 5 percent of GDP. Today, the US government consumes nearly 22% of GDP.

The Great Depression

The Great Depression changed not only our nation's psyche, but also our form of government.

Very few understood the magnitude of the Great Depression at its inception, the stock market crash of 1929. Without question, the United States had endured its share of economic calamities up to that point. These included a series of currency crises and economic depressions during the 1870s and a serious depression at the beginning of the twentieth century. But none had the impact of the Great Depression, given its worldwide scope.

President Herbert Hoover has been vilified by historians for his reaction to the Great Depression, but his actions have to be taken within the context of the time. Perhaps one of the most accomplished men ever to hold the office, Hoover was not paralyzed in office, as some have said. Rather, he was mindful of the restrictions imposed on the presidency by the Constitution and the limits of government to address a worldwide depression. Hoover understood the opportunities that the United States' laissez-faire system afforded to individuals, since he was largely a product of those opportunities.

Hoover grew up an orphan and graduated first in his class at Stanford University. Prior to becoming president, he was an accomplished engineer who traveled the world on business and made his fortune in mining. Retiring from private industry in his forties as a wealthy man, Hoover turned his attention and administrative skills to government. During World War I, Hoover took over the logistics of supplying Allied troops with munitions and manufactures from the United States. In doing so, Hoover directed a nation with vast resources and manufacturing capabilities, but also one that was not used to war. The US had not fought a significant war for over fifty years. Hoover handled the task adroitly, and should share a lot of the credit for turning the tide of World War I.

Hoover brought these considerable skills to the White House in 1929. But, despite his impressive resume, there was little to prepare him for the Great Depression. The collapse of the worldwide economy, which occurred within less than a year of his taking office, certainly was not his fault. Further, Hoover proposed many programs that would become the foundation of the New Deal, but as a traditionalist he stopped short of transcending the bounds of the Constitution. In particular, Hoover proposed public works programs to employ the millions who had lost their jobs, but recognized that these programs were borderline unconstitutional. After all, the Constitution provided Congress with very limited spending and legislative powers, and jobs works programs were certainly not among them. Despite popular history's take, economic growth and the stock market recovered somewhat during Hoover's final two years in office. Unfortunately, by this point the damage was done. Hoover's reputation as a high-handed executive was well established.

FDR's New Deal

Franklin D. Roosevelt entered office with the promise of more government activism and hope. A great orator, FDR began using radio to encourage a beleaguered nation. His first inaugural address is one of the greatest in US history. Taking his cue from Abraham Lincoln, FDR did not appeal to the darker side of humanity. He inspired, telling Americans that they had nothing to "fear but fear itself." In his first weeks as president, FDR took Hoover's government works programs and multiplied and expanded them. He then pushed these new and expanded programs through Congress. During his first one hundred days, FDR created almost all of the great public works programs of the New Deal, including the Agricultural Adjustment Act, Civilian Conservation Corps, Civilian Works Administration, Fair Labor Standards Act, Federal Deposit Insurance Corporation, Federal Housing Administration, National Labor Relations Act, National Youth Administration, Public Works Administration, Rural Electric Administration, Securities and Exchange Commission, Social Security Administration, Tennessee Valley Authority, and Works Progress Administration, to name a few. Despite his success,[1] most knew these laws would be struck down as unconstitutional by the Supreme Court.

New Deal Struck Down—FDR's End-Around of the Constitution

The Supreme Court nullified most of the legislation passed during FDR's first hundred days, largely vindicating Hoover's reticence on this front. Frustrated by the "old men" of the Supreme Court, the president undertook to make the most dramatic change to the nation's judiciary since its founding. FDR claimed that the nation's courts were too firmly in the grip of elderly judges because the US Constitution provided for the lifetime appointment of federal judges.

Not wanting to challenge the Constitution directly, FDR took a more subtle route. He proposed that Congress introduce legislation to appoint one additional judge to each court for every member of that court over the age of seventy. Although FDR's motives were dubious, this recommendation was entirely constitutional. Article I provides that Congress has absolute right to determine the composition of the judiciary and provide for the creation of courts. Congress could populate the courts however it chose.

Not coincidentally, six members of the Supreme Court were over the age of seventy, and almost all of these judges were hostile to FDR's New Deal initiatives. The president's proposal would give him the opportunity to appoint six additional justices. Since most of the New Deal cases had been decided 5-4 against FDR, the additional six judges would have given him a comfortable majority on the Supreme Court. While politically savvy, FDR did not anticipate the hostility generated by his proposal. Both Congress and the people viewed his effort for what it was: an end-around of the Constitution. Even as popular as FDR was, this tactic proved to be an overreach. Ultimately, facing the wrath of a deeply skeptical populace, Congress did not act on FDR's proposal.

Some historians view the "court-packing scheme," as it was popularly known, as a defeat for FDR. Far from it. The Supreme Court, not immune from political pressure, took note and began to take a more pragmatic view of FDR's New Deal legislation. In fact, after this proposal, FDR fared well in the Supreme Court battle on his New Deal programs. With this one bold move, FDR started a trend of increasing the power of the federal government, which has continued to this day. This is significant. If one part of government expands its power, that power has to come from somewhere else. And if the federal government has expanded its power, it is only logical that the losers have been the states and the people. Today, the United States has seen such a significant expansion in the power of the federal government that most people do not know or understand that there were once significant restrictions on the government's power.

CHAPTER 28

Constitutional Fidelity: Changing the Tone

As we have seen, the dramatic expansion of executive power and the federal government started in the 1930s under President Franklin D. Roosevelt. The gradual erosion of the separation of powers doctrine found in the Constitution has come in two basic forms. The first is the separation of powers between the various branches of the federal government. This is the area where most constitutional debates have occurred over the last several decades, as the president, Congress, and on rare occasions the Supreme Court have vied with one another for power.

But the more significant area was the encroachment of the federal government on the rights of the states and the people. This is the most fundamental and basic element of the Constitution. That is, the federal government is one of limited power and that all powers not expressly granted to the federal government were reserved for the states and people. The founders made this point in Amendment X (reservation of powers to states) and Amendment IX (reservation of rights for people). So, in the world of social contract theory, the delegation of powers originally went from the people to the various states and then from the states to the federal government. The founders wanted to ensure that the federal government was limited in all respects. The following schematic gives some sense of the distribution of power among the various constituents:

CHART 28-1

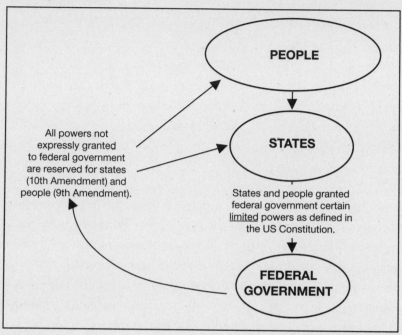

This distinction is critical to understanding how power should be shared in accordance with the Constitution.

Federal Government vs. State Governments

With the expansion of the federal government, the United States has seen a decline in the debate over the constitutionality of legislation. Most politicians have come to accept a federal government of unlimited powers, regardless of what the Constitution provides. In their minds, there is really not much to debate. Unfortunately, this has significant implications. As originally envisaged, our system of government sought to reduce regional squabbles by allowing states and the people to have a high degree of self-determination. The federal government was only to provide certain basic services (e.g., national defense, treaties, coining money, recognizing and enforcing patents, etc.).

While not perfect, this enabled a country with significant regional differences to prosper. Today, we still have many differences in mores and values among the various states and regions, but these differences are increasingly argued at the federal level rather than the state level. This elevates the stakes with regard to these differences, given that any resultant legislation does not impact just one state but all of them. If the battles were fought at the state level, each state could fashion legislation in a manner that best suited its populace. If an individual did not like the result, that person could move to another state that better suited his or her values.

The United States would be better served if Congress, the president, and the Supreme Court recognized that the federal government has limited, enumerated powers, and left the remaining issues to the states and people. Since the Constitution largely left moral issues to the states and the people, most of the "wedge" issues being debated in Washington would instead be debated in statehouses across the land. The result would be less partisanship on Capitol Hill and a country better tailored to the mores and values of its populace.

Deciding Wedge Issues

With that in mind, we should look at a few of the issues that have been hotly debated over the past thirty to forty years and address them in this context.

Abortion. The abortion debate has vocal participants on both the right and left, with the vast majority of Americans being stuck somewhere in the middle. The abortion debate is almost a textbook case of judicial interference into an area that should be reserved for the states and the people, with limited federal involvement. Before *Roe v. Wade,* the controversial Supreme Court decision that legalized abortion throughout the United States, the debate over abortion resided in the various statehouses across the nation. This is where it should be, because no federal issue is at stake. The "right to privacy," a right created out of thin air by the Supreme Court in *Roe*, is nowhere to be found in the Constitution. In fact, the "right to privacy," if such a right exists, should be determined at the state level, not the federal level.

The abortion debate centers on the right of a fetus versus the right of a woman. In the past, debates over social issues were resolved in the state legislatures, where elected representatives knew the mores and values of their constituents. In the case of abortion, depending on the mores of a particular state, laws either tilted toward significant protection of the unborn fetus or toward the protection of women. In more conservative states, the state legislature believed that life begins either at conception or shortly thereafter. Thus, an abortion at almost any juncture represents murder. Taken in this context, a woman's rights were significantly curtailed. She could not have an abortion under most circumstances. In most other states, the issue was much more nuanced. Their legislatures ruled that life did not begin at conception or shortly thereafter, but when the fetus started taking on the signs of being a person. That time ranged from taking on the appearance of a human being to showing signs of human life. These states permitted abortion in the first trimester but significantly curtailed the right thereafter. In the remaining states, a woman's rights significantly outweighed those of the fetus. Here the ability of the fetus to survive outside the womb was the principal issue. Until that time, a woman's right to live her life as she chose was paramount. In these states, abortion was typically permitted, even in late-term pregnancies.

When you boil the arguments down, the principal issue in the abortion debate is the age-old question of when life begins. That is a deeply personal and social issue that differs from person to person and state to state.[1] Within this context the states, not Congress or the federal courts, should make this determination.[2]

Gay Marriage. Like abortion, the issue of gay marriage or civil unions should be fought out in state legislatures across the land. However, unlike abortion, the issue is a bit more complicated. The gay marriage debate relates to the right of people to make contracts and the types of contracts a state will recognize. In most states, people have fairly broad rights to enter into contracts with one another, whether to provide for personal services, goods, marriage (or unions). But states also have a keen interest restricting the types of contracts or relationships into which its citizens enter. In the case of gay marriage, many states will recognize the right of gays to enter into state-sanctioned relationships, whether the relationships are defined as "marriage" or "civil unions." Their citizens believe that homosexuals should have the right to enter into state-recognized relationships. These relationships would confer the same rights and obligations as married heterosexuals, including the right to inherit from a spouse, medical benefits, community property, alimony, etc. In other states, citizens believe that homosexuals should not have these rights.

Again, the issue is best decided in each state, where people can petition their state governments based on their views. Each state legislature will likely find the best fit for the prevailing mores and values of that state. The wonderful thing about federalism is that it is not a one-size-fits-all form of government. The federal government does not dictate, from either the right or the left, but leaves moral and ethical issues to each of the constituent states, where local mores can prevail.

Stem Cell Research. President George W. Bush vetoed the stem cell research bill in 2006, stating that he believed life began at conception and that the bill was, by implication, immoral. Bush was right to veto the bill, but his action was based on the wrong grounds. The question of life is not a federal issue but a state one. So the issue of whether an embryo represents life should not be fought at the federal level. Rather than making a moral statement, President Bush should have said that the federal government had no business supporting such medical research, that this was an overreach by the legislature, and that he was vetoing the bill on constitutional grounds. Bush should have stated that this research should be conducted by the private sector and/or supported by the states. The private sector, whether nonprofits or for-profit institutions, has either a mission or a profit motive for supporting such research. States, if they choose, could support this research because their citizens believe in it or because they want to have a competitive advantage in attracting medical researchers to the state. Indeed, after Bush's veto, an outpouring of state and private sector money financed stem cell research. Stem cell research is booming as a result.

Separation of Powers among Branches of Federal Government: Fostering Accountability

General. The founders believed that the powers delegated by the people and states to the federal government should be clear and that each branch of government should provide a check and balance to the other branches. This was particularly the case with the executive branch, which became stronger under the Constitution (vis-à-vis the Articles of Confederation).

Executive Power, Explicit and Derivative. The Constitution provides each branch of government with certain explicit duties and responsibilities. In the case of the executive, these are found in Section II of the Constitution and include the ability to prosecute wars, enforce laws, and carry out foreign relations. In each case, a considerable amount of the power is largely derivative from powers provided to Congress. The second broad area of executive power is enforcing the laws of the United States. Here, the power of the president is entirely derivative of the power of Congress to enact laws.

At the inception of the Constitution, the powers of Congress were rather limited; that is, limited to the sixteen enumerated powers set forth in the Constitution. Accordingly, the president's power to enforce laws was similarly limited. With the vast expansion of congressional power since the New Deal, the president's power has expanded well beyond that originally contemplated.

In addition to seeing an expansion of executive branch power, the lines have also blurred among the various branches of government. For example, some suggest that the federal judiciary is now legislating from the bench and creating laws or rights from the Constitution where none exist.

The corollary to the notion of checks and balances is that each branch of government has certain constitutional responsibilities (sometimes shared) and should be judged or held accountable based on performance of those duties.

President Harry S. Truman seemed to have acknowledged this when he said, "The buck stops here." This was a simple statement that as chief executive of the government he had constitutional authority and responsibilities and he was not shying away from them. In branding the 80th Congress the "do nothing Congress," Truman laid down the gauntlet for his successful 1948 upset campaign against Thomas Dewey. The campaign highlighted congressional ineptitude, with a focus on holding Congress accountable for its lack of action on legislative matters. Today, the powers of each branch have expanded so greatly and have seeped into the spheres of the other branches, that it is difficult for the members of each branch to distinguish who is responsible for what. There are several good examples.

Iraq. President Bush has repeatedly said that "Congress looked at the same intelligence" as he did in authorizing the war in Iraq. This is not true, yet Congress has done nothing to dispute this notion. As head of the executive branch, the president, not Congress, is responsible for gathering intelligence and analyzing it. The executive branch gathered the intelligence on Iraq, interpreted it, and winnowed it down for Congress. It also conveyed the intelligence not only to Congress but to the public as a whole. The executive branch did not equivocate in the least. It did not acknowledge the uncertain nature of the intelligence. The president and vice president were "certain," leaving no room for doubt. The president then submitted a condensed report to Congress. Congress used this much smaller subset of intelligence to authorize the use of force against Saddam Hussein. It turned out to be wrong. The question is, who is responsible?

The president should have taken full responsibility for the intelligence failures and going to war on a false premise. After all, as the chief executive, he *is* responsible for this country's intelligence community. Congress authorized the use of force based on the intelligence he provided. President Bush has deftly shifted some of the blame for the faulty intelligence to Congress, stating that "Congress looked at the same intelligence." And Congress has let him get away with it, in part, I believe, because it appears very few members of Congress understand that the president, not Congress, is responsible for intelligence. This is not to say that Congress does not share any of the blame for Iraq. It does. It failed to scrutinize the intelligence proffered by the administration or to ask difficult questions. In addition, Congress failed to take its power to declare war seriously, as outlined in a previous chapter.

Judicial Legislation. Another area that has become increasingly problematic over the past fifty to sixty years is judicial activism, or judges "legislating" from the bench. *Roe v. Wade* is a good example. Justice Harry Blackmun created a right—the "right to privacy"—out of thin air, bypassing not only Congress but the state legislatures that had historically determined the balance between the rights of an unborn fetus and the rights of a woman.

To a certain extent, this decision is based on mores and cultural values, which shift from region to region. So rather than allowing the people, through their elected representatives, to decide the matter, the Supreme Court enacted a law from the bench. As a result, countless time and energy has been expended fighting the abortion battle on the national level. Both sides understand the consequences a shift in this law would have on the nation as a whole. These battles should be fought in the statehouses, where the stakes, while high, do not have national implications. The federal government can then focus on those things it does best: defense, foreign relations, etc.

Signing Statements. Signing statements are another area in which the president has overstepped his constitutional boundaries, straying into both the legislative and judicial spheres. A signing statement is a pernicious action on the part of the president. He signs a bill into law but attaches a statement with his comments on the law. Historically, the signing statement has been used sparingly, with presidents using it occasionally to clarify their views on a particular bill. President Bush has used signing statements to a greater extent than all other presidents combined. During his first term he signed five hundred bills into law with a signing statement appended.

In some instances, President Bush indicated that he is signing the bill into law yet believes a portion of the bill is unconstitutional. In these signing statements, he has stated that he will not enforce the unconstitutional portion of the bill. The Constitution does not, however, provide the president with the right to pick and choose what portion of a bill he wants to sign into law or what portion is constitutional. He must either sign the bill into law or not. And, based on his oath of office, if he believes that any part of a bill is unconstitutional, he is duty bound to veto it on those grounds.

By picking and choosing, the president usurps the powers of the legislature by modifying bills that come to his desk. He also encroaches on judicial powers by striking down portions of bills as unconstitutional rather than the bills in their entirety. It is surprising that Congress has allowed President Bush to get away with this obvious infringement on congressional and judicial authority. The practice of signing statements should be challenged in court. It is unconstitutional *per se*.

Declaration of War. As noted previously, the US Congress has largely abdicated its constitutional duty to declare war and has allowed the president increasing rights on this front.

Conclusion

As with the unwritten Roman constitution, the US Constitution has eroded over time, with more power concentrated in the hands of a few men and women in Washington and the executive branch. Since the delineation of rights between the people and the government tends to be a zero-sum game, the people have seen an erosion in their power and rights. There is no good solution to this trend, other than to elect officials who understand and respect the Constitution and are committed to governing in a manner consistent with its words.

Most conservatives believe the solution lies in nominating strict constructionist justices to the Supreme Court. In some ways they are correct. By nominating and confirming justices who respect the separation of powers—and also the delineation of power between the federal government and the states and people—the president and Congress could take a step in the right direction of restoring the constitutional balance of power. But this is merely the first step. The most significant step will be one required of Congress and the executive. Congress has significantly encroached on the power of the states. There must be a recognition of this fact and an effort to reduce the scope of power of Congress vis-à-vis the states. The same holds true of the executive branch.

CHAPTER 29

Congressional Apportionment

The political climate today is toxic and highly partisan but much less so than it was at the founding of the republic. But that does not make the current situation ideal or even desirable. The current political environment is a product of an insulated political class. The reelection rate among incumbent members of the House of Representatives—over 99 percent for incumbents seeking reelection in 2004[1]—is now rivaling that of the Soviet Politburo of old.[2] Worse yet, the number of "landslides" in House races (20% or greater margin of victory) has steadily climbed from 65 percent in 1992 to well over 80 percent in 2002. And the average margin of victory for incumbents was nearly 40 percent in 2002. While some point to campaign finance as the principal reason for the power of the incumbency, I would suggest that an even more powerful influence is at work: gerrymandering.

Gerrymandering

Gerrymandering is as old as the Constitution itself. To an extent, it is a product of the Constitution. As most know, "gerrymandering" is the act, or the "art," of drawing the boundaries of congressional districts in a manner that favors one party (usually the party in power) over another. Since congressional districts are drawn by state legislatures, the party controlling a particular state's legislature has the ability to draw congressional districts in a manner that favors that party. If left unchecked, state legislatures would draw districts in a manner where the majority party would gain a significant number of seats, even if the popular vote of that state was much narrower. Not surprisingly, federal courts have become involved in reviewing the redistricting process. This process occurs every ten years, after the census is published. Challenges to congressional redistricting are often based on the equal protection clause of the Fourteenth Amendment; that is, whether a citizen's right to vote (or the value of his or her vote) has been compromised vis-à-vis other citizens.

State legislatures have become quite adept at meeting the requirements of the Fourteenth Amendment while still achieving the desired goal of using congressional redistricting to favor one political party over another, resulting in an increasingly insulated political ruling class. In some cases, both parties are complicit, as are the courts.[3]

Here is how it works. Assume, for example, that Party A holds a slight majority in the Texas legislature. With this majority, Party A passes a redistricting plan that would give it a majority of seats in the Texas delegation to the US Congress. Most of these seats will be "safe" ones and drawn in such a way that the incumbent is unlikely to lose based on the composition of the district. To ensure that Party B does not object too much, Party A works with Party B to ensure that Party B has a number of very safe seats as well, insulating many of Party B's incumbents in seats that are likely to be won through lopsided votes by the constituents of Party B. Party A also throws in a handful of safe minority seats. The result is an allocation of seats roughly based on party popularity in Texas. The scheme passes constitutional muster, since courts roughly look at the apportionment of seats and number of minority seats in determining whether a redistricting plan comports with the Constitution. The result is a series of congressional districts that are homogeneous from a political standpoint and drawn largely along party lines. In these districts, incumbents have an overwhelming advantage and generally win reelection handily.

These homogeneous districts typically reward incumbents who cater to the prevailing ideology of the district. And, since the districts are homogenous, the incumbents are motivated to vote consistently and ardently along party lines, without compromise. After all, the biggest challenge the incumbent is likely to face is in the primary— if he or she is foolish enough to buck his or her party. Thus, gerrymandering results in a more partisan and ideologically driven Congress. Further, it creates a ruling class largely immune from defeat, unless members vote against their party or are engulfed in a scandal. With the impact of gerrymandering today, the party primary becomes the de facto race for the congressional seat. Since primaries are often won by the candidates who cater to the extreme elements of the party in question, most of the safe seats (about 95% of the total seats) are won by party hard-liners and ideologues. Worse yet, since their districts are drawn in a partisan manner, the candidates have little incentive to compromise or work across the aisle as in years past.

Solution to Gerrymandering

Iowa offers a sound manner to establish congressional districts. Enacted in 1980, Iowa's redistricting process provides that the Iowa legislature is responsible for enacting both state and congressional redistricting plans. With that said, the process is begun by a nonpartisan panel called the Legislative Services Bureau. The bureau is advised by a panel of five citizens. Four are selected by the state legislature. The fifth, the chairman, is selected by these four citizens. While the bureau may consult with the panel, it is not obligated to do so. The bureau must draft a plan based on four criteria, listed in order of importance:

1. population equality,
2. contiguity,

3. unity of counties and cities (maintaining county lines and "nesting" house districts within senate districts and senate districts within congressional districts), and
4. compactness.

The statute prohibits the use of political affiliation, addresses of the incumbents, previous election results, or any demographic information other than population growth. An important part of the process is keeping the public informed. Thus, after the first proposed plan is developed by the bureau, three public hearings are required to be held and citizens can request information from the bureau that outlines proposed district lines. If the legislature does not approve the first three plans offered by the bureau, it must itself approve an alternative plan by September 1, or the state supreme court will take responsibility for the state districts. The governor has veto power over plans, regardless of how they are developed.

The process has worked well. Since it was implemented in 1980, the legislature has accepted most of the bureau's plans. It has done so, even though some of the plans have been less than ideal for certain incumbent state legislative leaders and members of Congress, who are often placed in very competitive districts. The 1991 redistricting plan was approved by a Democratic legislature but was considered to widely favor the Republicans. Ultimately, the Republicans took over the Iowa state legislature and now hold a majority of the congressional seats as well. While this may not be ideal for the incumbent, it reflects the overall fairness of the process, given that in another state the incumbents would control the redistricting process and provide safe seats for themselves. Plans offered by the bureau are sometimes rejected, which happened in 2001. In that year, the legislature rejected the bureau's first plan but adopted its second, even though it placed some Republicans in tough new districts.

The result in Iowa has been a success. Four of Iowa's five congressional districts are relatively balanced between Republicans and Democrats constituents, which provides for competitive House races. In addition, as a result of competitive races, the Iowa congressmen are encouraged to take a more balanced approach to legislation in Washington, rather than taking intractable or highly partisan positions.

Apportionment of Electoral Votes

The current manner of electing presidents, through votes by the Electoral College, has worked reasonably well for nearly 230 years. Under the system, the Electoral College elects the president. Each state appoints electors. The Constitution requires that each state legislature determine how electors are to vote. Accordingly, each state has a law in place that instructs how their electors vote. Most states instruct their electors to vote for the candidate who wins the popular vote in their state. It is important to note that electors are not bound to do so, although it is almost unheard of for them to vote otherwise. If a candidate does not win a majority of the electoral votes across the entire United States, the election is then decided by the House of Representatives.[4]

Since 1789, the House of Representatives has decided only two elections: in 1800 it elected Thomas Jefferson over Aaron Burr, and in 1824 it elected John Quincy Adams over Andrew Jackson (who won the popular vote). Since almost all states apportion their electoral votes in a winner-take-all fashion, one trend has occurred and another is just beginning. The first trend is that since most states lean either Democrat or Republican, the presidential election is now decided among a handful of states that are split fairly evenly. These states include Colorado, Florida, Missouri, New Mexico, Ohio, and Washington. From election to election, others may come into play: Minnesota, Pennsylvania, Virginia, etc. But the vast majority of states are "nonfactors" in the presidential election, given that one party tends to dominate the state.

This means that if you live in Texas, as I do, your vote counts for very little. Texas is solidly Republican for now, and presidential candidates of both parties would be foolish to spend any time there, unless it is to raise money. The same holds true for California and New York, both Democratic strongholds. Thus, the three largest states in the Union are "nonfactors" in presidential elections. Rather than campaigning in any of these states, the candidates spend their time in Florida, Ohio, or other "swing" states, where the presidential election is likely to be decided.

The second trend is just beginning. It is starting in California, where there was a ballot initiative that would allocate the state's electoral votes based on the following: (a) one vote for each congressional district carried by the candidate and (b) two votes (electors relating to the senators) based on a candidate carrying the popular vote in the state. Maine apportions its elector votes in this manner. In isolation, this allocation of electoral votes makes sense. Currently, California is not "in play," so neither party's candidate campaigns there actively during the general election. If California apportions its electors consistent with Maine, suddenly a block of electoral votes frees up for a Republican candidate, making California a relevant state for both Republican and Democratic nominees. However, this creates a problem: it shifts the electoral balance. With California allocating its electoral votes differently than other major states, the electoral map tilts significantly toward a Republican candidate. This is why Republicans favored the California plan and Democrats opposed it. This effort was being undertaken via a state referendum, which would have to be passed by voters. The initiative to put the matter on the ballot failed, but the potential for similar initiatives in the future should be taken seriously since it would change the electoral map considerably.[5]

To avoid the potential for mischief (e.g., the California plan above), a more sensible plan would be to have a consistent manner for each state to allocate its electoral votes. Some believe that the president should be elected based on the popular vote across the United States. However, this flies in the face of the Virginia-Massachusetts compromise, which gives smaller states a modest degree of incremental representation. The Constitution was ratified on this premise, and it should be preserved. Further, it provides a modest incentive for presidential candidates to pay attention to smaller states.

A better system would be to adopt the Maine manner of allocating electoral votes in every state. This preserves the notion that smaller states gain a modest degree of incremental representation and provides each candidate an incentive to campaign in smaller states. However, it also makes voters in states that lean toward one party more relevant during the campaign. Candidates would be forced to campaign in more states, especially if congressional districts were drawn in a more balanced manner (as set forth above). It would also give states with smaller populations—such as Idaho, Montana, New Mexico—a disproportionate say in presidential elections, consistent with the logic of the Great Compromise[6]

PART VII

AMERICA 2020

- ■ Peering through the Looking Glass
- ■ America of Tomorrow

* * *

The purpose of the remaining chapters is to summarize the solutions to America's most pressing problems and paint an optimistic picture, rather than a bleak one, regarding America's future.

CHAPTER 30

Peering through the Looking Glass

Most Americans find some degree of comfort in blaming the politicians in Washington for this nation's problems, which range from immigration to our exploding entitlement system to our reliance on foreign energy. While convenient, the blame lies elsewhere.

Our Extreme Wealth Has Fostered Complacency

The United States is a representative democracy—a republic. The elected officials in Washington are representative of the nation as a whole, as painful as that might be to hear. Americans (me included) like low taxes and tax cuts, generous entitlement programs, and an expansive, national security umbrella. But we are not terribly interested in paying for it. We are more content to borrow the money from China and hand the bill to future generations. After all, if we *were* to pay for it, we would either need to increase taxes or reduce entitlements or national defense, notions contrary to orthodoxies of both political parties.

Republicans believe that tax cuts are the most important plank of the party's domestic agenda and will try to preserve them at all cost, even if it means going into hock to our largest global competitor. On the other hand, Democrats believe the current system of entitlements is sacrosanct and would not dream of touching Social Security or Medicare, although the United States cannot afford either program as currently structured. The dirty little secret is that Democrats, while railing against tax cuts, did little to stop them, and Republicans, while ranting about entitlements, actually expanded them substantially during Bush's first term. Both parties are complicit in the current bout of fiscal mismanagement.

Worse yet, many other problems are quite similar. Energy, for example, lies at the heart of global warming and our current foreign policy morass. Many people lament our reliance on foreign oil, but that does not stop them (including myself) from driving energy inefficient cars, living in larger than needed homes, and flying too much. Further, Americans have exhibited little interest in learning about other areas of the world, or even their own form of government, when doing so would, perhaps, provide them with a better view of foreign policy.

Before being too hard on ourselves, we should understand that America's complacency is largely a product of its extreme success. Just a hundred years ago, many people in this nation were worried about their next meal. Energy issues were largely nonexistent, because many Americans could not afford to adequately heat their homes. Air conditioning did not exist. Foreign policy did not matter much, since the United States was just emerging on the international scene. It was regarded by our more refined European brethren as a bumptious distant cousin—not entirely irrelevant, but not a real player on the international scene.

Much has changed over the past century. Today, starvation is nonexistent in the United States. We live in climate-controlled homes. Our lives are long, and the vast majority of Americans have decent to superlative medical care. And our wars, while gut-wrenching, are not as deadly as they were in the past. The United States has lost approximately 4,500 troops in Iraq and Afghanistan, a terrible loss. But the

US lost about 0.3 percent of its population in World War II and about 2 percent in the Civil War.[1] Adjusted for today's population, the losses would range from 1 million dead (World War II) to 6 million dead (Civil War).

Too Wedded to Orthodoxy

Americans are too wedded to the orthodoxy of their political parties and fail to consider options incongruent with these orthodoxies. Why should our foreign policy be one of nation building and spreading democracy at gunpoint, when most Americans do not particularly like other nations forcing their values on us? Are we safer if we trade and establish diplomatic relations with rogue regimes rather than isolating them? Why do we have military bases and a huge military presence throughout the world when we have two oceans that protect us? Why not focus our military on its historical role of securing our borders?

These are but a few questions that Americans should be asking. They form the basis of this book. It is time for Americans to think differently, even if it is counter to prevailing wisdom. Many believe that our founders represented conservative thought. Nothing is further from the truth. Our founders were radicals. The notion of a republic governed by the people was treasonous to most of the global powers of that era. Our founders gave thought to the important issues of their time rather accepting conventional wisdom, and the world is a better place for it. The next sections briefly outline the reasons why China may or may not eventually overwhelm the United States during the twenty-first century. It provides some reasons why Americans should be optimistic about our ability to compete with China, especially if we address some of our more pressing issues.

The Sino-American Challenge

China is the new emerging power bursting onto the world stage. However, all the talk about the emergence of China ignores one thing: China has been a historical power, boasting one of the largest economies *throughout* history. From AD 1000 to the twentieth century, China ranked as the world's largest economy. This all began to change in the nineteenth and twentieth century.

By 1950, the United States ranked as the world's largest economy, while China had experienced a sharp reversal. This trend continued throughout the remainder of the twentieth century and into the twenty-first, with the US economy easily surpassing those of the rest of the world.

Despite the United States' hegemony, China has gained ground, starting in the 1970s and 1980s. This growth accelerated sharply after the fall of the Bamboo Curtain, the most virulent form of Communism. With capitalism taking hold, China has grown rapidly over the past several years, with its economy generating growth of 10 to 11 percent of GDP per annum. The United States, long the fastest-growing *developed* nation, has grown at a respectable 3 percent per annum over recent years. By some measures, China has caught up to Germany and the United Kingdom in terms of economic strength, though one study shows a much smaller China, a point discussed below. Regardless of the study, one fact remains clear: China is booming and set to challenge America's dominance within the lifetime of many readers of this book.

China's emergence is giving rise to the notion that the twenty-first century might well be the "Sino century," one in which China will dominate the world both economically and perhaps even militarily. However, Americans should not view China's reemergence with resignation. China will prove the United States' greatest global competitor over the next several decades. Yet Americans should understand that we can compete with China, especially if we address some important problems in the manner set forth above.

The Lessons of Japan

Historian Paul Kennedy's book *The Rise and Fall of the Great Powers* outlines the life cycle of the great empires of the past five hundred years. These great empires see their military obligations expand and become more costly. Ultimately, their economy is not big enough to fund their military and domestic commitments and they have to borrow heavily to sustain them. Due to heavy borrowings, these nations see their economic and military might slip and see other, more fiscally responsible powers take their place. The most recent example is the decline of the British Empire and the emergence of America.

Over the long term, Professor Kennedy's thesis is sound; history provides no exception. My guess is that the United States will prove no such exception. The critical question to me is not whether the US may *eventually* decline, but whether it can maintain its primacy for some time to come. I believe that it can, even against China. When Professor Kennedy wrote his book, Japan was viewed much as China is today. Many people were almost resigned to the fact that Japan would "own" the United States. The Japanese went on a buying spree in the US, snapping up trophy assets. This added to the unease of many Americans. Japanese industry was the envy of the world. Its economic growth was staggering, and its companies were considered the best in the world. It was redefining capitalism with cozy, close-knit relationship with banks, manufacturers, and their suppliers. *Keiretsu*, the Japanese word for these relationships, became a standard staple of learning in US business schools, including the one I attended. Many Americans were convinced that Japan would soon rule the world.

Of course, shortly thereafter, Japan went into a steep decline from which it is now just emerging. At the same time, the United States began a decade-and-a-half surge. Concerns about Japan melted away. However, reviewing some of the reasons for Japan's rise and decline may offer some lessons about China's ascendancy and some of the problems it might encounter going forward. Japan's deep recession was caused by several things, two of which are worth noting. First, the much-admired *keiretsu* system was not as efficient as most thought. During the boom time, Japanese banks made loans to property speculators, business owners, and others who were not underwritten appropriately. Many of the loans were influenced by the relationships underpinning the *keiretsu* system rather than sound underwriting principles. This resulted in a misallocation of resources; that is, loans were made on inflated real estate values and to companies that were not credit worthy. The Japanese government and people were not willing to write off these loans and take the short-term pain associated with them. The loans stayed on the balance sheets of banks for years, even decades. Sick banks and companies were allowed to survive and compete with healthier ones, creating a stagnant business climate. In addition to the *keiretsu* system, the Japanese government, through the Ministry of International Trade and Industry, directed investment in Japanese industry and did not allow competition in many of its industries. And, through subtle coercion, many Japanese companies were forced to do business with one another.

So the root of the problem stemmed from a misallocation of resources due to state interference in business activities. Unfortunately for Japan, the length and depth of the recession was also likely due to government interference. In particular, rather than allowing the markets to direct the flow of capital and force the write-off of many of these bad loans and investments, the Japanese government intervened with easy monetary and fiscal policy. On the monetary policy side, the Bank of Japan began flooding the market with cheap money. The Japanese central bank cut interest rates to 0.5 percent in hopes of stimulating economic activity and propping up sick businesses. At the same time, the Japanese government began deficit spending in hopes of "priming the pump" of economic growth, causing public debt to spiral out of control. Japan's credit rating sank from AAA to an unheard of A2, the same as Botswana in 2001.[2] To make matters worse, Japan now faces with a demographic time bomb. While war, famine, or pestilence are common reasons for a decline in population, Japan recently became the first country to see its population decline as a result of demographic changes.

Despite these challenges and mistakes, Japan is fortunate. It is an industrialized country with a high GDP per capita and savings rate. These two factors make Japan's demographic problems—that is, its aging population—more manageable. It has the social welfare infrastructure in place to ease the burden of an aging population. Further, since Japan has invested heavily in sophisticated manufacturing and technology, workers can remain productive for longer periods of time, since the manual component of the labor force is relatively small. The United States, on the other hand emerged from its decade-and-a-half period of malaise in 1982, beginning a resurgence that lasted until 2000. Not coincidentally, this expansion rode the demographic wave caused by the baby boomer generation and technology innovations driven by American entrepreneurs. Focused more on manufacturing than innovation, Japan lagged far behind America in the development of new technologies that fueled the boom in America during the 1990s.

Like Japan, the United States suffered through a real estate bubble during the late 1980s and early 1990s. Unlike Japan, America worked through the crisis. The US government, forced bad banks out of business, and banks were forced to write off hundreds of billions of bad loans. This allowed sound banks and businesses to move forward and forced sick ones to go out of business. While Darwinian, the process worked, as evidenced by the US economic recovery and strength of the 1980s and 1990s. Quite simply, America's adherence to a market-driven economy provided its principal competitive advantage over Japan during the 1990s. It may, along with sounder governmental policy, provide the same fuel in its battle against China in the years to come.

China

Today, China is reminiscent of Japan of yesteryear. Its manufacturing base is expanding rapidly, and it is generating staggering growth through an export-driven model focusing on the United States as its market of choice. Like Japan, China has amassed large holdings of US dollar assets to keep its currency weak against the dollar and make its exports cheaper for Americans. Further, China has a great deal of governmental interference in its economy. Actually, China's government is much more involved in the development of its economy than Japan's government was. The result may well be similar to that of Japan: a big crash.

Governmental Interference. The misallocation of resources in China is thought to be staggering. No one knows for sure, since China provides little information on government activities. Real estate development and speculation has reached levels like those found in Japan during the 1980s. Loans and investments are being made by banks at the direction of the government, which controls the banks. This governmental interference has likely resulted in a misallocation of resources on a grand scale.

Some believe that for every dollar of foreign reserves accumulated by the Chinese government, the Chinese banks have a dollar's worth of bad debt on their balance sheets. That equates to nearly $1.4 trillion worth of bad debt, a staggering total. And it is unlikely that the Chinese will be any more willing than the Japanese to write this debt off anytime soon. At the same time, China is seeing the value of its dollar holdings decline due to a weakening dollar and it is also seeing its banks accumulate more bad debt. In the end, some or all of this debt will have to be written off.

The equity markets may also struggle and correct. Because the Chinese government controls both industry and the stock markets, it dictates the terms and conditions for equity investments in China. These are likely being made at prices that make little sense and/or in companies that do not merit the investment. The Chinese government is trying to "cool" the economy and investment fervor by raising interest rates, placing restrictions on investments, and raising reserve and capital requirements for banks. However, these measures have taken little steam out of the mania gripping the country. With a savings rate approaching 40 percent, the Chinese are now directing their money to the stock market and property holdings, much like the Japanese two decades before them.

And, like Japan before it, China is experiencing a bubble driven by governmental interference. The government directs which companies can go public and limits investment in these companies. This limits supply and inflates prices. Many of these companies are state owned and do not have transparent financial statements. Finally, Chinese cannot easily invest abroad, leading to them piling money into Chinese stocks and real estate. So with both Chinese and foreign capital being directed into just a handful of issues, China's stock market has soared, with valuations reaching Internet bubble (1980s Japan) levels. Indeed, the Chinese market surged by over 90 percent in 2007, following strong gains in 2005 and 2006. Ominously, it has sold off in 2008. This may be a portent of things to come. As with most emerging markets, China will go through periods of boom and bust, with a general upward trend. China is due for a crash, and it could be a significant one. Like the Japanese government, China might not allow the market system to work through the resultant mess. Instead, it may exacerbate the crash through governmental measures that often make matters worse, not better.

Demographic Problems. China has significant demographic issues. In what may be one of the biggest blunders of central planning in history, China adopted a "one-child policy" in 1980. Under this policy, the Chinese government mandated that couples could only have one child, which has resulted in a demographic nightmare. Whereas at one time China had an almost unlimited supply of people, particularly young ones, the trend will start reversing sharply by the mid twenty-first century. Based on current projections, China will have a *shrinking population by 2050*, rather than a growing one.

So, like Japan, China will face an aging population in the future. However, Japan's demographic problems are somewhat mitigated by the fact that it has a developed and industrialized society. Japan's wealth makes it possible for its population to age without there being a significant amount of dislocation. China, on the other hand, generates about $2,000 of GDP per capita. Even if China grows at 8 percent per year for the next forty-two years, it will still significantly lag the rest of the industrialized world in wealth per capita. So China may be the first country in history to age before it fully industrializes.

The United States and Japan have, to varying degrees, seen their citizens save enough for retirement. Even though China's savings rate is profound, the total amount being saved is relatively paltry. So rather than investing in infrastructure over the next forty years, China may well have to focus its savings on the retirement of 600 million Chinese, which will make the retirement of America's 80 million baby boomers pale in comparison. This problem will be compounded if China, like Japan before it, has a crash and a lengthy recession when this generation is nearing retirement. That is, if China goes into a ten-year recession after this period of euphoria, China would face a demographic problem without the resources necessary to address it. I doubt that China will go through the lengthy recession that Japan did, but Chinese policymakers have to start planning for the retirement of hundreds of millions of Chinese. They must provide for them, since most of them grew up during the Communist era and have greater expectations of the government.

Environmental and Natural Resource Issues. China, thus far, has been given a free pass on environmental problems fostered by its staggering growth. It is using coal and other fossil fuels for power generation, much like the United States and others. In addition, China is seeing extreme growth in the number of automobiles on the road. The anticipated growth in energy consumption, particularly of oil, is placing strains on the world's oil supplies and also accelerating global warming. With a large population and very few controls, China's pollution is the worst in the world.

China is addressing these impending shortages by securing vast amounts of natural resources from nations across the world, including rogue nations that the United States will not conduct business with (e.g., Iran). Not only is this providing China with access to supply, it is also providing it with growing influence in the developing world. However, the damage being done to the environment by China's growth is being increasingly noted by the West. Alone among major industrial powers, the United States has balked, along with China, at efforts by Europe and others to reduce emissions and global warming. The United States' position has given China much-needed cover to continue with its energy consumption and acquisition of energy supplies.

Inflation. Food Shortages. China is facing surging energy and food costs, fueling inflation. Inflation is eroding the purchasing power of its citizens and placing an onerous burden on its massive and largely impoverished population. This is particularly true of rural provinces, where wages do not rise as quickly as they do in the cities. China is taking steps to reduce inflation. One of the more effective steps would be to allow the yuan to appreciate more against the dollar. The risk here is significant: a slowdown, or worse, in its export-driven economy. If that were to occur, China might see unemployment rise in the cities and factories, and substitute unrest in the rural areas with the same in the cities.

Conclusion. China's growth has been nothing less than astounding, and it appears that nothing can stop it from becoming the world's leading industrial power. However, below the surface, China faces challenges in the decades to come. Most of these challenges will result from its government's significant role in driving the Chinese economy. These challenges include demographic issues, a result of the government's one-child policy.

Another issue relates to state-owned directives on investment, which dictate where capital will be allocated. In the history of modern economies, no major economy has emerged with such a strong degree of central planning. Ultimately, the government will either allocate resources inefficiently or in accordance with the demands of the people. In either case, bubbles will result and crashes will occur.

Finally, China lacks transparency; its government and companies do not provide as reliable statistics or data as the West. Investors are left to guess about the financial statements of the Chinese government and Chinese companies. While the Chinese government and many of these companies are likely healthy, there is no way of knowing for sure.

CHAPTER 31

America of Tomorrow

America will look very different in 2020 than today. We will either be in a position to maintain our global economic supremacy, ensuring the standard of living that most Americans not only desire but demand. Or, we will see our competitive position eroded and Americans' standard of living in decline along with it. The choices we make today and in the years to come will have a strong bearing on which direction America ultimately takes. By adopting the main proposals I've outlined in this book, I believe the United States can maintain its competitive advantage over China and other global competitors well into the future. But to do so, America must ensure that its economic base is strong and growing. Without that, Americans will see not only their standard of living decline, but also national security compromised as it struggles to pay mounting defense costs with a declining economic base. America's changing demographics, addiction to debt, and profound lack of prioritization relating to government spending come into play in reworking its immigration policies and restructuring its finances. Along with a reformulation of energy and foreign policy, these changes should place the United States on sound economic and national security footing well into the future.

Changing Demographics; Immigration

America has a significant competitive advantage over China and Europe: a growing population due to strong inflows of human capital from immigration. While the United States has to control its borders, immigration should remain America's great "free lunch," a transfer of wealth from emerging markets to the US of between $225 billion to $600 billion per annum. Immigration provides a central plank to shore up our tax base and our competitive advantage over other nations. Because of its immigration policies, the United States can expect a growing population through 2050. With that growing population, America we will become a "younger" country relative to many of its competitors.

Today, America's population is about 23 percent the size of China's. By 2050, America's population will be about 35 percent its size. Immigration has provided the United States with this demographic luxury. But we cannot be complacent. Other countries, notably Germany, have learned that the battles of the twenty-first century will be fought over not only increasingly scarce natural resources, but also over increasingly scarce human capital. Accordingly, Germany is developing plans to increase its immigration to support its aging population. We should expect other countries to follow suit. By virtue of its pluralistic and dynamic society, the United States has a huge competitive advantage on this front, but it should not be taken for granted. We thus must adopt the most liberal immigration policies in the world as soon as practicable if we intend to create an even more dynamic economy and a population base that will be the envy of the industrialized world.

A growing population will not only supply this nation with the labor it needs for economic growth, it will also provide an enhanced tax base to support a growing number of retirees and shore up Social Security and Medicare. By taxing the current 13 million illegal immigrants in this nation, the United States could generate approximately $50 billion per annum in additional tax revenues, which could help shore up Social Security well into the future.

Fiscal and Monetary Policy

America's finances are a mess. By most measures, the federal government is bankrupt. Until recently, the US government has showed a budget picture that was improving and deficits that were relatively modest. In doing so, the president and Congress passed a $150 billion "stimulus" package. Unfortunately, the budget picture provided by the president and Congress to the American public is more misleading than the one provided by Enron to its shareholders. By using a series of accounting gimmicks, the federal deficit for 2007 was cast as "only" $162 billion, about 1.5 percent of GDP and well below the thirty-year average. However, if you accrued for future costs under Social Security and Medicare, the budget deficit would have been over $4 trillion in 2007, or about 30 percent of GDP. Americans must hold the president and Congress to the same standards as corporate America and require our politicians to provide all Americans with reliable information on the state of this nation's finances.

Toward this end, I have proposed a constitutional amendment that would require Congress and the president to publish financial statements in the same manner as corporate America (no more financial gimmicks). The amendment would subject Congress and the president to the same penalties as corporate chieftains if they lied about the financial condition of this nation. Each American would receive the nation's financial statements on an annual basis. Armed with this information, Americans could begin the process of establishing spending priorities and developing a more cogent, pro-growth tax system. Toward this end, America should dramatically reform its tax system. The current system is far too complex. This complexity results in high compliance costs, tax avoidance, and distorts economic activity. Rates for a new, dramatically simplified system would be set to generate a targeted amount of revenues, say 20 percent of GDP. This is slightly higher than our current revenues. But then again, we are running deficits.

The new code would eliminate corporate taxes altogether, in recognition that this tax is not paid by corporations but is largely "passed" to consumers in the form of higher prices. Thus, the corporate tax falls more heavily on the poor, who tend to spend a higher percentage of their earnings on goods and services. Further, our corporate tax system, which has among the highest rates in the world, imposes a higher cost structure on American corporations. By eliminating corporate taxes, America's companies would be more competitive, keeping more jobs at home. Corporate tax revenues would be replaced by taxes on illegal immigrants, a carbon tax, and a tariff on oil imported from outside the NAFTA region.

The centerpiece of the new tax regime would be a dramatically simplified tax system for individuals, covering all their tax liabilities (personal, Social Security, and Medicare). There would be three tax rates on income, with the highest being capped at 40 percent. The working poor would pay no taxes at all. The system would eliminate all but three income tax deductions: interest on home mortgages, retirement savings, and a tax credit for children. The estate tax would be reformed to eliminate double taxation on estates by treating them as effective sales from the deceased to his or her heirs. And the tax rate on capital gains and dividends would be kept low to promote capital formation and investment.

Once we had a more rational system to *raise* revenues, we would need a more sensible way to allocate resources, while keeping the national debt within reasonable bounds. To do so, we would need to prioritize spending and learn to adhere to targets for overall indebtedness based on whether the nation is at peace or war. During peacetime, the United States should focus on reducing its debt as a percentage of GDP to some range between 50 and 70 percent of GDP, a manageable level. This would provide the United States with flexibility to increase debt during times of crisis or war, as we did during World War II when the debt grew from about 50 percent to well over 100 percent of GDP. Currently, our national debt is anywhere from 70 percent of GDP (fudged numbers) to 400 percent of GDP if calculated in accordance with GAAP (insolvency).

The US Congress and president would then allocate tax dollars in a more efficient manner based on national priorities. By reducing its military presence across the globe, the United States can, over time, reduce its military budget significantly. Further, the restructuring of Social Security and Medicare would dramatically slow the increase in spending contemplated under both these entitlement programs. Assuming this plan started in 2010 (cuts occurring over ten years thereafter) and assuming 3 percent GDP growth after inflation, the United States could reduce its national debt to 60 percent of GDP by 2020 and bring its budget into balance by 2020. By this time, America would have the strongest balance sheet of any major industrialized nation. By maintaining a relatively low debt load, the dollar would remain strong and one of the world's reserve currencies, providing Americans with a higher standard of living and a competitive advantage over its competitors.

Like fiscal policy, monetary policy should be radically reformed. Currently, the Federal Reserve sets short-term rates: the Fed Funds rate (the rate at which banks make loans to one another). Accordingly, central planning plays an important role in setting the cost of the most ubiquitous of all commodities: the price of money. In particular, the Fed Funds rate influences short-term interest rates (in effect, the cost of money) of almost all stripes, including mortgages, consumer credit, business loans, etc. It should come as no surprise that the Federal Reserve has failed in its attempt to appropriately price money, just as central planners have historically failed in their attempts to price other commodities. The latter part of the Greenspan era was punctuated by easy money policies that were analogous to those of the inflationary late 1960s and 1970s. To avert recession, Greenspan cut short-term rates to at or below 0 percent (after inflation) and held them there for nearly four years. Housing prices and other asset values soared because of plentiful cheap money. Once the

Federal Reserve raised rates to more normal levels and market participants started repricing risk (starting in 2006), asset values started collapsing shortly thereafter.

Today, the Federal Reserve is trying in vain to support collapsing asset values through yet more easy monetary policy. This time it will not work. Asset values will continue their free fall until they are reduced to fair value. Further, the Federal Reserve can lower rates to o percent and it will not help much. Asset values will continue to fall until they reach fair value. Thus, they have much further to fall. Banks will be reticent to loan money until they are finished writing off bad loans from the credit bubble. And consumers will start to save more, as they see their biggest asset (housing) fall in value and are faced with having to reduce their own debt loads. Hence, the chickens of easy monetary policy have come home to roost. The tonic to fix the problem is not more easy monetary policy, which will only prove inflationary. The cure is quite simple. It lies in allowing the market to establish short-term interest rates, just as it does long-term rates. While imperfect, the market has proven superior to central planning over time, and it is not as prone to political influence as are central bankers and central planners.

Although the Federal Reserve would not set short-term rates in this new framework, it would maintain a prominent role in monetary policy. Its mandate would be changed. Rather than focusing on maintaining high long-term employment and low inflation, which are often contradictory policy objectives, the Federal Reserve would focus on making sure that the US banking system was strong and that there was adequate liquidity for it. In doing so, the Federal Reserve would focus to a greater extent on asset inflation and deflation and use the banks' capital ratios and margin lending requirements to address asset bubbles or asset deflation.

In particular, if asset values rose or fell too quickly, the Federal Reserve would use a sliding scale to increase the capital requirements for banks or margin requirements for investors. This would have a more targeted effect of reducing liquidity in the market, and vice versa. In addition, the Federal Reserve could use its balance sheet to provide liquidity (loans) to banks facing a seizure of credit, as it has with its Treasury Auction and Securities Auction Facilities. Pursuant to these facilities, the Federal Reserve, which loans treasuries to banks that post less liquid securities as collateral. Also, if interbank lending freezes and interbank loan rates spike, the Federal Reserve should guarantee interbank loans for a fee. This will drive down interbank loan rates to more normal levels during times of crisis. Finally, the Federal Reserve, as a quasi-independent body, should also provide the markets with the most important financial data and statistics. In doing so, the Federal Reserve would take this very important role from the US government, which has a conflict of interest in providing such data.

Ultimately, the market should dictate the cost of money, based on supply and demand characteristics. Bubbles and inflation should be less prevalent, especially if the Federal Reserve uses capital and margin requirements to tamp down asset inflation or avoid asset deflation.

Energy and the Environment

As the largest emitter of greenhouse gases, the United States should take immediate steps to reduce them by imposing a carbon emission tax on all forms of carbon-based energy (the equivalent of $15 per barrel) and install a floor on the price of oil of $80 per barrel. We should also reduce our reliance on Middle Eastern oil by imposing a tariff on oil imported from nations outside the NAFTA region (e.g., $25 per barrel). This would recover a portion of the cost of maintaining a military presence in the Middle East. If America's defense costs in the region decline (as proposed), the tax would decline proportionately.

Further, domestic energy producers would have a more level playing field vis-à-vis Middle Eastern producers, which require a US military umbrella and should have to pay for it through a tariff on their production. Alternative energy would have a further price advantage over producers of fossil fuels if carbon emissions and the damage done to the environment associated with them were appropriately priced.

Finally, a floor on the price of oil would provide domestic producers and alternative energy solutions and technologies with the ability to plan and make capital expenditures. They could invest without fear that oil prices would fall precipitously.

The United States should focus on conservation as well. Obviously, higher prices would stunt demand growth. In addition to the strong influence of the market, the US should continue to impose energy conservation requirements on cars, homes, electric appliances, lightbulbs, etc. On the power generation front, we should *immediately* start a transition to nuclear power.

The last leg of the energy and environmental policy would be to promote research and development on an electric car. This "Energy Manhattan Project"— either financed or encouraged by the federal government—would bring together scientists across the nation in one locale to explore the promise of battery technology. If we found a battery technology that was cost effective, we would in effect have cut the Gordian knot so long as long as we got everyone behind nuclear energy, including the environmentalists. This "grand bargain" would eliminate the need to import foreign oil over the next twenty years and dramatically cut our carbon emissions within the next ten.

The world would watch the US commitment on this front. If we dramatically reduced the amount of fossil fuels consumed by 2030, the world would follow. Further, if we developed new technologies for solar, wind, and other forms of clean energy, we could become the global leader in "green" technologies, which would drive industry, jobs, and exports.

Foreign Policy. The United States needs to reclaim its proud tradition of an active foreign policy based on engagement, economic trade, and avoiding conflicts that are not in our national interest. The current generation of American policymakers will have to think differently about foreign policy and recapture the grand foreign policy tradition of George Washington. Washington advocated direct engagement with our enemies, a tack followed by Richard Nixon (China), Ronald

Reagan (USSR), Bill Clinton (Vietnam), and George W. Bush (Libya) to much success. It offers the surest path to a more stable world. Through engagement and trade, the United States will be in a much better position to influence rogue states than we are now.

There are several specific crisis spots that must be resolved. In Iraq, the United States should put a plan in place to provide for post-surge stability, one that requires cooperation from nations in the region, including major world powers and even Iran. The United States should recommend that Iraq be partitioned along ethnic and cultural lines. As for the countries that emerged after Yugoslavia's dissolution, there may be short-term pain. However, in the long term, the result will be three nations, each of which will have a relatively common cultural, ethnic, and religious composition. As with the splintering of Yugoslavia, the result will be greater stability in the region.

On the Israel–Palestinian issue, the United States should convene a regional peace conference that calls for restoring the pre-1967 borders of Israel, and for a shared capital of Jerusalem. A provision will also have to be made for some land swapping between the two sides. All Arab states and Iran will have to recognize Israel's right to exist and recognize Israel diplomatically. Critical to the success of such a conference would be a major aid package to both countries, with Arab nations and other world powers contributing. The anticipated $6 billion in aid would be split between Israel and Palestine, but each would be required to spend their money with the states that contributed, in proportion to the amounts of the percentages contributed.

By reclaiming its proud foreign policy tradition, the United States can offer the rest of the world strong leadership, a commitment to democracy, and economic prosperity, in sharp contrast to other emerging powers.

Military Policy

A new foreign policy would tie neatly into a reconfigured military that would not span the globe, as it did during the Cold War era. The new military would be smaller, more nimble, and better able to fight the battles of the twenty-first century.

By closing bases and reducing the number of military personnel stationed overseas, the United States would save money that could be used to reduce our massive budget deficits. Historically, the US has used its natural barriers, the Atlantic and Pacific Oceans, to its benefit. During the nineteenth century, the US military guarded the borders and established forts throughout the nation to guard civilians.

The newly configured US military would play a similar role today. The US military could secure our borders from illegal entry, consistent with the new, expanded immigration policy, and provide better security for strategic assets. In doing so, the United States would dramatically reduce the risk most Americans are concerned about: a terrorist attack on American soil. Isn't this the age-old rationale for a military?

The United States would still have bases abroad, but the bases would be strategically located in just a few troubled areas: the Far East, Indian Ocean, and Turkey, or the new Kurdish state on former Iraqi territory. This would give the US the ability to protect its interests in these theaters and provide ports for the US navy.

Part and parcel of America's military strategy would be maintaining its nuclear arsenal, a cost-effective deterrent to conventional war. US foreign policy would be noninterventionist but not passive. If a nation were harboring terrorists, that state could be subject to strikes from US bases either in the Middle East or Far East. In the unlikely event of a large-scale conventional war, the smaller US military could fight until troops were raised, either through an enlistment effort or conscription (as was the case in World War II). The new military would be more effective in fighting the foes of the twenty-first century and would do so at a much reduced cost—e.g., at 3 percent of GDP rather than 5 percent. The net result would be lower taxes and a better-protected country.

Maintaining the Republic

The US Constitution was set up to provide maximum freedom for the people and for most matters to be solved by local and state governments, rather than the federal government. The intention was to ensure that people could develop their talents and skills and improve their lives with as little governmental interference as possible, while still maintaining a degree of social order. The final aspect to ensuring that America is well run is to remain faithful to its constitution—and take the admonitions of our founders seriously. Americans should invest the time and energy necessary to gain a renewed understanding of this document, which can be regarded as the nation's "business plan." While not perfect, it provides the best plan ever devised for a government. The onus for understanding and acting on it falls on the American people, not the politicians. Once we demand that politicians follow the Constitution, they will.

Challenging Our Orthodoxies. Grand Bargains

If you have made it this far, you have probably agreed with some of my assessments and been uncomfortable with others. Indeed, in the years to come, Americans will be faced with choices that may run contrary to long-held beliefs and prejudices. Environmentalists may have to consider nuclear power as the only viable near-term option to global warming. Liberals will also have to accept that drilling along the coasts and in ANWR are near-term imperatives. Conservatives have to accept the realities of global warming as something beyond the fantasy of a few "tree huggers." They may even be required to accept a broad plan to develop an electric car to wean ourselves off Middle Eastern oil. Conservatives will also have to understand that allocating the cost of our Middle Eastern military presence to imported oil is grounded in classical economic theory and basic cost accounting. Also, that taxing carbon emissions is necessary to reduce greenhouse emissions and combat global warming.

Americans as a whole may have to come to grips with the contradiction between having low taxes and an expansive social infrastructure. Conservatives will have to accept that a death tax based on taxing the untaxed portion of an estate is fair and a wise way to raise revenues. Liberals will have to actually consider that taxing corporations is anticompetitive and regressive. Conservatives will have to come to grips with the idea that the US military cannot maintain bases throughout the world without subjecting the United States to the same fate as all other superpowers that overextend themselves militarily. Liberals, however, will have to accept that with this smaller military, the US would be foolish to give up its nuclear deterrent and its research on a missile defense.

Finally, the politicians in Washington may have to deal with the unpleasantness of telling Americans the truth about the state of this nation's finances. They should become subject to criminal prosecution just as executives at public companies are, if they lie to Americans about the state of this nation's finances.

Amazingly, none of these choices, in isolation or as a whole, require extreme sacrifices on the part of the American public, as long as we undertake them soon. Taxes would not have to go up dramatically, if at all. While Americans might have to save a little more for retirement, they would still have access to a pension and health care safety net if something went awry. Nevertheless, the choices are difficult, because they require us to challenge our own preconceptions, prejudices, and orthodoxies. Yet Americans have a proud heritage of challenging conventional wisdom and accepted orthodoxies, of striking well-reasoned compromises for the national good.

Over two hundred years ago, our founders challenged the prevailing wisdom of the time: the divine right of kings to rule over the people. In doing so, they developed a radical new form of government, considered liberal and treasonous by conventional orthodoxies of that era. Our founders documented their unorthodox views first in the Declaration of Independence and then in a document intended to govern a group of disparate and independent states, the Constitution. The adoption of this brilliant plan of government was the product of the Great Compromise and series of smaller ones along the way.

Notes

Introduction

1. Without question, the United States has faced other serious crises during its existence, ranging from the War of 1812 to the depressions throughout the nineteenth century to the Cold War. With the exception of the War of 1812, none of these threatened our very existence as a country or our way of life.

Chapter 1: The Powder Keg: An Explosion of US Debt

1. http://news.bbc.co.uk/2/hi/business/1626932.stm
2. http://www.heritage.org/Research/Economy/wm1204.cfm
3. http://www.cato.org/pubs/tbb/tbb-0510-26.pdf
4. http://finance.sympatico.msn.ca/investing/insight/article.aspx?cp-documentid=5750084
5. http://finance.sympatico.msn.ca/investing/insight/article.aspx?cp-documentid=5750084
6. $4 trillion GAAP deficit, divided by $13 trillion GDP (2006 estimate). https://www.cia.gov/library/publications/the-world-factbook/print/us.html
7. http://www.csmonitor.com/2008/0128/p01s04-usec.html
8. http://frwebgate.access.gpo.gov/cgi-bin/getdoc.cgi?dbname=110_cong_public_laws&docid=f:publ185.110
9. http://www.newyorkfed.org/markets/omo/dmm/fedfundsdata.cfm
10. http://www.newyorkfed.org/markets/omo/dmm/fedfundsdata.cfm
11. http://www.hsh.com/natmo2000.html
12. http://www.hsh.com/natmo2005.html

13. http://www.benengebreth.org/archives/2005/06/housing_priceto.php

14. http://www.swans.com/library/art14/mdolin31.html

15. http://www.iie.com/research/topics/hottopic.cfm?HotTopicID=9

16. http://www.chinadaily.com.cn/bizchina/2007-11/29/content_6287492.htm

17. http://www.eia.doe.gov/emeu/steo/pub/special/high-oil-price.html

18. http://www.uofaweb.ualberta.ca/chinainstitute/nav03.cfm?nav03=
47258&nav02=43884&nav01=43092

19, http://hubbert.mines.edu/news/Simmons_02-1.pdf

20. http://www.simmonsco-intl.com/files/ASPO%20World%20Conf.pdf

21. http://www.eia.doe.gov/emeu/international/reserves.xls

22. http://www.news.cornell.edu/stories/july05/ethanol.toocostly.ssl.html

23. http://www.ers.usda.gov/Briefing/Wheat/2008baseline.htm

24. http://www.ag.ndsu.edu/news/columns/livestockma/market-advisor-will-
2007-cattle-price-volatility-continue-in-2008

25. http://www.usatoday.com/money/industries/energy/2005-10-10-iraq-oil-
usat_x.htm

26. http://www.timesonline.co.uk/tol/news/world/iraq/article3285580.ece

27. http://www.fxstreet.com/fundamental/analysis-reports/energy-iran-forward-
curves-and-forecasts/2006-06-22.html

28. http://www.csmonitor.com/2008/0310/p16s01-wmgn.html

29. http://www.iranfocus.com/en/index.php?option=com_content&task=
view&id=6606

30. http://www.house.gov/jec/studies/2007/Straight%20of%20Hormuz%20Study.pdf

31. http://www.gpoaccess.gov/usbudget/fy04/pdf/hist.pdf. The deficits surged
from $1.5 billion in 1965, when the budget was roughly in balance, to nearly $25
billion in 1968. In 1969, the budget was "miraculously" balanced. However, the
"balanced" budget of 1969 was achieved due to President Johnson's decision in 1968
to include Social Security and all other trust funds in a "unified budget"
(http://www.ssa.gov/history/BudgetTreatment.html).

32 http://www.theatlantic.com/doc/200511u/nj_crook_2005-11-08

33. http://www.bloomberg.com/apps/news?pid=20601087&sid=
aHBPDpMwyUMI&refer=home

34. http://www.economist.com/opinion/displaystory.cfm?story_id=10215040

35. Yields on ten-year TIPs are generally around 2 percent plus inflation, which
would equate to an approximately 2 percent real rate of return for ten-year risk-free
notes (http://seekingalpha.com/article/65832-10-year-tips-vs-10-year-treasury-
which-is-the-better-choice.)

36. http://www.ukrainianjournal.com/index.php?w=article&id=6519
http://www.reuters.com/article/economicNews/idUSL203860120070520

37. http://www.telegraph.co.uk/money/main.jhtml?xml=/money/2007/08/07/
bcnchina107a.xml

38. http://data.ebonds.info//comments/31723/WhatDoesIt

MeantoBeaTrippleASovereign.pdf39. One credit rating service has indicated that unless the United States gets its entitlement programs under control, US government debt could face a downgrade over the long term.

39. http://www.reuters.com/article/bondsNews/idUSN1017237120080110
40. http://www.slate.com/id/2192377/

Chapter 2: The Economics of Demographics

1. Naohiro Ogawa and Rikiya Matsukura, "The Role of Older Persons' Changing Health and Wealth in an Aging Society: The Case of Japan," *United Nations Expert Group Meeting on the Implications of Changing Population Age Structure* (New York, NY and Mexico City, Mexico: Population Division, Department of Economic and Social Affairs, United Nations Secretariat: 31 August 31–September 2, 2005), 5.

2. BBC News World Asia-Pacific, "China's Aging Population," BBC News Online. Available from: http://news.bbc.co.uk/2/hi/asia-pacific/906114.stm. Internet; accessed April 1, 2007.

3. Since 1994, the United Nations Population Division has used the year 2050 in its most cited projections. Ben J. Wattenberg, *Fewer: How the New Demography of Depopulation Will Shape Our Future* (Chicago, IL: Ivan R. Dee, 2004), 83, 87.

4. Michael Meyer, "Birth Dearth," *Newsweek*, 27 September 2004, 7. Available from: http://www.msnbc.msn.com/id/6040427/site/newsweek/. Internet; accessed April 1, 2007.

5. http://robert.shimer.googlepages.com/US_unemployment.pdf . During the Great Depression and World War II, births declined as a percentage of the overall population and, in some years, in actual terms.

6. Wage inflation was accompanied, surprisingly, by an increase in unemployment. However, some have suggested that the higher unemployment rate during the 1970s (approximately 6.4 percent on average vs. 5.7 percent during the 2000s) was a product of an increasing number of young workers entering the workforce, causing the unemployment rate to be skewed upward.

Chapter 3: Immigration: America's "Free Lunch"

1. These numbers are based on the U.S. Department of Agriculture's report issued in April 2007, detailing the cost of raising a child from birth to the age of seventeen in a lower-income family in 2007. The range for lower-level income is defined as before-tax family income of $44,500 or less, with the average income being $27,800. The actual cost of raising a child born in 2007 to the age seventeen is $143,790. For ease of understanding, I have rounded this number up to $150,000, and used the age of eighteen as the base year for calculations (the age by which most people will have completed their high-school education but not begun their

university education. The average annual expenditure was calculated in the following manner: $150,000/18=$8.33$, or $8,300 (rounded down). For data on 2006 child-rearing costs for low-, medium-, and high-income families, see: Center for Nutrition Policy and Promotion, *Expenditures on Children By Families* (Washington, DC: United States Department of Agriculture, 2007), 5.

2. This assumes that parents "invest" two hours per day (between the two) in teaching a child the "basics," whether language or the basic acts necessary to function in society. This equates to roughly 1,000 hours per year. Given that America's per capita income is approximately $40,000 per annum ($20 per hour, based on a 2,000 hour work year), the aggregate investment on the part of parents represents approximately $14,600 per annum (730 hours multiplied by $20 per hour).

3. This number is current as of March 2005. See: Steven A. Camatora, "Immigrants to the United States-2002," *Backgrounder* (Washington, DC: Center for Immigration Studies, 2002), 1.

4. Currently, only 65,000 H-1B visas are issued each year. Congress should follow through on its plan to raise this number to 300,000. Bloomberg News, "Gates: End Limits on H-1B visas," *The Boston Globe*, 8 March 2007; available from http://www.boston.com/business/technology/articles/2007/03/08/gates_end_limits_on_h_1b_visas/?rss_id=Boston+Globe+—+Business+News. Internet; accessed 3 April 2007.

5. For the 2006–2007 academic year, the average cost of one year of education at a four-year private US college was slightly over $30,000 (including tuition and room and board) For simplicity it has been rounded down to $30,000 and multiplied by 4, yielding a total cost of $120,000 ($30,000 x 4=$120,000) for a four-year education. The average cost of a four-year public college was approximately $12,800 a year, and this had been rounded up to $13,000 and multiplied by 4, yielding a total cost of $52,000 ($13,000 x 4=$52,000) for a four-year education. After taking the average of these two numbers ($120,000 + $52,000=$172,000/2=$86,000), the average cost of a four-year college education in the United States is approximately $86,000. For a summary of the College Board's estimates of the cost of postsecondary education in the United States for the 2006–2007 academic year, see: http://money.cnn.com/2006/10/24/pf/college/college_costs/index.htm.

6. This explains our trade deficit much better than "dark matter" theory, which posits that our trade deficit is overstated because of IP, our educational system, etc. Focusing on the inflow of human capital is a more traditional way of explaining our imbalance (or lack thereof) and explains why we have run a deficit for so long. For a summary of dark matter theory and its effect on the current account deficit, see: Michael Mandel, "Dark Matter," BusinessWeek Online, 28 December 2005. available from http://www.businessweek.com/the_thread/economicsunbound/archives/2005/12/dark_matter.html. Internet; accessed 11 April 2007.

7. The United States has over 15 million immigrants, about 13 million of whom are undocumented or illegal. Assuming that it takes $150,000 to feed, clothe, and

educate a person from birth to age eighteen, this represents a tremendous transfer of wealth from the nations that have invested that capital to the United States.

8. Assumes: 75 percent of the 13 million illegal immigrants are in the workforce making $10 per hour working 2,000 hours per year. The average worker would make approximately $20,000 per annum and is assumed to pay 10 percent in federal income tax and 15.3 percent in Social Security and Medicare taxes.

9. Alan Sloan, "What Bush Didn't Say About Social Security," *Washington Post*, 31 January 2007, section, 2. available from: http://www.washingtonpost.com/wp-dyn/content/article/2007/01/29/AR2007012901848.html. Internet; accessed 5 April 2007.

10. For a description of President Bush's Comprehensive Immigration Reform proposal see: http://www.whitehouse.gov/infocus/immigration/. Internet; accessed 11 April 2007.

11. Paul S. Boyer, *Promises to Keep: The United States Since World War II* (Boston: Houghton Mifflin Co., 2005), 19-20.

12. Ibid., 75-76.

13. Stuart Anderson, *The Impact of Agricultural Guest Worker Programs on Illegal Immigration* (article online) (Arlington, VA: National Foundation for American Policy, 2003), 7.

14. Betty K. Koed, *The Politics of Reform: Policymakers and Immigration Act of 1965* (Ph.D. Dissertation, University of California, Santa Barbara, 1999), 284.

15. Anderson, *The Impact of Guest Worker Programs*, 7.

16. United Press International, "Fed Undercounts Illegal Aliens."

17. Section 1 of the Fourteenth Amendment of the US Constitution provides that "[a]ll persons born or naturalized in the United States, and subject to the jurisdiction thereof, are citizens of the United States and of the State wherein they reside." This would seemingly apply to the children of illegal immigrants. Obviously, at the time of the drafting of this section, the issue of illegal immigration was not as prominent as today. Accordingly, to address this issue, a constitutional amendment would be necessary to clarify that any person who enters this country illegally shall not become a citizen nor shall their children become citizens, except through naturalization.

Chapter 4: Social Security

1. http://www.gao.gov/financial/fy2007/guide.pdf

2. Social Security and Medicare combined shortfall/Current US population=$40 trillion/300 million people=$ 105, 333. The current US population is 301,719,066, according to the US Census Bureau on 1 May 2007: http://factfinder.census.gov/home/saff/main.html?_lang=en. Internet; accessed 1 May 2007.

3. $105,333 X 4= $421, 332.

4. These are the total assets in the Social Security Trust Fund as of 2007. See: http://www.ssa.gov/OACT/STATS/table4a3.html

5. US Congressional Budget Office, *Social Security: A Primer* (Washington, DC: Government Printing Office, 2001), 11.

6. Ibid.

7. US Congressional Budget Office, *The Outlook for Social Security* (Washington, DC: Government Printing Office, 2004); available from http://www.cbo.gov/showdoc.cfm?index=5530&sequence=0&from=0; Internet; accessed 21 April 2007.

8. "Social Security: Gambling with Your Future." [article-online] (Palo Alto, CA: Tuljapurkar Lab, Department of Biological Studies, Stanford University, no publication date given); Internet; accessed 21 April 2007.

9. United Press International "Fed Undercounts Illegal Aliens," Internet; accessed 4 April 2007.

10. Patrick L, "Norway 300 bln usd state pension fund to up equity allocation to 60 pct vs. 40," *Forbes.com* , 3 April 2007 [magazine on-line]; available from http://www.forbes.com/business/feeds/afx/2007/04/13/afx3609066.html; Internet; accessed 22 April 2007.

11. http://www.cato.org/pubs/ssps/ssp2.html.

12. Some have argued that the critical debate is the life span after one reaches retirement age. While this is important, there are two factors that should be taken into account. The first factor is the percentage of workers that reach retirement age. The second factor is the length of time that survivors live after they reach retirement age. It was unquestioned that once workers reached retirement, they lived lives just a few years shorter than those who reach retirement today. However, many more workers died before reaching retirement during that era and paid into Social Security prior to death, bolstering the program.

13. http://www.cato.org/pubs/ssps/ssp2.html.

14. http://www.californiahealthline.org/articles/2006/9/5/Higher-Life-Expectancy-Health-Care-Costs-Correlate.aspx

15. http://www.ssa.gov/OACT/TR/TR06/II_project.html

16. Ibid.

17. Appointed by President Bush on May 2, 2001, the Commission to Strengthen Social Security (CSSS) released its final report on December 21, 2001. The report can be downloaded from http://www.csss.gov/. Internet; accessed April 22, 2007.

Chapter 5: Saving for Retirement. Pension Reform

1. "Protecting The Nest Egg: A Primer on Defined Benefit and Defined Contribution Retirement Plans," *Council Primer* (Washington, DC: Council of Institutional Investors, no publication date given), 5.

2. This is the weighted median average rate of return for the two types of plans between 1988 and 2004. Alicia H. Munnell, Mauricio Soto, Jerilyn Libby, and John Prinzivalli, "Investment Returns: Defined Benefit vs. 401(k) Plans," *An Issue in Brief* 52 (Chestnut Hill, MA: Center For Retirement Research at Boston College, Summer 2006), 3.

Chapter 6: Medicare

1. http://www.gao.gov/financial/fy2007/guide.pdf

2. http://www.fairtax.org/PDF/WhatTheFederalTaxSystemIsCostingYou.pdf

3. http://www.photius.com/rankings/healthranks.html

4. Julie Bryant, "Frustrated Doctors Are Leaving Medicine Behind," *Atlanta Business Chronicle* (Atlanta, GA: American City Business Journals, Inc., 9 June 2000); available from http://atlanta.bizjournals.com/atlanta/stories/2000/06/12/story8.html?page=1. Internet; accessed April 27, 2007.

5. http://www.ahipbelieves.com/media/The%20Factors%20Fueling%20 Rising%20Healthcare%20Costs.pdf

6. "Automobile Insurance Comparisons." Available from http://www.tdi.state.tx.us/consumer/rgauto.html; Internet; accessed April 27, 2007.

7. Chad Terhune, "Guarded Health—Covering the Uninsured, But Only up to $25,000: Tennessee Experiment Goes Against the Grain as States Remake Care." *Wall Street Journal*, April 18, 2007 online article; available from http://online.wsj.com/article_email/article_print/SB117686046984573508-lMyQjAxMDE3NzI2NTgyNjUwWj.html. Internet; accessed 27 April 2007.

8. While there will be some who criticize the amount of the deductible as too high for working families, a deductible is a necessary element of the plan to ensure appropriate usage of medical services. Further, the deductible is necessary to keep costs in line for coverage. That is, if there is no deductible or a de minimis one, the policy would be cost prohibitive for most employers. There will be a safety net for many individuals in the form of Medicare.

9. $80 x 12 months = $960, or approximately $1,000 a year.

10. Total Annual Premium + Total Deductible = $1,000 +$1,000 = $2,000.

11. In a later chapter I will argue for the elimination of corporate taxes, which would solve this problem. This analysis assumes that this proposal is not adopted.

12. The current highest marginal rate is 35 percent. Assuming $3,000 in medical insurance paid by a corporation on behalf of a highly paid executive, the corporation deducts $3,000 as an expense. However, the executive does not pay taxes on the benefit provided. Accordingly, the lost revenues on the $3,000 benefit for the US Treasury are over $1,000, which is calculated as $3,000 multiplied by highest marginal rate of 35 percent.

Chapter 7: The Collapse of the Dollar

1. Financing government debt is particularly difficult for countries that cannot finance their external debt in their own currency, such as Argentina. These countries cannot borrow money in their own currency because investors fear these countries will just print more money to repay their debts if they run into financial trouble. This results in a collapse of the country's currency and, typically, inflation—an enemy of bond holders.

Consider the following illustration. If Argentina's government borrows in its own currency (the peso) and the Argentinian peso declines in value by 50 percent against the dollar, then an American who loans $1,000 to Argentina would only get $500 (because once you convert the Argentinian peso back to dollars, you have lost half of your money). To mitigate against the risk that a country will inflate its way out of a debt crisis, investors require that less creditworthy countries borrow in more stable currencies, often called "reserve" currencies. That is, Argentina would have to borrow in dollars.

Obviously, it is not positive for a borrowing nation to issue debt in another country's currency because the borrower runs an additional risk, namely, that its currency will decline relative to the reserve currency, thus making it harder for it to repay its debts. In the example above, if the Argentinian peso declines by 50 percent against the dollar and Argentina has issued debt denominated in dollars and not pesos, then Argentina will see its debt load increase by 200 percent as a result. This is what occurred in the latest Argentinian debt crisis in 2003.

2. In many cases, these countries believe that the US dollar will maintain its value over time, and by tying their currencies to the dollar, they are in effect creating currency stability in their country as well. To maintain the value of their currency vis-à-vis the dollar, these countries have to balance the supply of their currency relative to the dollar, and if their currency is appreciating too sharply, these countries have to accumulate dollars and issue more of their currency (in effect) to bring the relative value of the two currencies into balance. In addition, these countries central banks usually have to track the interest rate policies of the US Federal Reserve. Of late, this means that these countries have very low interest rates (stimulating inflation) and are having to accumulate s of dollars to keep the price of their currency depressed against the dollar.

3. http://www.post-gazette.com/pg/07008/752058-192.stm

4. http://www.industryweek.com/ReadArticle.aspx?ArticleID=13709

5. http://www.telegraph.co.uk/money/main.jhtml?xml=/money/2007/10/16/bcnchina116.xml

6. http://www.reuters.com/article/economicNews/idUSL203860120070520

7. http://www.mees.com/Energy_Tables/crude-oil.htm

8. https://www.cia.gov/library/publications/the-world-factbook/print/rs.html

9. In the interim, interest rates may remain low, or relatively low, as investors continue to view US treasuries as a safe haven. However, when investors begin to

realize that the dynamics of holding US treasuries means they lose money every year and that the US government's future obligations are massive, they will flee the US Treasury market.

Chapter 8: Fiscal Policy

1. http://www.cbsnews.com/stories/2007/03/01/60minutes/main2528226.shtml

Chapter 9: Accountability, Reporting, and Budgeting

1. While there has been a law in place to address this, Congress and the president have ignored it, preferring to publish inaccurate and misleading budgetary figures.

2. As it stands today, absent a crisis or a fit of honesty in Washington, there is little chance that a constitutional amendment would pass the House and Senate. (As required by Article V of the Constitution a constitutional amendment must pass by a two-thirds vote in the House and Senate and be ratified by two-thirds of the state legislatures). However, there is an alternative manner to adopt a constitutional amendment, which has not been used to date. The Constitution provides that the states may call a constitutional convention for the purpose of amending the Constitution. In this regard, a constitutional convention would be convened much like the original Constitutional Convention. At the constitutional convention, delegates from each of the states would deliberate in much the same manner as before and develop an amendment or a series of amendments to address the situation at hand.

Chapter 10: Tax Policy

1. H&R Block 2006 tax calculator used for calculation. Tax liability rounded down to nearest 1,000 (http://www.hrblock.com/taxes/tax_calculators/index.html).

2. Ibid.

3. http://www.irs.gov/pub/irs-soi/toder.pdf

4. Ibid.

5. Nobel laureate economist Gary Becker concluded that it takes approximately 2.6 billion man hours to prepare, file, and review (by the IRS) tax returns. Based on $40 per hour, Dr. Becker estimates the total tab, along with out-of-pocket costs, to be approximately $265 billion for 2005—over 20 percent of the overall individual tax revenues for the year. Please see http://www.taxfoundation.org/blog/show/1442.html.

6. Federal individual income taxes were $1.2 trillion in 2005. Using the IRS figure of between $86 billion and $118 billion yields a result of approximately 7 to 10 percent of individual tax revenues. Using Dr. Becker's figures, the percentage increases to over 20 percent (http://www.taxfoundation.org/blog/show/1442.html).

7. Calculated by taking the tax compliance costs of between $86 billion and $240 million and dividing that total by estimated 2007 US GDP of approximately $13 trillion in 2006. https://www.cia.gov/library/publications/the-world-factbook/geos/us.htm

8. http://www.epinet.org/content.cfm/webfeatures_snapshots_20050413

9. http://www.fairtax.org/PDF/TheImpactOfTheFairTaxOnCharitableGiving.pdf

10. http://www.heritage.org/Research/Taxes/wm327.cfm

11. http://www.irs.gov/businesses/small/article/0,,id=98968,00.html

12. Ibid.

13. A Congressional Budget Office study indicates that there is no conclusive evidence that a lower capital gains rate increased tax receipts over time. However, the last two rate cuts led to sustained higher revenues after the cut. The economy also tended to be stronger after the rate cuts, which also influences capital gains realizations. It is unclear how significant an impact a lower capital gains rate had on economic growth, although economic growth has seemed to be strong after each capital gains cut (http://www.cbo.gov/ftpdocs/70xx/doc7047/02-23-CapitalGains.pdf).

14. http://pages.stern.nyu.edu/~adamodar/New_Home_Page/datafile/spearn.htm

15. Ibid.

16. While some might argue that corporations are internalizing their cash flow to seize upon better and better investment opportunities, they have been doing almost the opposite. Over the past several years, corporations have continued to increase their cash holdings, rather than investing them or paying them out as dividends. With a more cogent tax regime covering dividends, corporations would be forced to either invest the capital in productive endeavors or return it to shareholders. Today, corporations can hide behind tax law on dividends to accumulate cash (arguing that it is not tax efficient to pay dividends) or make foolish investments, rather than returning it to shareholders (given the dividend tax).

17. http://en.wikipedia.org/wiki/Corporation_tax

18. Indeed, a Congressional Budget Office study found that 70 percent of corporate taxes are borne by domestic labor through lower wages or lost opportunities to foreign workers (who will see their productivity increase due to greater capital formation). The other 30 percent of the differential is borne by the corporation in the form of lower profits or is presumably passed on to the consumer in the form of higher prices of goods and services.

19. http://www.nytimes.com/2008/06/01/business/01view.html?_r=1&scp=1&sq=corporate+income+taxes&st=nyt&oref=slogin

Chapter 11: Monetary Policy

1. http://www.gold-eagle.com/gold_digest_02/powell120602.html

2. http://economics.about.com/library/glossary/bldef-liquidity-trap.htm

3. http://www.federalreserve.gov/aboutthefed/bios/board/default.htm

4. The chairman is appointed to a fourteen-year term as a member of the FOMC, although his term as chairman is only a four-year appointment (although he can be reappointed).

5. http://www.mises.org/story/1759

6. http://www.newyorkfed.org/markets/statistics/dlyrates/fedrate.html

7. Alan Greenspan made his comments in Jackson Hole, Wyoming, at an annual gathering of the Federal Reserve. He made these comments in a speech entitled "The Challenge of Central Banking in a Democratic Society:" http://www.federalreserve.gov/BoardDocs/speeches/1996/19961205.htm.

8. Alan Greenspan made this speech on January 13, 2000 (http://www.federalreserve.gov/boarddocs/speeches/2000/200001132.htm).

9. http://www.abc.net.au/news/newsitems/200307/s903871.htm

10. There could be cases where short-term rates might be higher than long-term rates, even if the Federal Reserved did not establish short-term rates. This might occur during an extreme liquidity crisis, where short-term borrowings become more valuable than long-term ones, driving up the price of capital. In such an event, the Federal Reserve should not intervene and reduce short-term rates. Rather, it should ensure liquidity among banks by making credit available to banks on favorable terms. Absent such events, the market should set both short- and long-term rates, as discussed below.

11. http://findarticles.com/p/articles/mi_qn4158/is_20051230/ai_n15982903

12. http://www.ny.frb.org/research/current_issues/ci2-7.pdf

13. http://article.nationalreview.com/?q=ZjhkYzcwMTVkYzMwNDUoZDhiMWE3ZjE4Y2Y3NGM3NTM

14. When the market does experience an inverted yield curve, the Federal Reserve should sit up and take notice, since it is likely to be driven by an extreme liquidity crisis and fear of recession.

15. Nominal interest rates were quite high during the 1970s. However, real interest rates (that is, the nominal interest rate less inflation) were quite low during this period. In fact, investors in both stocks and fixed income lost money in real terms, after inflation, during the period from 1966 through 1982 (measured by the returns on the ten-year Treasury and the S&P 500 over this time frame).

Chapter 12: The New Federal Reserve

1. This gave rise to one of the most famous lines from any politician, which Bryan uttered while accepting the Democratic nomination for president in 1876: "Do not press upon my brow a crown of gold, do not crucify mankind on a cross of gold."

2. Although deflation was the norm under the gold standard, there were occasions of inflation as well. Major gold and silver finds were always a cause of inflation. Inflation spiked 30 percent from 1850 to 1855 as a result of the California gold rush; http://eh.net/encyclopedia/article/whaples.goldrush.

3. http://www.occ.treas.gov/j

4. http://www.federalreserve.gov/releases/h3/hist/annualreview.htm# reservetranch

5. http://findarticles.com/p/articles/mi_m3937/is_2000_Sept-Oct/ai_80855422

6. http://www.bloomberg.com/apps/news?pid=20601087&sid=a3cNyC_p95 DE&refer=home

7. http://govinfo.library.unt.edu/npr/library/reports/dol17.html

8. Walter J. "John" Williams has been one of the leading critics of the data supplied to the public by the US government, particularly deficit figures, inflationary figures, and other economic data. His firm Shadow Government Statistics provides in-depth analysis of the figures provided by the US government. In some cases, Williams calculates current government statistics based on the manner in which the government used to calculate them (e.g., inflation) or applies conventional accounting standards to government figures to gain a better understanding of the true financial condition of the US government. His website is www.shadowstats.com, a useful source of information for those serious about understanding the true financial health of the US government and economy.

Chapter 13: Addressing the Current US Trade and Account Deficits

1. See note 1, Chapter 3.

2. This number is current as of March 2005. See Steven A. Camatora, "Immigrants to the United States—2002," *Backgrounder* (Washington, DC: Center for Immigration Studies, 2002), 1.

3. Currently, only 65, 000 H-1B visas are issued each year. Congress should follow through on its plan to raise this number to 300,000. Bloomberg News, "Gates: End Limits on H-1B visas," *The Boston Globe*, 8 March 2007; available from http://www.boston.com/business/technology/articles/2007/03/08/gates_end_limits_on_h_1b_visas/?rss_id=Boston+Globe+—+Business+News. Internet; accessed April 3, 2007.

4. See note 6, Chapter 3.

5. C. Fred Bergsten, "The Current Account Deficit and the US Economy: Testimony Before the Budget Committee of the United States Senate. February 1, 2007," *Speeches, Testimony, Papers* (Washington, DC: Peter G. Peterson Institute for International Economics, 2007); available from:

http://www.iie.com/publications/papers/paper.cfm?ResearchID=705. Internet; accessed April 5, 2007.

6. This is the US GDP for the fourth (final) quarter of fiscal year 2006, ending in April 2007. See http://www.bea.gov/national/index.htm#gdp. Internet; accessed April 8, 2007.

Chapter 14: The Issues Driving Energy Policy Have Expanded

1. http://www.guardian.co.uk/science/2007/feb/02/greenpolitics.climatechange

2. Professor Lovelock developed a device that detects chemicals through capturing electrons, which has enabled scientists to discover the dangers of DDT and the impact of chlorofluorocarbons in eroding the ozone layer. Please see http://www.alternet.org/environment/43606. Lovelock is best known for his Gaia theory, which provides that the earth is akin to a living organism and that changes to its delicate, self-regulating ecosystem threatens its very existence. In particular, the theory holds that the ecosystem is a self-regulating system comprised of all organisms on the planet—from rocks to the ocean to the atmosphere—and that any changes impact the system as a whole.

3. Based on his computer models, Lovelock believes that the earth is moving toward a "tipping point" on global warming that would accelerate the pace of global warming and be irreversible. According to Lovelock, the current surge in the earth's temperature is causing the death of algae that absorb carbon dioxide in the oceans and has diminished the ability of smaller plants on land to absorb carbon dioxide, both important defenses against the release of carbon dioxide in the atmosphere. In addition, global warming is melting the polar ice caps. This will cause water levels to rise to catastrophic levels, flooding major coastal cities.

As significant, the loss of ice mass means that the earth's "albedo," its ability to reflect light, is being reduced as the polar ice caps are replaced by more absorptive sea water. The earth cannot reflect light and heat as before and is now absorbing it, causing its temperature to rise. As the earth's temperature increases, the ice sheets across Siberia and elsewhere are also melting. In some areas, these sheets cover large areas of ancient degraded biomass, which would release harmful methane gases into the environment but for the ice sheets that encase them. With the protective sheets melting, there is nothing to stop the release of these harmful gases into the atmosphere.

According to Lovelock, some or all of these are enough to tip the earth, already teetering on the verge of disaster, toward a catastrophically warmer state. The increase in temperature will make it difficult, if not impossible, to grow enough food to sustain humankind; only a determined effort will result in humans surviving at all. In the best case scenario, Lovelock believes that a small fraction of the earth's population will survive—200 million of the 6 billion total population. But that is only if leaders act immediately to make the Artic inhabitable, it being one of the few places on earth that will have a temperate enough climate for human life.

4. There are some who view global warming skeptically, in some cases with persuasive evidence. One alternative theory holds that the earth is emerging from a "mini ice age" that started in the 1700s, and it is just now trending back to normal, warmer temperatures. Another theory points toward activity on the surface of the sun that has caused other planets to increase in temperature of late, so it is logical that the earth would warm as well.

5. In 2002, White House Press Secretary Ari Fleischer said that "conservation"

was not a priority for the administration and was a "personal choice" for each American. While true on both fronts, the administration has changed course over the past couple of years, particularly in the face of the hostilities in the Middle East and surging energy prices.

Chapter 15: Liberals vs. Conservatives

1. A study conducted by Cornell University ecologist, David Pimentel, indicates that corn ethanol requires 29 percent more fossil energy to produce than the fuel it produces. Switch grass requires 45 percent more and wood biomass 57 percent more. In short, "producing ethanol or biodiesel from plant biomass is going down the wrong road, because you use more energy to produce these fuels than you get … from combustion of these products." So rather than reducing the United States' dependence on foreign energy and global warming, ethanol does just the opposite. Further, by promoting these energy-inefficient products through subsidies (about $.50 per gallon), the government is actually promoting global warming and dependency on foreign oil.

2. Corn is used in sodas (corn syrup), as feed for livestock, in cereals, and in other basic foods, such as tortillas. Since the cost of corn has surged, these and other products have experienced rapid price increases. Tortillas, for example, have increased by about 60 percent since September 2006.

3. http://www.solarblog.com/

4. The length of time it takes to recoup the investment through energy savings.

5. Potentially, the homeowner might recoup some of the cost on the sale of the home, but it is equally likely that the homeowner will suffer a loss on the investment. So, viewed from a purely cost and return on investment perspective, the typical homeowner installing solar power is generally making an poor economic decision.

6. http://tonto.eia.doe.gov/FTPROOT/service/sroiaf(2004)04.pdf

Chapter 16: Energy Plan: Near Term

1. http://tonto.eia.doe.gov/FTPROOT/service/sroiaf(2004)04.pdf

Chapter 17: The "Manhattan Project" for Energy Independence: Longer Term

1. The outline in the previous chapter represents the intermediate step over the next ten years. America needs to appropriately cost fossil fuels to promote discovery of domestic energy sources (fossil fuels and alternatives) and promote conservation. America's defense umbrella provides a significant subsidy to Middle Eastern producers vis-à-vis domestic producers. Further, America should impose a carbon tax on fossil fuels to take into consideration the environmental costs of using fossil

fuels over cleaner-burning fuels. The higher price of oil, along with energy conservation measures (phased in over ten years), should at least slow the increase of our reliance on foreign oil and carbon emissions. But this alone is not enough.

2. The energy itself must be transportable. Coal, natural gas, etc. are the energy sources, and they are used at power plants to generate electricity. Then, electricity is transported through the "grid" (power lines) to provide electricity to homes, office buildings, etc. This is different from cars. The power source itself must be transportable, since the car has an engine, a mini power plant, to transform energy into power in order to propel the car.

3. http://www.ncpa.org/pub/bg/bg159/

4. Natural gas cannot be transported in its natural, gaseous state, except through pipelines. Therefore, natural gas imports from overseas must be cooled and converted into a liquid before being loaded on a ship for transportation to the United States. Once here, the liquefied natural gas (LNG) is pumped from the ship into a facility that heats and regasifies the liquid natural gas (LNG facility) into its natural state. It is then shipped to end markets via America's gas pipeline system. Since natural gas is highly combustible, the cooling and heating process poses dangers, which is why the permitting process for LNG facilities in and around US coastal cities runs into such fierce opposition.

5. http://www.eia.doe.gov/cneaf/electricity/page/co2_report/co2report.html

6. http://www.nei.org/resourcesandstats/documentlibrary/reliableandaffordableenergy/graphicsandcharts/usnucleargeneratingstatistics/

7. http://news.bbc.co.uk/1/hi/health/4283295.stm

8. http://www.euronuclear.org/pdf/HSC-Statements.pdf

9. http://www.nei.org/resourcesandstats/nuclear_statistics/usnuclearpowerplants/

10. *OECD/IEA NEA 2005*; please see http://www.uic.com.au/nip08.htm; US 2003 cents/kWh. Discount rate 10 percent, forty-year lifetime, 85 percent load factor.

11. http://www.uic.com.au/nip08.ht

12. Over time, natural gas may increasingly become a substitute for gasoline refined from oil for larger fleets, such as buses, UPS trucks, etc. It is cleaner burning and the US produces a significant amount of natural gas. To make this viable, the United States would have to increase nuclear power generation to offset the diversion of natural gas to transportation.

13. America currently generates approximately 17 percent of its electricity from nuclear power, saving approximately 700 million metric tons of carbon dioxide per annum. If the US boosted its nuclear power generation to 70 percent, that would be another 50 percent worth of nuclear power, which would equate to taking another 2,000 million metric tons of carbon dioxide out of the atmosphere each year (assuming the same rate). http://www.eia.doe.gov/kids/energyfacts/sources/non-renewable/nuclear.html

14. If you believe, as I do, that President Bush's decision to invade Iraq was based, at least partially, on the desire to secure Middle Eastern energy supplies, it is important to put the cost in the context of that war. The cost of the Iraqi War will likely be $1 trillion before it is all over.

A $1 trillion in nuclear plants would have resulted in three hundred new plants, which would have provided over 50 percent of this nation's energy needs in the coming years. This would have greatly reduced our need to burn oil for home heating, thereby reducing our dependence on foreign oil. Further, it would have significantly reduced our carbon emissions and allowed us to reduce our greenhouse emissions by as much as 30 percent. On another front, a $1 trillion investment would have more than likely yielded much more efficient alternative fuel solution, whether solar, wind power, cold fusion, or more efficient batteries for cars.

It is quite true that one should not cry over spilt milk, which brings me to the next point: if we believed the administration's rhetoric about an Islamic threat against the United States, shouldn't we invest a $1 trillion to eliminate the one leverage point that Middle Eastern countries have over the US oil? That is, should this nation, as a part of its war on terror, use the proposed oil tax that I have outlined above to finance a new "Manhattan Project" to find a substitute for fossil fuels?

Chapter 19: Defining the Enemy and Why They Are Fighting

1. Pape, Robert A., *Dying to Win: The Strategic Logic of Suicide Terrorism,* (Random House, 2005), page 65, citing Ronald Reagan, *An American Life* (New York: Simon & Schuster, 1990), p. 465.

2. I believe we are fortunate that the war does not center on Muslims "hating our freedoms." If it did, the United States would have just a few poor options to win such a war. First, Americans could give up those freedoms, which is not very likely. Second, the United States could convince the Arabs of the folly of their ways. If that is our current strategy, it, too, is failing and it is unclear whether military action is the best means to achieve this. Finally, the United States can win on the battlefield and kill all Arab extremists, or at least kill them in enough quantities to weaken them and convince the remainder that it is not worth the fight. Demographics are working against America here: the Islamic population is booming and intelligence reports indicate that our policies and activities are, if anything, increasing the number of Islamic fanatics, not reducing them. As a society, America will also have difficulty accepting the number of deaths associated with this strategy. A war based on Islamic hatred of our freedoms would be doomed to failure.

3. http://www.timesonline.co.uk/tol/news/world/us_and_americas/article1386812.ece

Chapter 20: New Foreign Policy

1. http://www.geocities.com/TimesSquare/1848/vietnam.html

2. The one arguable success of the saber/sanctions model is Libya. Libya sought to normalize relations with the West after fifteen years of sanctions, which started after the bombing of the airliner over Locherbie, Scotland. Through negotiations begun during the Clinton administration and spearheaded by Tony Blair of England, Libya agreed to acknowledge its role in the bombing and pay reparations to the families of those lost in the bombing, in exchange for the normalization of relationships with the West.

Chapter 21: Reconfiguring the US Military

1. To the extent the United States believes that certain humanitarian missions are necessary, it should supply troops to a newly reconfigured NATO, which will address these matters on a global basis and through consensus (at least on the part of the NATO members). The members of the US military would volunteer for NATO duty, though the US government would pay for its contribution of troops and hardware. Members of the military would volunteer to ensure that the mission corresponds with their view of their duty.

Some members of the military may not believe in the cause associated with nation building, believing that their enlistment in the US military was to protect and defend the US from national security threats. Others may believe in the humanitarian missions that would be associated with NATO. But, again, the important consideration is that NATO would address humanitarian issues, rather than unilateral action on the part of the US. This has bred hatred and animosity against the US.

2. http://www.afghanconflictmonitor.org/2008/03/pew-poll-result.html

3. http://www.historyplace.com/unitedstates/vietnam/index-1969.html

4. http://www.pollingreport.com/iraq.htm

5. This represents the approval ratings of President Nixon's policies in Vietnam. http://www.historyplace.com/unitedstates/vietnam/index-1969.html

6. http://www.isreview.org/issues/40/vietnamIII.shtml

7. http://www.washingtonpost.com/ac2/wp-dyn/A44837-2004Apr26?language=printer

8. http://www.npr.org/templates/story/story.php?storyId=10782562

9. Once the United States gained some degree of economic development and a larger population, the invasion of the United States became impractical and almost impossible. Instead, the US, with a relatively small army, consolidated the remainder of North America through wars with the American Indians and Mexico without fearing intervention by another great power.

The passage of time does not seem to have eroded the benefits of having the ocean barriers. The invasion of the US is even more unthinkable today that it ever has been. The barriers provided by the Atlantic and Pacific Oceans means that an invasion force would be detected relatively quickly after departure and would be an easy target in the middle of one of these vast bodies of water. Indeed, Great Britain has not been invaded for nearly a thousand years due to protective barrier of the English Channel. The reason is quite simple: it is difficult to bridge even a small body of water without overwhelming military superiority.

In the obverse, D-Day in World War II illustrates just how difficult that it is. The United States and its allies had to assemble the greatest armada and invading force in history to cross the channel and launch an invasion against a significantly weakened Germany. Despite having the element of surprise, the invasion still nearly failed.

10. Includes spending from all departments on defense and defense related matters, such as the $20 billion or more spent by the Department of Energy to maintain the nuclear arsenal, and the $150 billion to $200 billion per annum spent on Iraq and Afghanistan.

Chapter 23: Addressing the Palestinian Issue: The New Marshall Plan

1. Interestingly, two groups of ancient Jews—the Zealots and Sicarii—used suicide terrorism to fight Roman rule and occupation in the first century AD, again illustrating that the use of suicide terrorism is a means used by weak foes against stronger ones (http://www.economist.com/displaystory.cfm?story_id=2329785).

2. http://www.iht.com/articles/2007/07/29/news/saudi.php; http://www.guardian.co.uk/Iraq/Story/0,,2100698,00.html

3. http://www.jewishvirtuallibrary.org/jsource/Society_&_Culture/newpop.html

4. http://www.arabicnews.com/ansub/Daily/Day/980227/1998022735.html

5. http://en.wikipedia.org/wiki/Demographics_of_Saudi_Arabia

6. http://www.nationmaster.com/country/iz-iraq

7. http://www.worldstatesmen.org/Iran.htm

8. http://en.wikipedia.org/wiki/Arab_world

Chapter 24: Addressing Iraq and Afghanistan

1. See National Intelligence Estimate on the State of Iraq dated August 2007.

2. Ibid.

3. This is the key distinction with the Democrats' plan, which provides for troop withdrawals without a plan to allow for an orderly dissolution of Iraq. While the results may be the same—the creation of three independent states—the process would be deadlier and bloodier. The US can hopefully provide a framework for a more orderly dissolution, saving lives and money.

4. In 2005, I wrote an editorial for a local paper, in which I owned an interest, calling for the implementation of this plan.

5. http://www.nydailynews.com/news/wn_report/2007/05/10/2007-05-10_troops_keep_comin_to_afghanistan.html

Part VI Introduction: The Constitution and Electoral Policy

1. The "social contract" theory proposes that people, in their natural state, hold all rights; the state is an artificial creation without any authority until delegated its authority and rights by the people. The people delegate some of their rights to the state in consideration for certain services they could not provide individually, such as the rule of law, judicial system for adjudicating rights, common defense, etc.

2. For the sake of brevity, the word "founders" is a composite. In using it I assume the prevailing view of the founders. Of course, their views were as varied as the men themselves; many of their views do not always agree with the general principles outlined in this section. Rather than providing a series of qualifications and explaining some of the differences (unless important) between the founders on these issues, I have discussed the prevailing views.

Chapter 25: Rome as a Guide

1. http://www.vroma.org/~bmcmanus/socialclass.html

2. Through its relatively liberal immigration policies, the United States has taken yet another page out of its forebears' book, attracting the best and brightest throughout the world.

3. The most successful of these opportunists was a Roman general named Sulla, who led an army into Rome more than forty-five years before Caesar did. Sulla's legions were met in Rome with shock and disbelief. After all, the Roman constitution required generals to lay down their arms and disband their armies before entering the city. Sulla ruled the republic as dictator for nearly ten years before handing back power peacefully in 80 BC. This precedent was a portent of things to come.

4. The Rubicon River represented the boundary at which Roman generals were supposed to leave their armies and return to Rome as citizens, unarmed and unthreatening to the state.

Chapter 26: The US Constitution and the Forgotten Amendments

1. The doctrine of judicial review would not become firmly established until 1803 in *Marbury vs. Madison*, when the founder of the American Supreme Court, Chief Justice John Marshall, brilliantly established the right of the Supreme Court to pass on the constitutionality of laws passed by Congress and signed into law by the president.

2. http://www.infoplease.com/ipa/A0005921.html

3. Ibid.

Chapter 27: The Constitution and the New Deal

1. http://www.vw.vccs.edu/vwhansd/HIS122/NewDeal.html

Chapter 28: Constitutional Fidelity. Changing the Tone

1. Perhaps the greatest constitutional struggle in this nation's history involved slavery. The issue in dispute, however, was not the constitutionality of slavery in the South, which at the time, was legal. The issue was the spread of slavery into new states. The Southern states wanted to maintain parity among slave and nonslave states, believing that if this parity was disturbed the Southern states had a right to nullify (withdraw from) the Union. The Northern states rejected the doctrine of nullification, believing that once created, the Union could not be dissolved. The North's victory in the Civil War ended the debate over the nullification theory.

2. The Terry Schiavo case also deserves to be noted. In that case the Florida courts ruled repeatedly that Ms. Schiavo was severely brain damaged and it was her desire to be taken off life support. The case reached Congress, which went into special session to try to pass legislation to stop her being taken off life support. Ultimately, Congress's action was too late, although its interference in the matter was deeply unpopular among the American people. The people appear to have instinctively viewed this as congressional overreach into a matter that should have been determined by the state and/or the husband.

Chapter 29: Congressional Apportionment

1. http://www.thisnation.com/question/016.html

2. In order to wring out some of the volatility, a rolling three-term cycle is used, providing remarkable insight into the power of the incumbency of recent years and the impact on gerrymandering.

3. The only complicating factor with gay marriage is the "full faith and credit" clause of the Constitution, where states have to recognize legal and legitimate contracts entered into and sanctioned by another state. In this case, a gay couple could marry lawfully in one state and then move to a state that does not permit gay marriage. That state would be required to recognize the gay marriage as legitimate. This doctrine has resulted in some uncomfortable situations in the past. For example, some states recognize marriage contracts between very young couples, while others do not. A couple could get married at a young age in one state and move to a state that does not recognize their marriage. The second state would have little recourse but to recognize that marriage. These occurrences are small in number and the price to be paid for federalism.

4. Courts typically review districts to ensure that the equal protection clause has been respected. In general, the courts have held that this clause requires districts to be drawn in such a way that political parties and other groups are appropriately represented. Over time, the use of the equal protection clause has resulted in districts that are either "safe" Republican districts, Democratic districts, or minority districts.

5. Each state has a number of electors equal to the number of senators (two) and representatives (based on population) that serve in Congress. This gives smaller states a modest degree of disproportionate representation, given the original framework of the Constitution. Accordingly, the smallest state in terms of population (Montana) has three electors: two for its two senators and one for its one House representative. California, on the other hand, has 55 electors (two Senators; 53 members of the House), or one for every 670,000 citizens (based on a 37 million population in 2006; http://quickfacts.census.gov/qfd/states/06000.html). Thus, based on population, Montana residents, with one elector for every 314,000 residents, get 100 percent greater representation in the election of presidents than does California.

While seemingly unfair, this is in line with the Virginia-Massachusetts compromise. In drafting the Constitution, large states believed that each state should get a number of representatives in the national legislature based on each state's population. Smaller states, fearing that their voice would be diluted, believed that each state should get the same number of representatives, regardless of population. The Virginia-Massachusetts compromise split the difference, permitting large states to have greater representation in the House (which controlled spending, taxes, etc.) and for every state to have equal representation in the Senate (which had more control over the ratification of treaties, confirmation of court nominees, etc.).

6. Even if the measure passed, it is questionable whether the measure would be constitutional; the Constitution is quite clear that state legislatures control the allocation of electoral votes. The California legislature, given that it is controlled by Democrats, would likely oppose such a change. If the electoral votes in California are largely split, it means that a Democrat would have to win Florida plus another state to maintain parity.

7. The Great Compromise occurred during the Constitutional Convention in 1787, and provided that the state delegations to the House of Representatives be allocated based on population (favoring large states) and that each state have two US Senators regardless of population (favoring small states).

Chapter 30: Peering through the Looking Glass

1. http://members.aol.com/usregistry/allwars.htm. The US population during the Civil War was about 31 million and about 132 million in 1945.

2. http://www.ifsc.co.bw/archives.htm